STUDENT TEXTBOOK

The World's
Happiest Kept Secret

CHAIRMAN
Rabbi Moshe Kotlarsky

PRINCIPAL BENEFACTOR
Mr. George Rohr

EXECUTIVE DIRECTOR
Rabbi Efraim Mintz

ROSH CHODESH SOCIETY DIRECTOR
Mrs. Shaindy Jacobson

AUTHOR
Rabbi Mordechai Dinerman
in consultation with
David Pelcovitz, PhD

COURSE DEVELOPMENT
Mrs. Mushka Grossbaum
Mrs. Rochel Holzkenner
Rabbi Yanky Raskin
Rabbi Naftali Silberberg
Casey Skvorc, PhD
Rabbi Yanki Tauber

EDITORIAL BOARD
Mrs. Malky Bitton
Mrs. Shula Bryski
Mrs. Shaindy Jacobson
Mrs. Chanie Wilhelm
Mrs. Yehudis Wolvovsky

CURRICULUM COORDINATOR
Mrs. Rivki Mockin

RCS ADMINISTRATOR
Mrs. Baila Goldstein

(888) YOUR-JLI/718-221-6900 ext. 117 or 160
www.myRCSociety.com

**THE ROHR
JEWISH LEARNING INSTITUTE**

gratefully acknowledges the
pioneering support of

George and Pamela Rohr

Since its inception, the Rohr JLI has been a beneficiary
of the vision, generosity, care, and concern
of the Rohr family.

. . . .

In the merit of the hundreds of thousands of hours of
Torah study by JLI students worldwide, may they be blessed with
health, *Yiddishe nachas* from all their loved ones, and extraordinary
success in all their endeavors.

ADVISORY BOARD OF GOVERNORS

YAAKOV AND KAREN COHEN
Potomac, MD

YITZCHOK AND JULIE GNIWISCH
Montreal, QC

BARBARA HINES
Aspen, CO

ELLEN MARKS
S. Diego, CA

DAVID MINTZ
Tenafly, NJ

DR. STEPHEN F. SERBIN
Columbia, SC

LEONARD A. WIEN, JR.
Miami Beach, FL

PARTNERING FOUNDATIONS

AVI CHAI FOUNDATION

CRAIN-MALING FOUNDATION

THE DIAMOND FOUNDATION

ESTATE OF ELLIOT JAMES BELKIN

FRANCINE GANI CHARITABLE FUND

GOLDSTEIN FAMILY FOUNDATION

KOHELET FOUNDATION

KOSINS FAMILY FOUNDATION

MAYBERG FOUNDATION

MEROMIM FOUNDATION

MYRA REINHARD FAMILY FOUNDATION

THE ROBBINS FAMILY FOUNDATION

RUDERMAN FAMILY FOUNDATION

WILLIAM DAVIDSON FOUNDATION

OLAMI—WOLFSON FOUNDATION

WORLD ZIONIST ORGANIZATION

YEHUDA AND ANNE NEUBERGER PHILANTHROPIC FUND

THE ZALIK FOUNDATION

PRINCIPAL BENEFACTOR

GEORGE ROHR
New York, NY

PILLARS OF JEWISH LITERACY

KEVIN BERMEISTER
Sydney, Australia

SHAYA BOYMELGREEN
Miami Beach, FL

PABLO AND SARA BRIMAN
Mexico City, Mexico

ZALMAN AND MIMI FELLIG
Miami Beach, FL

YOSEF GOROWITZ
Redondo Beach, CA

SHLOIMY & MIRELE GREENWALD
Brooklyn, NY

DR. VERA KOCH GROSZMANN
S. Paulo, Brazil

HOWARD JONAS
Newark, New Jersey

HERSCHEL LAZAROFF
Monsey, NY

JENNY LJUNGBERG
New York, NY

DAVID MAGERMAN
Gladwyne, PA

YITZCHAK MIRILASHVILI
Herzliya, Israel

BEN NASH
New Jersey

EYAL AND AVIVA POSTELNIK
Marietta, GA

LEE AND PATTI SCHEAR
Dayton, OH

ISADORE SCHOEN
Fairfax, VA

YAIR SHAMIR
Savyon, Israel

LARRY SIFEN
Virginia Beach, VA

SPONSORS

MARK AND REBECCA BOLINSKY
Long Beach, NY

DANIEL AND ETA COTLAR
Houston, TX

RABBI MEYER AND LEAH EICHLER
Brooklyn, NY

YOEL GABAY
Brooklyn, NY

BRIAN AND DANA GAVIN
Houston, TX

SHMUEL AND SHARONE GOODMAN
Chicago, IL

CAROLYN HESSEL
New York, NY

MICHAEL AND ANDREA LEVEN
Atlanta, GA

JOE AND SHIRA LIPSEY
Aspen, CO

JOSEF MICHELASHVILI
Glendale, NY

RACHELLE NEDOW
El Paso, TX

PETER AND HAZEL PFLAUM
Newport Beach, CA

ABE PODOLAK
Princeton Junction, NJ

MOSHE AND YAFFA POPACK
Fisher Island, FL

HERCHEL AND JULIE PORTMAN
Denver, CO

DR. ZE'EV RAV-NOY
Los Angeles, CA

CLIVE AND ZOE ROCK
Irvine, CA

ZVI RYZMAN
Los Angeles, CA

ALAN ZEKELMAN
Bloomfield Hills, MI

MYRNA ZISMAN
Cedarhurst, NY

JANICE AND IVAN ZUCKERMAN
Coral Gables, FL

בס"ד

THIS COURSE IS DEDICATED
IN LOVING MEMORY OF

Hindi Krinsky-Kanarfogel

לעילוי נשמת מרת **הינדא לאה** ע"ה
בת יבלחט"א הרה"ת **מנחם מענדל** שי'
ו' אלול, תשע"ח

. . . .

A rare individual, Hindi radiated pure joy from within, illuminating everyone
and everything around her—making the world and the people within it happier
and holier in perpetuity. Her joy lives on in her loving family and numerous
accomplishments, and is etched in our hearts for eternity.

May her love, passion, and dedication for Jewish education serve as an everlasting
foundation upon which her beautiful family will continue to build forever.

May our dear friends Reb Mendel & Miriam and all their
loved ones merit the immediate fulfillment of
"והקיצו ורננו שוכני עפר—arise and awake . . . and sing. . ."
—Isaiah 26:19

May they go from strength to strength and enjoy health, happiness,
nachas from their loved ones, and success in all their endeavors.

לאורך ימים ושנים טובות

. . . .

DEDICATED BY YOUR FRIENDS

When it hurts to look back and you're afraid to look ahead,
look beside you, and we will be there.

TABLE OF CONTENTS

ENDORSEMENTS

For a long time, when policy makers and educators asked me to develop programs or curricula to increase well-being in various field settings, I told them that there was not enough rigorous research to support such an endeavor. The day has come, however, that we are ready to apply the findings of positive psychology to the wider world! RCS's *Code to Joy* is a thoughtful, impressive effort to accomplish just that. I wish I could take this course myself!

SONJA LYUBOMIRSKY, PHD
Professor of Psychology at the University of California, Riverside
Author of The How of Happiness *and* The Myths of Happiness

The Rosh Chodesh Society's *Code to Joy* brings together modern research in positive psychology and ancient Jewish wisdom. This marriage between theology and science can bring about significant positive change in individuals and communities.

TAL BEN-SHAHAR, PHD
Lecturer, Interdisciplinary Center, Herzliya, Israel
Author of Happier *and* The Question of Happiness

As a meaning scholar, I firmly believe that the best parts of our own humanity are drawn to a deep and true encounter with what really matters in life. RCS's *Code to Joy* is a rich, accessible effort, embedding the science of positive psychology within the invaluable treasure of cultural and spiritual wisdom to facilitate the quest for meaning and fulfillment.

MICHAEL F. STEGER, PHD
Associate Professor, Colorado State University
Editor of Purpose and Meaning in the Workplace *and* Designing Positive Psychology

The Rosh Chodesh Society's *Code to Joy* presents an exciting integration of Jewish wisdom and several highly effective practices currently used in psychology. As a professional who has specialized in working with people whose life circumstances require unusual resiliency, I believe the combination of a Jewish spiritual approach along with positive psychology strategies promises to have far-reaching effects on individuals and their families. Both approaches are powerful alone in terms of enhancing well-being and together are likely to be synergistic in their impact.

LAURA MARSHAK, PHD
Professor of Counseling,
Indiana University of Pennsylvania
Psychologist, North Hills Psychological Services
Author of Married with Special-Needs Children

I'm grateful to Professor Pelcovitz and the Rosh Chodesh Society for the gift of this essential and pioneering course on positive psychology. It will not only benefit us as individuals striving to lead a happy, creative, and joyful life; it's teachings will also enhance our families, communities, and the world we live in, as we learn new strategies to deal with stressful times.

HARRIET LERNER, PHD
Clinical Psychologist
Lawrence, Kansas
Author of The Dance of Anger *and* Marriage Rules

Code to Joy provides a wonderful blueprint to help those who feel trapped in the past and to help release them to be in the moment. It is no secret. The pull of living in the past leads us into depression, while the preoccupation with the future keeps us anxious. Real calm and joy can only come from the present and being in the moment. I love this course and its step-by-step guide to achieve new feelings of positivity and optimism. It is practical and achievable.

MARK L. BRENNER, PHD
Adjunct Professor, Pepperdine University
Founder of Parent Fitness Training

Code to Joy helps us take this positive research and make it come alive. If more people were effectively educated on these topics, a revolution would occur as the world would know that happiness is a choice.

SHAWN ACHOR
Author of The Happiness Advantage *and* Before Happiness

Once again, the Rosh Chodesh Society has hit the psychological bulls-eye. At a time when our vulnerability is increasing and our unease growing in the wrong direction, this course tackles the challenges to our well-being in a thoughtful, sensitive, and effective manner. A truly wonderful and helpful endeavor.

RABBI REUVEN P. BULKA, PHD, CM
Adjunct Professor, The College of the Humanities—Carleton University
Rabbi, Congregation Machzikei Hadas
Ottawa, ON, Canada

A proper education should include more courses like this one, which takes up basic questions of morality that are important to live a successful, mindful life.

ELLEN LANGER, PHD
Professor of Psychology, Harvard University
Author of Mindfulness *and* Counterclockwise

Positive psychology can only penetrate the individual in a lasting manner if it is consistent with their worldview. Therefore, aligning the scientific knowledge with cultural and spiritual roots is a wonderfully creative way to ensure long-term impact.

ILONA BONIWELL, PHD
Principal Lecturer and Course Leader of MAPP, Anglia Ruskin University,
Oxford, UK
CEO, Positran, Paris, France
Author of Positive Psychology in a Nutshell
Editor of The Oxford Handbook of Happiness

Positive psychology has shown the importance of activities and feelings such as thankfulness, forgiveness, and helpfulness in promoting positive mental health. Religion, spirituality, and virtue are starting to take their rightful place as scientifically and clinically sound sources of happiness. Building on exciting recent discoveries in positive psychology, participants in this course will discover strategies based on Jewish spiritual values for enhancing happiness. The Rosh Chodesh Society, Professor Pelcovitz, and all concerned can be congratulated for this initiative, which will make these important strategies accessible and usable for all taking part.

KATE MIRIAM LOEWENTHAL, PHD
Emeritus Professor of Psychology,
Royal Holloway, University of London
Professor of Abnormal Psychology, NYU London

COURSE FOREWORD

BY DAVID PELCOVITZ, PHD

I am honored to write the foreword for the Rosh Chodesh Society's course *Code to Joy: The World's Happiest Kept Secret,* an inspiring course that provides a synthesis of current findings from the field of positive psychology integrated with ancient Jewish wisdom. This melding of modern research with insights informed by Jewish learning can provide invaluable understanding and direction toward living an ethical, happy, and fulfilling life.

The relatively new discipline of positive psychology has signaled a paradigm shift in the mental health field. Instead of focusing on what is wrong with an individual, positive psychology systematically studies how to actively nurture strengths. At a practical level, this leads to empirical investigations into how to understand and promote happiness rather than alleviate depression. Positive psychologists are less interested in anger, while more concerned about forgiveness; they are more likely to try to understand gratitude rather than cynicism. One of the founders of positive psychology, Dr. Martin Seligman, points out that when parents dream of how they want their child to be as an adult, their focus is not on raising a child who is not depressed or anxious but on a child who embraces life with joy and enthusiasm.

This focus is very familiar to students of *Chasidut, Musar* (ethical teachings), and *Hashkafah* (Jewish thought). Traditionally, Jewish practice and learning have placed a great deal of emphasis on living a life filled with joy, gratitude, and virtually every other area that is the focus of positive psychology. Jewish texts are replete with wisdom that foreshadows many of the empirical findings of research and explores what it means to nourish positive emotion. A more nuanced understanding of the wisdom that Jewish thinkers have expressed about these virtues over the millennia would serve to enrich the field of positive psychology. Likewise, the emerging science of techniques on how to nourish these traits in educational, family, personal, and business settings may enhance Jewish thinking and living.

Surveys of American parents over the past thirty years consistently find that they view preparing children to become responsible citizens as one of the most important goals of education. An array of studies conducted over the last decade find that values emphasized by positive psychology are at least as important in predicting long-term success in children as are grades. For example, self-discipline is twice as good a predictor of high school grades as IQ. Furthermore, happy adolescents earn substantially more money as adults than their less happy counterparts. Researchers have also found that the skills and values imparted by an approach informed by positive psychology have been found to differentiate flourishing corporate teams, relative to stagnating teams, in the business world as well as predict greater satisfaction and success in one's personal relationships. For example, in the realm of marriage, an extensive series of studies conducted by John Mordecai Gottman and his colleagues have documented that a five-to-one ratio of positive to negative interactions is necessary for marriages to thrive.

I teach a required course on Jewish perspectives in positive psychology at the Azrieli Graduate School of Jewish Education at Yeshiva University. The reaction of my students to this course has consistently been excitement at how applying the lessons of positive psychology in Jewish settings shows much promise as an effective approach to leading a more fulfilling life. The designers of *Code to Joy* have brought together this approach in a highly effective and accessible manner. They have skillfully summarized the recent advances in positive psychology, while at the same time presenting the wisdom of Chasidic thought and Torah insights. All of this is done in a practical manner that can help bring higher levels of fulfillment and values-driven living into our daily lives.

DAVID PELCOVITZ, PHD
Gwendolyn & Joseph Straus Chair in Psychology and Jewish Education,
Azrieli Graduate School of Jewish Education and Administration,
Yeshiva University

Just Over Yonder?

FINDING HAPPINESS IN LIFE'S GIFTS

*What matters most is how we appreciate
our life circumstances and how regularly
we express that appreciation.*

THE HAPPINESS ADVANTAGE
SELF-MASTERY

Exercise 1.1

1. To what degree do our circumstances (family, resources, career, etc.) impact our overall happiness?

2. What are some of the challenges to living a life of happiness?

3. One can be happier if . . .

4. What are some of the benefits of living happily?

Question for Discussion

Why does happiness have so many positive side effects?

Text 1

RABBI SHNE'UR ZALMAN OF LIADI, *TANYA*, CH. 26 ⊕

בְּרַם כְּגוֹן דָא צָרִיךְ לְאוֹדוֹעֵי כְּלָל גָּדוֹל.

כִּי כְּמוֹ שֶׁנִּצָחוֹן לְנַצֵּחַ דָּבָר גַּשְׁמִי, כְּגוֹן שְׁנֵי אֲנָשִׁים הַמִּתְאַבְּקִים זֶה עִם זֶה לְהַפִּיל זֶה אֶת זֶה, הִנֵּה אִם הָאֶחָד הוּא בְּעַצְלוּת וּכְבֵדוּת, יְנֻצַּח בְּקַל וְיִפּוֹל, גַּם אִם הוּא גִבּוֹר יוֹתֵר מֵחֲבֵרוֹ.

כָּכָה מַמָּשׁ בְּנִצָחוֹן הַיֵּצֶר, אִי אֶפְשָׁר לְנַצְחוֹ בְּעַצְלוּת וּכְבֵדוּת הַנִּמְשָׁכוֹת מֵעַצְבוּת וְטִמְטוּם הַלֵּב כְּאֶבֶן, כִּי אִם בִּזְרִיזוּת הַנִּמְשֶׁכֶת מִשִּׂמְחָה וּפְתִיחַת הַלֵּב וְטַהֲרָתוֹ מִכָּל נְדְנוּד דְּאָגָה וָעֶצֶב בָּעוֹלָם.

RABBI SHNE'UR ZALMAN OF LIADI (ALTER REBBE)
1745–1812

Chasidic rebbe, halachic authority, and founder of the Chabad movement. The Alter Rebbe was born in Liozna, Belarus, and was among the principal students of the Magid of Mezeritch. His numerous works include the *Tanya*, an early classic containing the fundamentals of Chabad Chasidism; and Shulchan Aruch HaRav, an expanded and reworked code of Jewish law.

This should be made known as a cardinal principle:

The internal spiritual battle waged against one's negative impulses is similar to a physical wrestling match. If two individuals are wrestling with each other, each striving to fell the other, but one is lazy and lethargic, he will fall and be easily defeated, even if he is stronger than his opponent.

The same applies regarding the conquest of one's impulses. It is impossible to defeat them from a state of laziness and heaviness, which stem from sadness and a dull heart. They can be defeated only from a state of enthusiasm, which derives from happiness and a heart free of any trace of worry and sadness.

SELF-REVELATION

> ## Text 2
> RABBI SHALOM DOVBER SCHNEERSOHN,
> *SEFER HAMAAMARIM* 5657, PP. 221–222

טֶבַע הַשִּׂמְחָה הוּא לִפְרוֹץ גֶּדֶר. דְּהַיְינוּ כָּל הַגְדָּרָה וְהַגְבָּלָה שֶׁבַּנֶּפֶשׁ, טֶבַע הַשִּׂמְחָה הִיא לִפְרוֹץ הַהַגְדָּרָה וְהַהַגְבָּלָה הַהִיא . . .

דְּכָל כֹּחַ כְּשֶׁבָּא לִידֵי גִילּוּי וְהַמְשָׁכָה . . . הֲרֵי הוּא בָּא בְּאֵיזֶה צִיּוּר, שֶׁנִּתְגַּלָּה בְּאוֹפֶן כָּזֶה וְכָזֶה, וְהַצִּיּוּר הוּא הַהַגְבָּלָה . . . וְהַשִּׂמְחָה פּוֹרֵץ גֶּדֶר הַהַנְהָגָה הָרְגִילָה, מִפְּנֵי שֶׁמּוֹצִיאָה עֶצֶם הַכֹּחַ מִן הַהֶעְלֵם אֶל הַגִּילּוּי, וְעַל יְדֵי זֶה הוּא יוֹצֵא מֵהַנְהָגָתוֹ הַגְדוּרָה.

RABBI SHALOM DOVBER SCHNEERSOHN (RASHAB)
1860–1920

Chasidic rebbe. Rabbi Shalom Dovber became the 5th leader of the Chabad movement upon the passing of his father, Rabbi Shmuel Schneersohn. He established the Lubavitch network of *yeshivot* called Tomchei Temimim. He authored many volumes of Chasidic discourses and is renowned for his lucid and thorough explanations of kabbalistic concepts.

The nature of joy is to breach barriers. That is, joy tends to break through the various limitations and restrictions of the human character. . . .

When the faculties of a person first emerge from a state of potential . . . they each take a certain definition and shape. . . . Human joy breaks through this default state. When we are joyous, we tap into and reveal the deeper but latent potential of our character, and we are then empowered to behave in a different, enhanced manner.

DIVINE MIRROR

Text 3
ZOHAR 2:184B ⏣

תָּא חֲזֵי: עָלְמָא תַּתָּאָה קַיְימָא לְקַבְּלָא תָּדִיר . . .
וְעָלְמָא עִלָּאָה לָא יָהִיב לֵיה אֶלָּא כְּגַוְונָא דְּאִיהוּ קַיְימָא. אִי
אִיהוּ קַיְימָא בִּנְהִירוּ דְּאַנְפִּין מִתַּתָּא, כְּדֵין הָכִי נָהֲרִין לֵיה
מֵעֵילָא, וְאִי אִיהוּ קַיְימָא בַּעֲצִיבוּ, יָהֲבִין לֵיה דִּינָא בְּקִבְלֵיה.
כְּגַוְונָא דָא (תְּהִלִּים ק, ב) "עִבְדוּ אֶת ה' בְּשִׂמְחָה", חֶדְוָה דְּבַר
נָשׁ מָשִׁיךְ לְגַבֵּיה חֶדְוָה אַחֲרָא עִלָּאָה.

Come and observe! Our world is always ready to receive [the spiritual flow that emanates from above]. . . .

The upper world provides in accordance with the state below. If the state below is joyous, abundance flows from above; but if the state below is one of sadness, the flow of blessing is constricted.

Therefore, "Serve G-d with joy" (Psalms 100:2).

ZOHAR
The seminal work of kabbalah, Jewish mysticism. The *Zohar* is a mystical commentary on the Torah, written in Aramaic and Hebrew. According to the Arizal, the *Zohar* contains the teachings of Rabbi Shimon bar Yocha'i, who lived in the Land of Israel during the 2nd century. The *Zohar* has become one of the indispensable texts of traditional Judaism, alongside and nearly equal in stature to the Mishnah and Talmud.

Text 4

RABBI MOSHE LEIB OF SASOV, *LIKUTEI RAMAL*, VAYETSEI 🧍

הַשִּׂמְחָה . . . מַדְרֵגָה יוֹתֵר מִבְּכִיָה.
כִּי לְהַבְּכִיָה פָּתוּחַ הַשַּׁעַר, כְּמוֹ שֶׁאָמְרוּ חֲכָמֵינוּ זִכְרוֹנָם לִבְרָכָה
(בָּבָא מְצִיעָא נט, א) "שַׁעֲרֵי דְמָעוֹת לֹא נִנְעָלוּ". אַךְ הַשִּׂמְחָה
מְשַׁבֵּר הַמְחִיצָה וְהַגוּדָא.

RABBI MOSHE LEIB OF SASOV
1745–1807

Chasidic rebbe. Rabbi Moshe Leib was a prominent disciple of Rabbi Shmelke of Nikolsburg, and later went on to be one of the greatest disseminators of Chasidism throughout Eastern Europe. He was famous for his love and care for the downtrodden and was known as "the father of widows and orphans." One of his descendants published his teachings, a commentary on the Talmud and the Torah, in the 20th century.

Joy . . . is loftier than tears.

The heavenly gates remain open for our tears, as the Talmud says (Bava Metsi'a 59a), "The gates of tears are not locked." Joy, however, demolishes and pulverizes the [supernal] walls and barriers.

HAPPINESS VS. *SIMCHAH*

Exercise 1.2

Subjective Happiness Scale

SONJA LYUBOMIRSKY, *THE HOW OF HAPPINESS*
(NEW YORK: PENGUIN PRESS, 2008), P. 33

For each of the following statements and/or questions, circle the point on the scale that you feel is most appropriate in describing you.

1. In general, I consider myself:

    1   2   3   4   5   6   7
    not a very happy person / a very happy person

2. Compared with most of my peers, I consider myself:

    1   2   3   4   5   6   7
    less happy / more happy

3. Some people are generally very happy. They enjoy life regardless of what is going on, getting the most out of everything. To what extent does this characterization describe you?

    1   2   3   4   5   6   7
    not at all / a great deal

4. Some people are generally not very happy. Although they are not depressed, they never seem as happy as they might be. To what extent does this characterization describe you?

    1   2   3   4   5   6   7
    not at all / a great deal

Thousands of people have taken this questionnaire and scientists have compared their scores. Here's how to arrive at your score.

First, reverse the score of the last question (but not the other three) as follows: A score of 7 becomes 1, a score of 6 becomes 2, etc. Then add the four numbers and divide them by four.

Older adults average a score of 5.6. The college-age score is a bit below 5. Of course, to determine that your score is not transient, you need to do this exercise more than once, over the course of a few months.

Text 5

TAL BEN-SHAHAR, HAPPIER: LEARN THE SECRETS TO DAILY JOY AND LASTING FULFILLMENT (LONDON: MCGRAW-HILL, 2008), PP. IX–X

In the United States, rates of depression are ten times higher today than they were in the 1960s, and the average age for the onset of depression is fourteen and a half compared to twenty-nine and a half in 1960. A study conducted in American colleges tells us that nearly 45 percent of students were "so depressed that they had difficulty functioning." Other countries are following in the footsteps of the United States. In 1957, 52 percent in Britain said that they were very happy, compared to 36 percent in 2005—despite the fact that the British have tripled their wealth over the last half century. With the rapid growth in the Chinese economy comes a rapid growth in the number of adults and children who experience anxiety and depression. According to the Chinese Health Ministry, "The mental health status of our country's children and youths is indeed worrying."

While levels of material prosperity are on the rise, so are levels of depression. Even though our generation—in most Western countries as well as in an increasing number of places in the East—is wealthier than previous generations, we are not happier for it. A leading scholar in the field of positive psychology, Mihaly Csikszentmihalyi, asks a simple question with a complex answer: "If we are so rich, why aren't we happy ?"

TAL BEN-SHAHAR, PHD

Noted teacher of positive psychology. Ben-Shahar currently teaches at the Interdisciplinary Center, Herzliya, Israel. He taught the largest course at Harvard University on positive psychology, and he consults and lectures around the world on the topics of leadership, education, ethics, happiness, self-esteem, resilience, goal setting, and mindfulness. He is the author of the international best sellers *Happier* and *Being Happy*, which have been translated into 25 languages.

Text 6
TIKUNEI ZOHAR 22 📖

וְאַתְוָון בְּשִׂמְחָ"ה אִיהִי מַחֲשָׁבָ"ה.

The letters forming the Hebrew word *"besim-chah"* (with joy) are the same letters that spell *"machshavah"* (thought).

TIKUNEI ZOHAR

An appendix to the *Zohar*, the seminal work of kabbalah (Jewish mysticism). *Tikunei Zohar* consists mostly of seventy kabbalistic expositions on the opening verse of the Torah. It was first printed in Mantua in 1558.

HEDONIC TREADMILL

Text 7

RABBI BACHYA IBN PAKUDAH, *CHOVOT HALEVAVOT,*
INTRODUCTION TO *SHAAR HABECHINAH*

וּמָשָׁלָם בְּזֶה לְתִינוֹק, שֶׁמְּצָאוֹ אִישׁ אֶחָד מֵאַנְשֵׁי הַחֶסֶד
בַּמִּדְבָּר, וְחָמַל עָלָיו, וַיַּאַסְפֵהוּ אֶל בֵּיתוֹ, וַיְגַדְּלֵהוּ, וַיַּאֲכִילֵהוּ,
וַיַּלְבִּשֵׁהוּ, וַיִּתְנַדֵּב עָלָיו בְּכָל הַטּוֹב לוֹ, עַד שֶׁהִשְׂכִּיל וְהֵבִין
אוֹפַנֵּי דַּרְכֵי טוֹבָתוֹ.

וְאַחַר כֵּן שָׁמַע הָאִישׁ הַהוּא עַל אָסִיר שֶׁנָּפַל בְּיַד שׂוֹנְאוֹ,
וְהִגִּיעֵהוּ אֶל תַּכְלִית הַצַּעַר, וְהָרָעֵב, וְהֶעָרוֹם יָמִים רַבִּים,
וְנִכְמְרוּ רַחֲמָיו עַל צַעֲרוֹ, וּפִיֵּיס לְשׂוֹנְאוֹ, עַד שֶׁהִתִּירוֹ וּמָחַל לוֹ
אֶת דָּמָיו, וַיַּאַסְפֵהוּ הָאִישׁ אֶל בֵּיתוֹ, וְהֵיטִיב לוֹ בְּמִקְצָת הַטּוֹב
אֲשֶׁר הֵיטִיב בּוֹ לַתִּינוֹק.

RABBI BACHYA IBN PAKUDAH
11TH CENTURY

Moral philosopher and author. Ibn
Pakudah lived in Muslim Spain, but
little else is known about his life.
Chovot Halevavot (Duties of the Heart),
his major work, was intended to be a
guide for attaining spiritual perfection.
Originally written in Judeo-Arabic
and published in 1080, it was later
translated into Hebrew and published
in 1161 by Judah ibn Tibbon, a scion
of the famous family of translators.
Ibn Pakudah had a strong influence
on Jewish pietistic literature.

A parable:

There was once an infant found in the desert by a kindhearted individual. This benevolent person took pity on the child, carried him home, brought him up, fed him, clothed him, and provided him generously with all that was good, until the child was old enough to understand and comprehend the many benefits he had received.

The same benefactor heard of someone who had fallen into the hands of his enemy and had for a long time been treated with extreme cruelty, starved, and kept naked. The benevolent person appeased the enemy and convinced him to free the prisoner and forgive his debt. The kind individual brought the man to his home, but the kindness provided to this man was a fraction of the kindness shown to the infant.

Text 8

MIDRASH, *KOHELET RABAH* 1:13

אֵין אָדָם יוֹצֵא מִן הָעוֹלָם וַחֲצִי תַּאֲוָתוֹ בְּיָדוֹ.
אֶלָּא אִן אִית לֵיהּ מְאָה, בָּעֵי לְמֶעְבַּד יַתְהוֹן תַּרְתֵּין מָאוָון. וְאִן אִית לֵיהּ תַּרְתֵּי מָאוָון, בָּעֵי לְמֶעְבַּד יַתְהוֹן אַרְבְּעָה מְאָה.

We don't manage to leave this world with even half of our desires fulfilled.

When we have one hundred, we want to turn it into two hundred; when we have two hundred, we want to make of it four hundred.

KOHELET RABAH

A Midrashic text on the Book of Ecclesiastes. Midrash is the designation of a particular genre of rabbinic literature. The term "Midrash" is derived from the root *d-r-sh*, which means "to search," "to examine," and "to investigate." This particular Midrash provides textual exegeses and develops and illustrates moral principles. It was first published in Pesaro, Italy, in 1519, together with 4 other Midrashic works on the other 4 biblical *Megilot*.

Questions for Discussion

1. What is the cause for this human trait?

2. What are the benefits of this trait?

3. What are its drawbacks?

THE HABIT OF GRATITUDE

Text 9

RABBI SHALOM DOVBER SCHNEERSOHN,
SEFER HAMAAMARIM 5659, P. 5

כְּשֶׁמְדַבֵּר דִּבְרֵי אַהֲבָה, שֶׁהַדִּיבּוּר מְקַבֵּל אָז מִמְּדַת אַהֲבָה
שֶׁבְּנַפְשׁוֹ, הִנֵּה אָנוּ רוֹאִין שֶׁהַדִּיבּוּר מוֹסִיף אוֹר בְּהָאַהֲבָה,
שֶׁעַל יְדֵי שֶׁמְדַבֵּר בָּהּ מֵאִיר בּוֹ הָאוֹר הָאַהֲבָה בְּיוֹתֵר וּמִתְפָּעֵל
בְּיוֹתֵר בְּנַפְשׁוֹ בְּאַהֲבָה וְחִיבָּה לְהַדָּבָר הַהוּא . . .
וְכֵן הוּא בְּכָל הַמִּדּוֹת: כְּשֶׁאֵינָם בָּאִים בְּדִּיבּוּר, יִתְקַטֵּן וְיִתְמַעֵט
הִתְפַּעֲלוּת הַמִּדּוֹת עַד שֶׁמִּתְעַלְּמִים לְגַמְרֵי. וּלְהֵיפָךְ עַל יְדֵי
שֶׁבָּאִים בְּדִּיבּוּר, מִתְרַבִּים וּמִתְרַחֲבִים בְּיוֹתֵר.

When a person pours feelings of love into words, the act of speaking these words fuels and intensifies the love. Through speaking about it, the emotional energy radiates with more passion, and the person is aroused with more love and fondness for the beloved. . . .

The same applies to all emotions: When they are not expressed through speech, they are reduced until they completely dissipate. When they are expressed verbally, they augment and grow considerably.

Text 10a
DEUTERONOMY 26:8–10

וַיּוֹצִאֵנוּ ה' מִמִּצְרַיִם בְּיָד חֲזָקָה וּבִזְרֹעַ נְטוּיָה וּבְמֹרָא גָּדֹל, וּבְאֹתוֹת וּבְמֹפְתִים.
וַיְבִאֵנוּ אֶל הַמָּקוֹם הַזֶּה, וַיִּתֶּן לָנוּ אֶת הָאָרֶץ הַזֹּאת אֶרֶץ זָבַת חָלָב וּדְבָשׁ.
וְעַתָּה הִנֵּה הֵבֵאתִי אֶת רֵאשִׁית פְּרִי הָאֲדָמָה אֲשֶׁר נָתַתָּה לִי ה'.

G-d brought us out from Egypt with a strong hand and with an outstretched arm, with great awe, and with miraculous signs and wonders.

He brought us to this place, and He gave us this land, a land flowing with milk and honey.

Now, behold, I have brought the first of the fruit of the ground that You, G-d, have given to me.

Text 10b
IBID., VERSE 11

וְשָׂמַחְתָּ בְכָל הַטּוֹב אֲשֶׁר נָתַן לְךָ ה' אֱלֹקֶיךָ וּלְבֵיתֶךָ.

And you shall rejoice in all the good that G-d has given you and your family.

Text 11

MIDRASH, *TANCHUMA*, KI TAVO 1 (ℹ️)

צָפָה מֹשֶׁה בְּרוּחַ הַקּוֹדֶשׁ וְרָאָה שֶׁבֵּית הַמִּקְדָשׁ עָתִיד לֵיחָרֵב וְהַבִּכּוּרִים עֲתִידִין לִיפָּסֵק, עָמַד וְהִתְקִין לְיִשְׂרָאֵל שֶׁיִהְיוּ מִתְפַּלְלִין שְׁלֹשָׁה פְּעָמִים בְּכָל יוֹם.

Moses foresaw that the Temple would be destroyed and the offering of the first fruits would cease. He therefore ordained that the Jewish people should pray three times a day.

TANCHUMA

A Midrashic work bearing the name of Rabbi Tanchuma, a 4th-century Talmudic sage quoted often in this work. "Midrash" is the designation of a particular genre of rabbinic literature usually forming a running commentary on specific books of the Bible. *Tanchuma* provides textual exegeses, expounds upon the biblical narrative, and develops and illustrates moral principles. *Tanchuma* is unique in that many of its sections commence with a halachic discussion, which subsequently leads into nonhalachic teachings.

Text 12

SIDDUR, PRAYER UPON RISING IN THE MORNING (ℹ️)

מוֹדֶה אֲנִי לְפָנֶיךָ מֶלֶךְ חַי וְקַיָם, שֶׁהֶחֱזַרְתָּ בִּי נִשְׁמָתִי בְּחֶמְלָה. רַבָּה אֱמוּנָתֶךָ.

I thank You, living and eternal King, for mercifully restoring my soul within me. Your faithfulness is great.

SIDDUR

The siddur is the Jewish prayer book. It was originally developed by the sages of the Great Assembly in the 4th century BCE, and later reconstructed by Rabban Gamliel after the destruction of the Second Temple. Various authorities continued to add prayers, from then until contemporary times. It includes praise of G-d, requests for personal and national needs, selections of the Bible, and much else. Various Jewish communities have slightly different versions of the siddur.

Text 13

ROBERT A. EMMONS, *GRATITUDE WORKS!*
(NEW YORK: WILEY, 2013), PP. 23–24

In 1998 my colleague Mike McCullough and I designed a program of research to examine the effect of a gratitude practice on psychological and physical well-being. In our first study, we randomly assigned college student participants one of three tasks. . . . They either briefly described, in a single sentence, five things they were grateful for (the gratitude condition), five hassles (the hassles condition), or five events or circumstances that affected them (events condition). Hassles are relatively minor, everyday stressful circumstances such as not being able to find a babysitter, dealing with the rising price of gas, doing laundry, misplacing one's wallet. The time frame for each of these was the past week. Participants completed these exercises along with a variety of other measures of health and happiness once per week for ten consecutive weeks. . . .

The results were quite striking. . . . Participants in the gratitude condition felt better about their life as a whole and were more optimistic about the future than participants in either of the other control conditions. To put it into numbers, they were a full 25 percent happier than the other participants. Those in the gratitude condition reported fewer health complaints and even spent more time exercising. . . . Something as simple as counting blessings once a week resulted in significant emotional and health benefits.

ROBERT EMMONS, PHD
1958–

Professor of psychology. Emmons teaches at the University of California, Davis, and is a leading scientific expert on the psychology of gratitude. Emmons is the founding editor in chief of *The Journal of Positive Psychology* and the author of multiple volumes on the subject of gratitude, including *Thanks! How Practicing Gratitude Can Make You Happier.*

CONCLUSION

Exercise 1.3

1. On a scale of 1–10, how proficient am I at being grateful for the things I have?

2. What do I find most challenging about being grateful and expressing gratitude?

3. What piece of advice can I give myself to overcome this challenge?

4. In what way can I grow over the course of the next month in terms of feeling and expressing more gratitude?

Key Points

1. Happiness leads to success in many areas of life, because:

   a) It is easier to accomplish difficult tasks from a state of enthusiasm and happiness.

   b) While we are blessed with many talents and strengths, their full power often remains dormant. Joy drives our potential to flow outward.

   c) When we are happy, we create joy in the divine realm. This supernal ecstasy results in the flow of increased blessings.

2. The letters forming the Hebrew word *besimchah* (with joy) are the same letters that spell *machshavah* (thought). Happiness is a product of our thought processes and attitudes—not our circumstances.

3. Abundance and success do not necessarily lead to more happiness, because:

   a) When we have been surrounded by a superabundance of blessings since our youth, we tend not to notice them.

   b) Furthermore, when we obtain something new, we experience a spike of joy. But as we quickly adapt to the fresh circumstance, the joy withers away. This is why humans have an unquenchable thirst for more—we crave a repeat of that temporary spike of joy.

4. When emotions are not verbally expressed, they are diminished and they dissipate. When they are verbally expressed, they flourish and are amplified. By focusing on and talking about the blessings in our lives, we foster happy emotions; by focusing less on what we are missing, we allow our negative feelings to dissipate.

5. Ritualizing gratitude at fixed intervals allows us to reap happiness from that which we have. Judaism has a built-in system of rituals that facilitates a steady expression of gratitude for all of the blessings in our lives.

6. We ought to be grateful not only for the gifts we have, but also for the fact that they are provided by someone who cares. Realizing that G-d loves us and cares for us is, perhaps, an even greater source of happiness than the gifts themselves.

APPENDIX
AFFLUENCE AND HAPPINESS

Text 14

SUNIYA S. LUTHAR, "THE CULTURE OF AFFLUENCE: PSYCHOLOGICAL COSTS OF MATERIAL WEALTH," *CHILD DEVELOPMENT* 74:6 (2003)

One of the first empirical studies to provide a glimpse into problems of affluent youth was a comparative investigation of low-income, urban 10th graders and their upper socioeconomic status (SES), suburban counterparts. . . . The sample included 264 suburban students who were mostly from Caucasian, white-collar families, and 224 inner-city youth who were predominantly minority and of low SES. . . . Affluent youth reported significantly higher levels of anxiety across several domains, and greater depression. They also reported significantly higher substance use than inner-city students, consistently indicating more frequent use of cigarettes, alcohol, marijuana, and other illicit drugs.

SUNIYA SUNANDA LUTHAR, PHD

Professor of psychology. Luthar is currently at Arizona State University and is professor emerita at Columbia University's Teachers College. Her books include *Children in Poverty, Developmental Psychopathology,* and *Resilience and Vulnerability in Childhood.* She served as associate editor of the journal *Developmental Psychology,* and currently serves as associate editor for the journal *Development and Psychopathology.*

MATTER OF PERSPECTIVE

Text 15

CHANIE GORKIN, "WORST DAY EVER?" WWW.POETRYNATION.COM

Today was the absolute worst day ever

And don't try to convince me that

There's something good in every day

Because, when you take a closer look,

This world is a pretty evil place.

Even if

Some goodness does shine through once in a while

Satisfaction and happiness don't last.

And it's not true that

It's all in the mind and heart

Because

True happiness can be attained

Only if one's surroundings are good.

It's not true that good exists

I'm sure you can agree that

The reality

Creates

My attitude

It's all beyond my control

And you'll never in a million years hear me say that

Today was a very good day.

Now read it from bottom to top, the other way,

And see what I really feel about my day

CHANIE GORKIN
1998–

In 2015, when Chanie Gorkin was in eleventh grade at Beth Rivkah High School in Crown Heights (Brooklyn, NY), she wrote a poem for a school assignment. The poem subsequently went viral on social media.

HEDONIC TREADMILL

Text 16

SONJA LYUBOMIRSKY, *THE HOW OF HAPPINESS*
(NEW YORK: PENGUIN PRESS, 2008), P. 140

As we acquire income and consumer goods that we desire, (e.g., gadgets, computers, cars, homes, or swimming pools), our aspirations simply rise to the same degree, thereby trapping us in a hedonic treadmill.

In one study that surveyed people over a thirty-six-year period, respondents were asked how much income was needed by a family of four to "get along." The higher the person's income, the more they estimated was required for a family of four. Remarkably, the estimate for "get along" income increased almost exactly to the same degree as did actual income, suggesting that the more you have, the more you think you "need."

SONJA LYUBOMIRSKY, PHD

Leading expert in positive psychology. Dr. Lyubomirsky is professor of psychology at the University of California, Riverside. Originally from Russia, she received her PhD in social/personality psychology from Stanford University. Her research on the possibility of permanently increasing happiness has been honored with various grants, including a million-dollar grant from the National Institute of Mental Health. She has authored *The How of Happiness* and, more recently, *The Myths of Happiness*.

ADDITIONAL READINGS

A LIGHTNING ROD TO THE SPIRITUAL REALMS

Rabbi Shloma Majeski

The positive potential of *simchah* is highlighted by the Maggid of Mezeritch's interpretation[1] of the teaching in *Pirkei Avos*:[2] "Know what is above you." Literally, the *Mishnah* is teaching us always to be conscious that, allegorically speaking, in the spiritual realms there exists an eye that sees everything we do, an ear that hears everything we say, and a hand that records everything that takes place.

The Maggid of Mezeritch extended the meaning of this teaching. He would say: "Know that everything above," all that transpires in the spiritual realm, is "from you," dependent on your conduct. Each of us influences what goes on in the spiritual realm. And so, when a person is happy, he not only lifts the spirits of the people around him, but he generates joy in the spiritual realm as well.

Let us explain the dynamics at work: One of the most fundamental concepts discussed in the *Kabbalah* and in *Chassidic* philosophy is the interrelationship between the spiritual realm and our material reality. The *Zohar*[3] states that our material world parallels the spiritual realm. It is like a mirror reflecting an object or person before it. When one sees a person moving a hand in the mirror, one realizes that standing in front of the mirror is an actual person who is moving his hand. Even when we cannot see the person himself, the image in the mirror is sufficient.

Similar concepts apply with regard to the interrelation between the physical and spiritual realms. Our physical realm mirrors spiritual reality. Everything taking place on our plane has a parallel within and gives us an understanding of the workings of spiritual existence. Although we may not be directly conscious of spiritual reality, we can understand many things about it from the parallels we see in our world.

This concept also has a deeper dimension. When we are speaking of a mirror and a person, we are talking about two separate, unrelated entities; one merely reflects the other. With regard to the spiritual and the physical, it is not that the spiritual realm is one form of existence and the physical realm another, with G-d creating them to correspond to each other. In this instance, the two are more closely related. Our material existence is merely an extension of the spiritual.

We do not have a proper analogy to illustrate this. One of the closest examples we have is the relationship between the soul and the body. Our Sages tell us[4] that just as the soul fills up the body, G-d fills up the world. Therefore, if we want to develop a better understanding of the interaction between G-d and the world or in different words, the spiritual realm and the physical realm we can focus on the relationship between the body and the soul, the *neshamah* and the *guf*.

The activity of a person's soul is reflected in his body. If a person is anxious, you can tell by looking at him. One look at his eyes and his facial expression tells the whole story. The same is true

RABBI SHLOMA MAJESKI

Scholar of Chasidic philosophy. Rabbi Majeski serves as the dean of Machon Chana Women's Institute in Crown Heights, Brooklyn, and is the author of *The Chassidic Approach to Joy* and *A Tzaddik and His Students*.

1 Cited in *Or HaTorah al Aggados Chazal*, p. 112b.
2 2:1; See *In the Paths of Our Fathers*, p. 43 (Kehot, N.Y., 1994).
3 I, 38a, 205b; c.f. *Berachos* 58a; *Zohar* I, 197a, III, 176b.

4 *Berachos* 10a.

when he is angry and when he is sad. And surely this is true when he is happy. When a person is truly *b'simchah*, his face radiates joy. For what a person experiences internally expresses itself in his physical form.

It has to be this way. The soul and the body function as a single entity. Although they have different sources, as long as a person is alive, his body and his soul share a single identity, and the body expresses what is happening within the person's soul.

A similar concept applies with regard to the interaction between the spiritual realm and the physical realm. When we see something happening in the physical realm—for example, it is raining—what we are seeing is, in essence, a reflection of what is taking place in the spiritual realm. In the spiritual realm, there is a great outpouring of kindness, and that becomes manifest in our world as rain.

And this holds true for all the events that take place in our world, a snowfall, a wind, an earthquake. From the most unusual to the most mundane, everything that occurs in our world is a result and a reflection of something that is taking place in the spiritual realm.

There is, however, a dual nature to the dynamic of causation. Just as what happens in our material realm is a result of what is taking place in the spiritual realm, what takes place in the spiritual realm can be determined by the events of our world. This is the meaning of the teaching of the Maggid of Mezeritch mentioned above. He explained that the *Mishnah* in *Pirkei Avos* is telling us to: "Know that what is above," the goings on in the spiritual realm, "is from you," dependent on our conduct. We mortals determine the nature of the influences active in the spiritual realm.

Why does man have this potential? Because "man was created in the image of G-d."[5] Needless to say, this does not mean that G-d has the same physical form as man; G-d is infinite and He has no body or shape whatsoever.[6] *Chassidus* and *Kabbalah*, nevertheless, explain that

there is a spiritual counterpart to all our bodily features. G-d does not possess eyes, but He possesses a means of perception that operates in a more complete way than we could possibly comprehend in a manner comparable to our power of sight. He does not possess a mouth, but He possesses a means of expression that corresponds to our power of speech. Similarly, every element of our being has its counterpart in the spiritual realm.

And so, when we move our hands, we are also activating the spiritual counterpart of our hands. Everything we do, all of our activities and everything that goes on in our lives in this physical realm, has an effect in the spiritual world.

In particular, there are three phases in this cycle: our deeds, the effect that activity has in the spiritual realm, and the reflection of the activity within the spiritual realm in our material world.

For example, when someone is not well, G-d forbid, and a friend decides to give charity in his merit, the friend's gift activates G-d's attribute of *chessed* (kindness) in the spiritual realm. This in turn becomes manifest in our world in the improvement of the sick person's condition.

The Baal Shem Tov explains a similar idea,[7] commenting on the verse,[8] "G-d is your shadow." Literally, the verse tells us that just as a shadow protects us from the sun, G-d shields us. The Baal Shem Tov, however, offers an extended interpretation, explaining that just as a shadow mirrors a person's actions, the nature of the influence that flows from G-d to the world will be a reflection of the nature of our activities.

This same idea is reflected in the Maggid's interpretation of the *Mishnah*, "Know what is above you," that "what is above" is dependent on "you." Everything that happens in the spiritual realm is determined by our behavior, because whatever we do activates the counterpart in the spiritual realm. And that spiritual activity brings about changes in our world. When I show compassion to another person that motivates G-d to show compassion.

5 *Genesis* 1:27.
6 See *Rambam, Mishneh Torah, Hilchos Yesodei HaTorah* 1:7–12.

7 *Keser Shem Tov, Hosafos* 60.
8 *Tehillim* 121:5.

Let us take another example of this idea. When two people marry, their union reflects the creation of a similar bond in the spiritual realm. For within the spiritual realm, there are two aspects: one referred to as *Malchus*, which reflects the feminine dimension, and another, referred to as *Zaer Anpin*, which reflects the masculine dimension. When a man and woman marry, they bring about a union between these attributes in the spiritual realm. This union, in turn, encourages the flow of positive influence to our material world.

Similar concepts apply with regard to speech. Everything said in our realm activates a counterpart in the spiritual realm. So when we say good things, positive influences are generated in the spiritual realm. And if, G-d forbid, we say unfavorable things, negative influences are generated.

This is one of the explanations of our Sages' statement,[9] "Do not regard the blessing of an ordinary person lightheartedly." We know that blessings given by a *tzaddik*, a righteous person, can bring about miraculous changes in our lives. But the truth is that whenever anyone gives a blessing, the blessing has power. For the person's statements create effects not only in our world, but in the spiritual realm. When he speaks words of blessing, he is actually generating a blessing in the spiritual realm. And that blessing can effect change in our world.

(The converse is also true. And for this reason, the Torah forbids cursing another person. For this can also, Heaven forbid, have an effect.)

Our thoughts also effect changes in the spiritual realm. In this world, thought has no apparent effect, but the dynamic of spiritual causation is such that every expression of our being, be it thought, speech, or action, creates a spiritual effect. And that spiritual effect can later bring about changes in our world. Indeed, we find that intense thought about another person has often produced very positive effects.[10]

There was once a *chassid* whose son was very ill. After a prolonged illness, the physicians finally told him that there was no hope. There was nothing more they could do; they did not know if the child would live.

The *chassid* was devastated. He hurried to Lubavitch and approached the Tzemach Tzedek, the third Lubavitcher Rebbe. Overcome with grief, he could barely mouth his request for a blessing.

The Rebbe answered him briefly in Yiddish: *Tracht gut, vet zein gut.* "Think positively, and the outcome will be good."[11]

As the *chassid* walked out of the Rebbe's room, he pulled himself together. He put himself in a state of mind that radiated utter confidence. He knew G-d could help him and cure his son. And he believed that this would happen.

When he came home, he was told that there had been a sudden change in his son's condition. The physicians had no explanation, but the child had definitely taken a turn for the better. When the *chassid* inquired, he was told that the change took place at exactly the time that he visited the Rebbe.

The story shows us that thinking positively produces two effects:

a) when a person is in high spirits, he functions better; and

b) thinking positively itself brings about positive change. By envisioning good in one's mind, one creates positive spiritual influence that enables that picture to materialize.

This is the basis of the *Chassidic* explanation of one of the most fundamental principles of Judaism, *bitochon*. *Bitochon* means confidence and trust that G-d will help. That G-d can help us at any given time is a point of faith, and one that is very easy to accept. After all, if He is G-d, He is capable of doing anything He wants. *Bitochon* means more than that; it expresses our trust and confidence that He will actually help.

Bitochon is not euphoric escapism; it does not absolve an individual of taking responsibility for his future, and acting accordingly. It means that as a person acts, he realizes that his efforts are dependent on G-d's providence, and he relies on G-d and trusts Him totally.

---

9 *Berachos* 7a.

10 *Likkutei Dibburim*, Vol. I, p. 6 (English translation).

11 See *Sefer HaSichos 5687*, p. 113 and sources cited there; explained in *Likkutei Sichos, Parshas Shemos 5751*.

Besides giving a person the confidence and inner strength to face challenges, this approach also generates positive Divine influence. When a person trusts and relies on G-d, G-d creates situations that will allow him to use his energies in positive and beneficial ways.[12] Our positive thoughts serve as catalysts that promote favorable circumstances for us.

Now we can appreciate the importance of *simchah*. When a person is genuinely happy and sees things in a positive way, he creates *simchah* in the spiritual realm, for "everything that happens above is dependent on you."

The joy that is activated in the spiritual realm is not self-contained, but flows outward, bringing joy to many others in our world. When we are *b'simchah*, in both a physical and spiritual way, we bring joy to ourselves, our families, and all the people around us.

As we explained in the previous chapter, this joy is not a passive potential. On the contrary, "joy breaks through barriers," destroying all the obstacles and difficulties that may present themselves.

When a person is happy, he stands above all his personal limitations and weaknesses. He can do things that he ordinarily could not do. He can forgive his worst enemy. His joy generates inner energy that breaks through and shatters any barrier that stands in his way.

When a person creates joy in the spiritual realm, the same thing happens. In the spiritual realm, there are also limitations and barriers, for G-d has chosen to establish a natural order through which He controls our world. Just as there are rules of nature that govern the physical world around us, there are principles of causality that govern the effects produced by our conduct. For as above, everything we do generates an effect in the spiritual realm that in turn produces an effect within our world. On the most general level, these rules follow the following principle:[13] When a person does good, he receives benefits that enable him to continue in this path. If he fails to do good, he will suffer difficulties that make it obvious to him that he should change his ways. These are the patterns of causation that G-d chose to establish in the spiritual realm.

Nevertheless, when a person is *b'simchah*, he creates joy in the spiritual realm; G-d Himself is, so to speak, also *b'simchah*. This causes G-d to reveal a transcendent dimension that is not bound by the laws of causation mentioned above. In simple terms, this means that G-d will give great blessings and make positive things happen, even though normally these blessings would not be granted.

When, G-d forbid, there is a situation where something is not going right, we must realize that this is a result of the laws of causation that G-d established. We must, however, also realize that by radiating *simchah*, we can awaken *simchah* above, and effect a radical change in the situation before us.

This demonstrates the power our joy possesses. With *simchah* we can change the makeup of the spiritual realm, and in this manner, bring blessing and all forms of good to ourselves, our families, and to the entire Jewish people.

The Chassidic Approach to Joy (New York: Sichos in English, 1996), pp. 97–105
Reprinted with permission of the publisher

---

12 See *Sefer HaIkkarim*, Discourse 4, Chapter 47.

13 See *Rambam, Hilchos Teshuvah* 9:1.

CELEBRATING LIFE

Rabbi Jonathan Sacks

NOT TAKING LIFE FOR GRANTED

It happened on our honeymoon. We had decided to go to Switzerland. I had always wanted to see the mountains, to climb high and breathe the chill air. It was beautiful in theory, and it was no less lovely when we arrived. The valley was bathed in light. The mountains looked down on us in majesty.

The next day we got ourselves ready for a climb and went outside. The mountains had disappeared, the one thing we had not reckoned on had happened. It was raining. The mountains had retreated behind a covering of low cloud. Gamely, for a few days, we climbed, wrapped in mist and dampness through which nothing could be seen. Eventually we decided it was too miserable. 'Let's try somewhere else', we said. So we hitchhiked down to Italy where we found the sun.

We stayed in a little coastal town called Paestum, an ancient place with some fine Roman ruins. And the sea. Rarely had it seemed more inviting than just then, after the gloom of Switzerland. The trouble was . . . I could not swim. It was not that I had never tried, but somehow I just could not get the hang of it.

As we sat on the beach and looked out across the water, however, I realized that the shore must be sloping very gently indeed. People were far out into the sea and yet the water was only coming up to their knees. It looked safe just to walk out, and so it was. I walked out to where

RABBI LORD JONATHAN SACKS, PHD
1948–

Former chief rabbi of the United Kingdom. Rabbi Sacks attended Cambridge University and received his doctorate from King's College, London. A prolific and influential author, his books include *Will We Have Jewish Grandchildren?* and *The Dignity of Difference*. He received the Jerusalem Prize in 1995 for his contributions to enhancing Jewish life in the Diaspora, was knighted and made a life peer in 2005, and became Baron Sacks of Aldridge in 2009.

I had seen people standing just a few minutes before and the water gently lapped against my knees. Then I started walking back to the shore. That was when it happened. Within minutes I found myself out of my depth.

How it happened I am not sure. There must have been a dip in the sand. I had missed it on my way out, but walked straight into it on my way back. I tried to swim. I failed. I kept going under. I looked around for some possible source of rescue. The other people bathing were a long way away—too far to reach me, I thought, too far to even hear. Besides which, we were in Italy. As I went under for the fifth time, I remember thinking two thoughts: 'What a way to begin a honeymoon!' and 'What's the Italian for "help"?'

It is difficult to recapture the panic I felt. Clearly someone rescued me, or I would not be writing now. At the time, however, it did seem like the end. As far as I can reconstruct that moment in my memory, I had already reconciled myself to drowning when someone, seeing me thrashing about, swam over, took hold of me and brought me to the shore. He deposited me, almost unconscious, at the feet of my wife. I was too shocked to do or say anything. I never found out his name. Somewhere there is someone to whom I owe my life.

It changed my life. For years afterwards, I would wake in the morning conscious of the fact that but for a miracle, I would not be here. Somehow that made everything easier to bear. Our life has had difficult times. It has had moments of crisis. Public life is full of stress and not everyone who lives it has a thick skin. People often ask me, 'How do you bear it?' The answer is simple. That day, on an Italian beach, I learned that life, which I so nearly lost, had been given back to me. It is difficult to feel depressed when you remember fairly constantly that life is a gift.

This is why, every morning, I say with real feeling the traditional Jewish prayer on waking up: 'I thank you, living and everlasting King, for restoring my soul to me in compassion, great is your faithfulness.' Thank you G-d, for giving me back my life.

It was then that I realized something I should have understood long before. Faith is not a complex set of theological propositions. It is simpler and deeper than that. It is about not taking things for granted. It is a sustained discipline of meditation on the miracle of being. 'Not how the world is, but that it is, is the mystical,' said Wittgenstein. Not how we are, but *that* we are, is cause for wonder, and faith is the symphony on that theme.

We are here. We might not have been. Somehow that makes every day a celebration, for at the core of that mystical awareness is the discovery that life itself is the breath of G-d....

GIVING THANKS

Oliver James's book *Britain on the Couch* tells a depressing story. Quite simply, we have become more depressed. Twenty-five-year-olds today are between three and ten times more likely than their parents to have suffered some form of depressive illness. We have become, in James's phrase, a 'low serotonin society'—serotonin being the chemical register in the brain of general states of well-being.

Depressive illness is tragic and needs serious medical attention. James's book though, raises a larger question. Can there be, he asks, something in our culture that has given rise to this sudden increase? Admittedly, it will not explain individual cases, only trends, but the question is real and has a long history. Just as there can be a physically unhealthy society, so there can be a psychologically unhealthy one.

James argues that part of the blame lies with the chaos of intimate relationships, especially in the breakdown of the stable two-parent family. No less important, though, are the kinds of emotions favoured by a commercial, competitive society. 'Advanced capitalism,' he says bluntly, 'makes money out of misery and dissatisfaction.'

Paraded daily before us on our television screens and in our newspapers are images of perfection, people who are more beautiful, thin, clever, or attractive that we will ever be. Ours is a culture of artificially created longings. We are invited to resolve the tension by buying this, or

wearing that, or going there. Unhappiness is good for business. It just happens to be bad for people.

At this stage, the religious believer wants to protest that it need not be like this at all. It is not a matter of opposing capitalism and all its works. It has, after all, made possible much of what makes life more dignified for more people than ever before. Economic growth and technological progress have allowed us to treat disease, conquer absolute poverty and extend the possibilities of travel and communication. Never before has so much been available to so many. The best cure for nostalgia is to imagine going to the dentist in any previous historical era. There is nothing wrong in celebrating the achievements of advanced societies.

There is, however, one spiritual discipline which religion once gave us and which we still need. It is the simple act of saying 'thank you' to G-d. There are prayers in which we ask G-d for the things we do not have, but there are others in which we simply thank G-d for the things we do have: family, friends, life itself with its counterpoint of pleasure and pain, the sheer exaltation of knowing that we are here when we might not have been.

To thank G-d is to know that I do not have less because my neighbor has more. I am not less worthwhile because someone else is more successful. Through prayer I know that I am valued for what I am. I learn to cherish what I have, rather than be diminished by what I do not have. A third-century rabbi put it simply. 'Who is rich?' he asked. Not one who has much, but 'one who rejoices in what he has'.

There is no single route to happiness, just as there is no single cure for depression, but the daily discipline of thanking G-d for what we are and what we enjoy is the most ancient form of what is today called 'cognitive therapy'. Making a blessing over life is the best way of turning life into a blessing.

Celebrating Life: Finding Happiness in Unexpected Places (London: Continuum International Publishing Group, 2003), pp. 7–9, 14–16
Reprinted with permission of the author

GRATITUDE

Rabbi Raphael Pelcovitz

David Pelcovitz, Phd

What is the origin of the name "Jew," *Yehudi*? Why are we not called "Hebrew," *Ivri*, or "Israelite," *Yisraeli,* as we were classified in earlier times? The reason, according to our teachers, is because the root of the name Yehudah is *hodaah,* to thank, to express gratitude. Judah was the fourth son of Leah and she felt a profound sense of gratitude when he was born. There was a tradition that Jacob was destined to have twelve sons, who would comprise the twelve tribes of Israel. Since Jacob had four wives, it was assumed that each wife would be allocated three sons.

When Leah gives birth to a fourth son, she is overwhelmed with a sense of thanksgiving:

> She conceived again, and bore a son and declared, "This time let me gratefully praise Hashem"; therefore she called his name Judah; then she stopped giving birth.[1]

RABBI RAPHAEL PELCOVITZ

Rabbi emeritus, author, and teacher. Rabbi Pelcovitz served as the pulpit rabbi and community leader of Congregation Kneseth Israel (the White Shul) in Far Rockaway, New York, for more than 50 years. He authored a number of books in which he presents ideas from Jewish thought in a compelling and comprehensible way. He also co-authored 2 books with his son, Dr. David Pelcovitz.

DAVID PELCOVITZ, PHD

Psychologist, teacher, and author. Dr. Pelcovitz, who received his PhD from the University of Pennsylvania, has published and lectured extensively on a variety of topics related to education, parenting, and mental health. He is currently the Straus Professor of Psychology and Education at the Azrieli Graduate School, Yeshiva University. His books include *Balanced Parenting* and *Life in the Balance*, both written in collaboration with his father, Rabbi Raphael Pelcovitz.

Rashi comments:

> "I have taken more than my share, so I now need to give thanks."

A Jew must always feel this same sense of gratitude to G-d, continually recognizing that he is the recipient of heavenly blessings. This attribute is the antithesis of a sense of entitlement. A Jew must acknowledge that he is a debtor who owes so much to his past—to his forebears and his progenitors; he is not a creditor to whom something is owed. This attribute of gratitude is reflected in his name, his identity, and shapes his essential character: *Yehudi.*

Another indication of the enormous importance that Jewish thought places on our obligation to express gratitude is the following *midrash*:

> In the future, all offerings will be abolished except for the thanksgiving-offering. All prayers will be abolished except for prayers of gratitude.[2]

Given the central role that offerings and prayer serve in Jewish life, this *midrash* is teaching us the central significance of gratitude. The need to express gratitude will remain even at a time that other spiritual duties and obligations will no longer be necessary.

Our Rabbis teach us that a key aspect of the experience of bringing the *korban todah* (thanksgiving-offering) is the social component. When one brought a thanksgiving-offering—which was offered after being saved from a life-threatening situation—he was required to bring 40 loaves of bread, 10 each of four different forms. One of each kind was given to the Kohen, leaving 36 loaves to be consumed within a time frame including that day and the ensuing night.

1 *Genesis* 29:35.
2 *Vayikra Rabbah* 9.

The medieval classic commentator on the Torah, the Sforno,[3] explains that this was to ensure that at the time that one expressed gratitude for his good fortune, one had no choice but to make this a social event. Included in this occasion was sharing one's food while recounting to others the story of the life-saving incident.

In *Alei Shur*,[4] Rabbi Wolbe further develops this interpersonal component of gratitude. He discusses the importance of overtly expressing feelings of gratitude to others as a means of fanning the flames of love and friendship between one Jew and another. He cites the Talmud[5] which states that if one gives bread as a gift to a child, it is important to inform the child's parents who gave the gift. As Rashi explains, identifying the source of this kindness evokes feelings of love and gratitude between Jews.

The need to express one's gratitude is also noted by secular thinkers. British novelist and academic C.S. Lewis said:

I think we delight to praise what we enjoy because the praise not merely expresses but completes the enjoyment; it is its appointed consummation.[6]

Gratitude has an individual, more personal, component. In addition to the need to overtly express feelings of appreciation to those who have been kind to us, we also have to internally nourish an emotional awareness of gratitude toward G-d. The only segment of the *Amidah* (or *Shemoneh Esrei*, the 19-blessing prayer recited three times a day) that can't be delegated to the *chazzan* during his repetition of the *Shemoneh Esrei* is *Modim*: the part of this prayer that focuses most directly on expression of gratitude to G-d for all that He has done for us as individuals and as a people. This is because when it comes to giving thanks to G-d, we can't delegate to others. Each individual has to articulate his own declaration of gratitude in a manner that fosters an internal recognition of gratitude.

Rabbi Wolbe also discusses this facet of gratitude, which is more related to individual as opposed to interpersonal growth. He elaborates on the *midrash*[7] that explains that Aharon, not Moshe, invoked the plagues that involved water and land. The reason for this was because it wasn't proper for Moshe to show any signs of ingratitude to the water that saved his life as an infant, or to the earth that allowed him to hide the Egyptian he killed when defending his fellow Jews. Obviously inanimate objects have no feelings that need protection. The reason why Moshe had to delegate these plagues to his brother was to develop in himself feelings of gratitude toward the vehicles of his salvation.

This aspect of gratitude was seen in a very concrete and moving way by those who visited Rabbi Yisroel Zev Gustman at Yeshivah Netzech Yisroel in Jerusalem. Rabbi Gustman always insisted on carefully caring for the trees and bushes in his garden, even though his students frequently offered to help him perform these seemingly menial gardening chores. He explained that during the war, he hid from the Nazis in a forest where the shelter of the bushes and the fruit of the trees repeatedly saved his life. He felt that caring for these trees and bushes was a necessary expression of gratitude to these instruments of his survival.

Further insight into the primary importance of the expression of gratitude is provided by the following analysis of Rabbi Joseph Soloveitchik regarding the connection between gratitude, prayer, and man's sustenance from nature.[8] In the Torah's discussion of the Creation, the following passages describe the creation of vegetation and precipitation:

Now all the plants of the field were not yet on the earth, and all the herbs of the field had not yet sprouted; for Hashem G-d had not sent rain upon the earth, and there was no man to work the soil.[9]

3 *Leviticus* 7:12.
4 Rabbi Shlomo Wolbe, *Alei Shur*, Volume II, p. 279.
5 *Beitzah* 16a.
6 Lewis, C.S. (1996). *Readings for Meditation and Reflection*. New York: HarperOne.
7 *Shemos Rabbah* 9:9.
8 Rabbi Hershel Schachter (1994). *Nefesh HaRav—Torah from Rabbi Joseph B. Soloveitchik*. Hoboken, NJ: Ktav.
9 *Genesis* 2:5.

Rashi, on this verse, points out that rain didn't come to earth until man was there to pray for it. In essence, Rashi says, the "switch" for rain is activated by prayer and gratitude, not the other way around:

Why didn't it rain? Because man wasn't there to work the land, and there was no one to recognize the benefit of rain. When man came and recognized that rain was a necessity for the world, he prayed for it and rain came down, allowing trees and grass to grow.

Rashi interprets the lack of rain and vegetation to the lack of recognition on anyone's part to acknowledge the goodness and beneficence of G-d. When Adam was created, he recognized and acknowledged the great blessing and benefit of rain. Subsequently, when Adam prays for rain, his prayers serve as a trigger for rain to fall and that results in the growth of vegetation. All this is alluded to in the word *siach ha'sadeh*—the plant of the field. The word *"siach,"* translated as vegetation of the field, refers not only to vegetation but also to prayer. We find this term in reference to Isaac's prayers, where the term *lasuach* is used.[10] The meaning of these verses, according to Rabbi Soloveitchik, is that since there was no concept of prayer in the world until the creation of man, there was no spark to ignite the force of rain. This phenomenon can only occur when man acknowledges and expresses his gratitude for this gift.

PSYCHOLOGICAL PERSPECTIVE

Secular thinkers also describe the central role that gratitude has in living a moral life. Cicero, the ancient Roman philosopher, described gratitude as a cornerstone of all values, writing that: *"Gratitude is not only the greatest of virtues, but the parent of all the others."*[11]

At first glance, being thankful does not logically seem to be of such central importance relative to the many other virtues for which people strive. Nevertheless, recent psychology research on the impact of building gratitude into one's life clearly confirms the importance of cultivating this trait. Studies have found numerous benefits that stem from building the capacity for gratitude into daily living. Those who regularly express gratitude are more likely to be forgiving, generous, agreeable and less likely to be narcissistic and selfish.[12] Research repeatedly confirms that those with high scores on measures of gratitude also score high on measures of happiness. In one study, 95 percent of individuals describe feeling happy when expressing gratitude and over 50 percent say that expressing gratitude made them feel *extremely happy.*[13]

From the viewpoint of parents and educators, a number of benefits result from teaching our children to be thankful. As a purely practical matter, when children express gratitude it makes it more likely that their benefactor will continue to act kindly toward them in the future. Perhaps more importantly, from the perspective of character education, the expression of gratitude also makes it more likely that the recipient will be generous to others.[14] Interestingly, this research finding suggests that a pathway to teaching our children to be giving and charitable is inculcating in them the value of *hakaras ha'tov,* gratitude. Perhaps by focusing their attention on thankfulness for what they receive, we develop their ability to give.

INGRATITUDE

A story was told to me (RP) by a congregant, regarding his father who was a prominent member of a Brooklyn synagogue many years ago:

His father was an extremely kind and generous man who did favors for countless people. He noticed that a fellow congregant, whom he considered a friend, was acting strangely toward him, conveying a general attitude of resentment. Troubled by this behavior he said

---

10 Ibid. 24:63.

11 Marcus Tullius Cicero, *Selected Works*, Penguin Classics (1960).

---

12 McCullough, M. & Emmons, R. (2004). *The Psychology of Gratitude*, Chapter 7, Oxford, UK: Oxford University Press.

13 Emmons R. & McCullough, M. (2003). Gratitude, optimism and health, counting blessings. *Journal of Personality and Social Psychology, 84,* p. 377.

14 Peterson & Stewart (1996). Antecedents and contexts of generativity. *Psychology and Aging, 11,* 21–33.

to him: "Reb Yankel, why are you angry at me? I haven't done you a favor yet!"

This congregant told me that he learned a great lesson from this episode: When doing a kindness for another, there is often a duality of emotions created between the recipient of a favor and the benefactor.

Researchers have found that most individuals find feelings of indebtedness to be unpleasant. Many individuals are uncomfortable with feeling dependent on others. A favor creates an inherent sense of discomfort; it forces one to reciprocate and feel obliged. The recipient is now a debtor, he owes his benefactor and that makes him uncomfortable, so he tries to minimize and belittle the favor. Rabbi Shimshon Dovid Pincus points out that the Hebrew expression for ingratitude—*kafui tov*—is related to the Hebrew word *kafah*, meaning to be forced or pressured. For example, the Rabbis tell us that if an individual resists fulfilling an obligation in a religious court, the court is authorized to pressure him until he acquiesces. The term for this is *kofim oso*—they pressure or force him. Similarly, when the Jews were given the Torah at Sinai and were reluctant, at first, to accept, the *Midrash* says *kafah aleihem*—G-d suspended the mountain over them, threatening to annihilate them unless they agreed. Based on this, Rabbi Pincus submits[15] that, frequently, when a favor is done for a person, he feels obligated and even pressured to pay back the debt of gratitude that he owes to his benefactor. This creates a sense of imbalance, an uncomfortable feeling of dependence fueled by a sense of indebtedness and a need to reciprocate. This character trait is traced by the Sages to the beginning of time and to Adam at Creation.

Instead of expressing gratitude when given the gift of Chavah, the first woman, Adam blames her when confronted by G-d after defying His command to not eat the fruit of the Tree of Knowledge. Adam's first line of defense when

accused of eating this fruit is to blame her by saying:

The woman whom You gave to be with me gave me of the fruit of the tree. . . .[16] The Talmud[17] comments on this episode by pointing out the irony of how swiftly gratitude can turn to ingratitude.

Rabbi Yechezkel Sarna[18] describes how a tendency toward ingratitude is built in as a default setting in the basic nature of man. He cites a *midrash* that explains why the word *adam* is used in the passage describing the punishment meted out to the generation that built the Tower of Bavel: *Hashem descended to look at the city and tower which the bnei Adam built.*[19] This *midrash* explains that the inherent nature of man includes, as mentioned above, this tendency toward a lack of gratitude. Instead of expressing eternal gratitude for having been saved from the deluge, this subsequent generation rebels against G-d. They build a tower, which our Sages explain was motivated by a desire to storm the heavens and prevent G-d from sending future destructive forces upon mankind. Apparently the innate sense of gratitude that one should feel toward his benefactor is tinged with an underlying sense of thanklessness. Therefore, one has to be very careful to not allow this innate tendency toward being a *kafui tov* to overtake him.

The following anecdote illustrates this tendency:

A grandmother is watching her grandchild play on the beach when a huge wave comes and washes him out to sea. She lifts her eyes to heaven and pleads, "Please, G-d, save my only grandson, bring him back!" A big wave washes the boy back onto the beach, good as new. The grandmother looks up to heaven and accusingly says: "He had a hat."

Our sense of gratitude is often incomplete. There is a tinge of the "ingrate" in us, because we somehow feel that what has been granted to us is incomplete.

15 *Tiferes Shimshon Al HaTorah, Chukas.*

16 *Genesis* 3:12.
17 *Avodah Zarah* 5a.
18 Rabbi Yechezkel Sarna, *Delillas Yechezkel.*
19 *Bereishis Rabbah* 38:9 (on *Genesis* 11:5).

Rabbi Yitzchak Hutner, reflecting the writings of the *Maharal* on the seriousness of ingratitude, writes of the seriousness of failing to be grateful:

When a person receives a benefit from his fellow, a seed of chesed is planted in his world. If the nature of chesed is functioning healthily and properly, this seed cannot but give rise to additional chesed. But if the person is an ingrate, it is as if he uproots the sprouting of chesed with his bare hands. Without a doubt, uprooting a planting of chesed is even more antithetical to the essence of chesed than is simply being uninvolved in matters of chesed. . . . An ingrate damages and destroys the very attribute of chesed. . . . One who is ungrateful to his fellow, it is as if he is ungrateful to G-d, because his denial is a response not just to the particular act of chesed that was done for him, but also to the attribute of chesed in the broadest sense.[20]

In light of this interpretation of ingratitude, it is not surprising to find the following statement made by the *Maharal*:

It is forbidden to do acts of chesed for one who will not respond with gratitude. For this reason, it didn't rain until man was created to pray for the rain.[21]

To the extent that ingratitude is viewed as heresy, the *Maharal's* position is understandable. One is not allowed to put an individual in a position where he is, in essence, ungrateful to G-d and simultaneously undermining one of the basic building blocks of humanity.

HABITUATION

The enemy of gratitude is habituation. The way the human brain works is that we quickly become accustomed to even the most spectacular of gifts.

I (DP) gave a paper at a beautiful resort in Hawaii. Surrounded by magnificent waterfalls, spectacular scenery, and unforgettable sunsets, I engaged one of the hotel staff in

conversation. *I asked him if it is possible to ever get used to working in such a remarkable setting. He answered: "To me this is just a job, I don't notice the beauty anymore. I drag my feet coming to work every Monday morning just like everybody else."*

Related to this aspect of human nature is the unfortunate reality that we tend to be least grateful to those who are closest to us. Research on the psychology of gratitude has found that people tend to be more grateful for the unexpected. Human nature is such that we experience less gratitude for favors done for us by family and close friends than when somebody who we are less close to does the same favor.[22]

The tendency toward habituation is also seen in the relationship between man and G-d. In the classic work *Duties of the Heart* (*Chovos HaLevavos*), Rabbeinu Bachya details the reasons for our ingratitude to G-d:

People . . . grow up surrounded with a superabundance of Divine favors which they experience continuously, and to which they become so accustomed that they come to regard these as essential parts of their being, not to be removed or separated from themselves during the whole of their lives. When their intelligence develops and their mental faculties become strong, they foolishly ignore the benefits the Creator has bestowed on them and do not consider the obligation of gratitude for Divine beneficence, for they are unaware of the high degree of the boon. . . .[23]

Contrast this to the following incident that beautifully illustrates how, in the face of an extremely stressful chronic situation, individuals can show gratitude for even the most basic human experience:

At a retreat for families of children with severe cognitive and physical limitations, I (DP) met with a family who had an 8-year-old daughter

20 *Pachad Yitzchak, Rosh Hashanah,* # 3, translated by Dr. Shai Held.

21 *Gur Aryeh,* Genesis 2:5 *"v'ein makir b'tovosam."*

22 McCullough, M. & Emmons, R. (2004). *The Psychology of Gratitude,* Oxford, UK: Oxford University Press.

23 *Duties of the Heart* (*Chovos HaLevavos*), Introduction to Section Two, translation by Moses Hyamson (1999). New York: Feldheim.

who was born with such profound brain damage that she was unable to speak or engage in even the most basic self-care functions. Her mother told me that for the first four years of her daughter's life she was unable to sit up, and the family was given little hope that this most basic of human activities would ever be possible. The child's parents heard of a program overseas that offered intensive physical therapy for their daughter's condition, having some limited success in working with these children. After years of visits to this program their daughter was now able to sit up. The parents called over the counselor who was caring for their daughter at the retreat and with intense excitement showed me how this 8-year-old daughter was now able to see the world from the perspective added by her newfound ability to sit. The girl flashed a million-dollar smile at her parents who met the smile with tears of pride and gratitude.

The obvious lesson taught by these remarkable parents is that it is possible to have gratitude for even the most basic of gifts given to us on a daily basis. The challenge is finding a way, under normal circumstances, to continually remind ourselves, as Rabbeinu Bachya writes, of the "*superabundance* of Divine favors which we experience continuously." Developing awareness of what to be grateful for even when life is going smoothly can require conscious effort and constant practice. As noted by Rabbi Sarna, without practice, this trait will not flow naturally from man's innate tendencies. The default setting is habituation.

DEVELOPING A HABIT OF ATTENTION: FINDING BEAUTY AND MEANING IN THE MUNDANE

The passage in the Torah regarding gifts to the poor while working in the fields is incongruously placed in the middle of the Torah's section discussing the various festivals and holidays in the Jewish calendar. After teaching us the laws regarding Pesach and Shavuos, followed by the laws of Rosh Hashanah, Yom Kippur, and Succos, there is a strange and incongruous interruption in the theme of the Torah's text by the insertion of the commandment regarding gifts to the poor:

When you reap the harvest of your land, you shall not remove completely the corners of your field as you reap and you shall not gather the gleanings of your harvest; for the poor and the proselyte shall you leave them; I am Hashem, your G-d.[24]

What is the significance of this interpolation? The *baalei Mussar* explain that when a Jew makes his pilgrimage to Jerusalem on one of the festivals, he is exposed to one of the highpoints of the Jewish experience. He senses the excitement and vibrancy of tens of thousands of Jews gathered from the four corners of Israel, joining in the observance of a Pesach and Shavuos. As a spectator, he stands in awe and reverence beholding the service of the Priests and the beautiful music and singing of the Levites. He is truly on a high and inspired beyond description. Reality, however, must soon set in when he leaves the holy city and goes back to his workshop or farm and is suddenly cast from the heights of spirituality to the physical, material life of the craftsman or farmer. He is challenged to retain spirituality in his mundane, day-to-day activities. That is why the Torah injects the laws of sharing one's produce with the less fortunate in the midst of the festival portion. It reminds the Jew that the moments of exhilaration and spiritual highs must be carried over and applied to the fields and mundane living. The commandments of G-d are common to both arenas. The material and the physical can be infused and informed by the spiritual experiences that he had when he went on his pilgrimage.

By the same token, what inspired the non-Jew to reject his way of life and his beliefs and decide to convert to Judaism? In Jewish theology we never encourage proselytizing; on the contrary, we try to dissuade a non-Jew from converting, explaining to him the rigorous disciplines he will be subjected to as a member of the Jewish faith. We are always very frank and open with him regarding the strictures of Jewish law. Still it seems strange that while we give him

24 *Leviticus* 23:22.

instructions in the fundamentals of Judaism if we are convinced of his sincerity to become a convert, the Talmud tells us that of all of the commandments of the Torah it is these obligations to the poor that we must teach a convert before the process of conversion is complete:

> If a prospective proselyte comes to a Jewish court to convert to Judaism in the present era . . . we inform him of the sin of failing to observe the laws of leket (leaving gleanings for the poor), shichchah (leaving forgotten sheaves for the poor), and pe'ah (the part of the harvest left over in the corner of the fields).[25]

Why is such importance given to this particular commandment? It is to teach the convert that while the inspiration that motivated him to convert is understandable—emanating either from a charismatic teacher or his experience witnessing special Jewish events, such as the majesty of the Jewish holidays or Jewish practice in the home on a Shabbos or festival—this enthusiasm and exuberance can easily ebb and wane when he must confront the reality of day-to-day living. It is for this reason that we teach him the laws that operate when he has come down from the mountain of spiritual heights to the field of the routine. We are teaching him that Jewish ideals are expressed in the tedious and the mundane, even as it is true of the special majestic moments of life. This may well be termed "the ordeal of the ordinary," which must in all frankness be taught to the prospective proselyte.

DEVELOPING A HABIT OF ATTENTION

Breathing is the most natural and reflexive continuous action of a person. The Sages, noting the similarity between the Hebrew word *neshamah* (soul) and the Hebrew word *neshimah* (breath), comment on the verse, *Let all souls praise G-d,*[26] man should praise and thank the Almighty for every breath.[27] This is the ultimate example of their awareness of continually

working on the need to overcome the tendency toward habituation.

Psychologists tell us that the antidote to habituation is consciously being mindful of how fortunate one's condition is and how it could have been otherwise.

While not easy, we can develop a habit of awareness, a habit of attention.

Gregg Krech, an author and counselor who specializes in the psychology of gratitude,[28] walks us through a disastrous Monday morning that is destined for catastrophe from the moment the alarm clock fails to wake us, all the way through to a near-death experience driving to work. The series of mishaps culminates when faced with an angry tirade from the boss after arriving so late for work. It is only when things go wrong that our attention is grabbed. It takes such an "out of the ordinary" event to bring us to an awareness and appreciation of a "normal" day. Krech points out: "What would happen if we turn the story around and experience a day when the alarm goes off as intended and you arrive at work without unexpected traffic or accidents?" How do we cultivate an approach to life that pays attention to the expected?

Perhaps the most potent antidote to habituation, from a Jewish perspective, is the daily experience of prayer. One-third of the prayers in the daily service address the theme of gratitude. What can be a more powerful answer to the challenge posed by Krech than thanking G-d three times a day with words expressing gratitude for the "miracles that surround us every day"? Of course, this too is a challenge. It is difficult to concentrate on the meaning of words said during prayer, and many experience the need to emotionally connect to the meaning of these words as a continual challenge. However, as we discussed, there are multiple spiritual and emotional benefits that emerge from concentrating on connecting to prayer in a manner that cultivates a habit of attention to that for which we should be grateful.

25 *Yevamos* 47a.
26 *Psalms* 150:6.
27 *Bereishis Rabbah* 14.

28 Krech, G. (2001). *Naikan: Gratitude and the Japanese Art of Self-Reflection.* St. Paul, MN: Stone Bridge Press.

Rabbi Chaim Shmulevitz[29] discusses the dangers of *tardeimas ha'heirgeil*, the deep sleep brought on by habituation. Overcoming this requires that we cultivate a fresh look at what has become too familiar. He illustrates this with the following incident depicted in the Talmud:

> *Rav Alexandri went to the marketplace and called out: "Who wants life, who wants life?" All the people came and gathered round him saying: "Give us life!" He then quoted to them, "Who is the man who desires life and loves his days so that he may see good in them . . . Guard your tongue from evil and your lips from speaking deceit."*[30]

What was Rav Alexandri telling people that they didn't already know? Among the practical lessons that Rav Alexandri was teaching was that when widely known information to which we might have become habituated is presented in a novel way, we can view it with fresh eyes in a manner that develops the habit of attention to what has otherwise become ordinary.

CYNICISM

An enemy of gratitude is cynicism. To the extent that gratitude requires a focus on the positive, cynicism is characterized by sarcasm, suspicion, and scorn.

There is an interesting question posed by the *Meshech Chochmah* regarding the passage in the Torah that describes the punishment of a man who cursed G-d:

> *And Moses spoke to the Children of Israel, and they took the blasphemer to the outside of the camp, and they stoned him to death; and the Children of Israel did as Hashem had commanded Moses.*[31]

The *Meshech Chochmah* asks why it says "as commanded"; after all, the Jews did many things at Hashem's command. Why single out the incident of the blasphemer for saying this?

He answers that a cynical complainer can cool off one's enthusiasm. The blasphemer scoffed

regarding the miracle of the Showbread. "Do you serve a king week-old bread?" he asked mockingly. There is always a danger when one is exposed to a complainer that a seed of doubt is planted regarding one's zeal and commitment to what one is doing. The passage therefore tells us that the complaints of the blasphemer did not impact the enthusiasm of the Jews in carrying out G-d's command in performing the mitzvah of the Showbread. It does not refer to the carrying out of the sentence, but to their retention of loyal obedience to G-d's commandment that had been challenged by the sinner.

SECULAR PERSPECTIVES ON CYNICISM

Research in the workplace has found that cynicism thrives when one feels disappointed in oneself or others, and becomes disillusioned because of being treated in a manner that breeds distrust, frustration, and resentment.[32] It is not surprising that when cynicism dominates in a family or one's job, motivation is sapped and antagonism increases.[33]

Reality television programs and sitcoms are often replete with cynical remarks, particularly when younger characters interact with their elders. What is particularly alarming is how common it is on sitcoms for children to be depicted as being chronically cynical, portraying this type of worldview as admirable and worthy of emulation. The findings of the Josephson Institute systematically document how this influence has impacted our children. In their 2009 survey of over 7,000 participants, the Josephson Institute of Ethics found alarming trends documenting the rise of cynicism in the United States. This institute has been taking the moral pulse of residents of the United States every two years since 1992. In their most recent survey, they report evidence that "The hole in the moral ozone seems to be getting bigger—each new generation is more likely to lie and cheat than

29 *Sichos Mussar, Maamar* 97.
30 *Avodah Zarah* 19b, *Psalms* 34:13–14.
31 *Leviticus* 24:23.

32 Mirvis, P. & Kanter, D. L. (1991). Beyond demography: A psychographic profile of the workforce. *Human Resource Management, 30*(1), 45–68.
33 Mirvis, P. & Kanter, D. L. (1989). Combating cynicism in the workplace. *National Productivity Review, 8*(4), 377–394.

the preceding one."[34] Adolescents, in 2009, were found to be five times more likely, and young adults three times more likely, than those over 40, to cynically endorse the belief that one must lie and cheat in order to be successful in life. This is a particularly ominous finding since their research confirmed that those who believe that cheating is necessary are significantly more likely to cheat or lie when they become adults. Those who cheat as adolescents were also found to be significantly more likely when adults to lie to their spouses, customers, employers, and insurance companies. It is of note that in this survey, participants who said that religion is an important part of their life tend to be less cynical than those who say that religion is not important (13 percent vs. 18 percent). The obvious take-home message is that this alarming trend can be checked to the extent that parents and educators shield children from excess exposure to media that glorify cynicism. Needless to say, parents, educators, and other adults in a child's life must always be aware of their vital function as role models and act accordingly. Following some of the suggested recommendations below regarding cultivating gratitude should also serve to lessen the tendency toward cynical attitudes and behavior.

RECOMMENDATIONS FOR FOSTERING GRATITUDE

1. ***Counting One's Blessings***—An important study regarding the benefits of gratitude suggests an intervention that can help to effectively build awareness of what we should be grateful for in our daily lives.

In this study, over the course of ten weeks, participants were assigned to one of three groups:

a Subjects who were asked to write about five things they were grateful for during the past week.
b Participants were asked to enumerate five hassles from the past week.
c Subjects were asked to list five events that affected them.

In the ensuing period, research participants who were assigned to the gratitude group felt better about their lives as a whole, were more optimistic about the future, reported fewer health complaints, and exercised more.

The actual script used in this study is informative:[35]

At the beginning and end of each day, list five things for which you are grateful, and then take a few minutes to meditate on the gift inherent in each. One means of elucidating this sense of appreciation is the use of the following sentence stem: "I appreciate ___ because ___." In the first blank, list the person, event, or thing for which you are grateful, and in the second blank state the reasons for each of the things for which you have expressed gratitude. Discuss the effects of one week of this practice with a classmate, and tweak the exercise as you wish.

More recently, researchers have found that this technique is as beneficial for children and adolescents as it is for adults.[36] For example, in one study, adolescents were given the following instructions:

There are many things in our lives, both large and small, that we might be grateful about. Think back over the past day and write down up to five things in your life that you are grateful or thankful for.

In that study, the adolescents experienced improved levels of optimism, life satisfaction, and overall satisfaction with school relative to adolescents in a comparison group. In a review of the research measuring the efficacy of this technique,[37] researchers summarize seven studies that found significant increases in feelings of well-being when one thinks about what they

---

34 Character Study Reveals Predictors of Lying and Cheating, Press release. Josephson Institute of Ethics, October 29, 2009.

35 Script from *Emmons & McCullough* (2003).

36 Froh, J. J., Sefick, W. J. & Emmons, R. A. (2008). Counting blessings in early adolescents: An experimental study of gratitude and subjective wellbeing. *Journal of School Psychology, 46,* 213–233.

37 Wood, A., Froh, J. J. & Geraghty, A. (2010). Gratitude and well-being: A review and theoretical integration. *Clinical Psychology Review (30),* 890–905.

should be grateful for in this systematic manner. Of course, it isn't necessary to write down what one is grateful for on a list. Going around the table during Friday-night meals and asking family members to share what they are grateful for that week can reap similar benefits. This has the added advantage of increasing family members' knowledge of details about each other's life—a benefit that has independent advantages according to research in family psychology.[38]

2. ***Direct Expression of Gratitude***—Directly expressing thanks leads to even more dramatic benefits. In a study done by Seligman and his colleagues,[39] adults were given one week to write and then deliver a letter of gratitude in person to someone who had been especially kind to them but had never been properly thanked. Happiness levels of the individuals who carried out this exercise increased substantially for a month after they paid the visit to their benefactor.

A teacher was speaking to an 11th-grade student who said that her love of learning came from a third-grade teacher whose enthusiasm for teaching continued to inspire the student even eight years later. The teacher asked: "Did you ever thank your third-grade teacher or even let her know of the way she changed your life?" When the student answered, "No," the teacher immediately asked her to go into a private area of the school office to write a note expressing her gratitude to the teacher. Both the student and the recipient of the note described the experience as deeply meaningful.

3. Research has found that overcoming the natural tendencies that serve as impediments to gratitude can help cultivate a personality that is more likely to be grateful. The following characteristics serve as impediments to gratitude:

a ***Self-preoccupation***—When one is so engrossed in their individual life-dramas, little

room is left for one to notice the needs of others. This calls for developing the muscle of empathy and awareness of the needs and suffering of others, even when pulled into the inevitable hassles that accompany daily life. In his biography of his teacher, Rav Yerucham Levovitz, Rabbi Wolbe relates a memorable story about the extent of his teacher's empathy. Rabbi Levovitz was told that a Jewish man was arrested by the Russians and accused of being a spy, an extremely serious offense that often resulted in the execution of the prisoner. It was reported that the level of Rabbi Levovitz's anguish was so great that when he awoke the morning after hearing the news, his beard had turned white.

b ***Expectation***—Human nature is to expect whatever one has become accustomed to. We tend to no longer be grateful or attentive to something that is expected and routine. What gets our attention is when the expectation is not met. A possible antidote is to develop the habit of paying attention to the lessons learned when our expectations are not met. When one is confronted with periods of illness instead of expected good health, once one's health returns, it is doubly important to try to hold on to the feelings of gratitude for good health. Likewise, on a more mundane level, when luggage is lost by the airline and one has to live for several days without all the clothing one is accustomed to, he can redouble his efforts to more fully appreciate his wardrobe once the luggage is returned.

c ***Entitlement***—The feelings of entitlement that often accompany the many luxuries of day-to-day life in an affluent society serve to block our awareness of how grateful we should be for the many gifts we regularly experience. When feelings of entitlement dominate, gratitude will, by definition, take a backseat. The antidote is to pay attention to the daily life of those less fortunate than we are. Periodic exposure to those living in poverty or with illness and disabilities, or those living in countries where basic civil liberties aren't respected, can serve as an important antidote to entitlement.

---

38 Gottman, J. (1999). *The Seven Principles for Making Marriage Work.* New York: Random House.

39 Seligman, M. E. P., Steen, T. A., Park, N. & Peterson, C. (2005). Positive psychology progress: Empirical validation of interventions. *American Psychologist, 60,* 410–421.

4 **Journal Keeping**—As noted earlier, systematically writing about what one is grateful for can have powerful benefits. There are many disciples of the early *baalei Mussar*, such as Rabbi Yisroel Salanter, Rabbi Yitzchak Blazer, and others, who have transmitted to their students either orally or in their writings that these great *Mussar* teachers had a practice of keeping what was called a *pinkus*—a notebook or diary—on their nightstand. They would record their experiences of the day and the lessons they learned from that day's activities, before retiring for the night.

In other cultures as well, such as Japan, there is a similar practice called *"Naikan."* This is a way of life for many, marked by structured self-reflection that, in that culture, helps develop a sense of gratitude.

Practitioners of *Naikan* ask themselves the following three questions related to gratitude during their daily meditation:

1. What have I received from others?
2. What have I given to others?
3. What troubles and difficulties have I caused others?

Whether in writing or thought, a daily *cheshbon hanefesh* (self-assessment) that includes reflection on our levels of gratitude and transcendence of self-involvement can be an important aspect of developing this trait.

5. Although at first glance admitting to our mistakes is not linked to gratitude, on a deeper level cultivating such non-defensiveness can also help nourish a sense of gratitude. As Gregg Krech says: "As long as I am humbled by my own mistakes or limitations, I am more likely to receive what I am given with gratitude and a true sense of appreciation for the giver as well as the gift."[40]

6. Parents should remember the importance of modeling gratitude in order to teach their children. Since it is so difficult to maintain gratitude toward those to whom we are closest, continually reminding ourselves to express gratitude to one's spouse, family members, and close friends is an important component of educating our children in this important trait. As noted in our book, *Balanced Parenting*, instilling gratitude—by taking an extra moment to thank a salesclerk at the store, or tipping the paperboy for getting the paper on the porch every day—lets our children see that gratitude is part of the daily repertoire of social interaction.

Children should be reminded to thank parents for what they may take for granted; for example, help with homework, a lift to a friend's house, or taking them out to dinner. Parents should resist any tendency to inadvertently sabotage this lesson by responding with phrases like: "Don't mention it." Instead, the child should be praised for expressing gratitude. Acting as a role model by expressing gratitude to others, in front of your child, is another powerful lesson in instilling this core value.

Life in the Balance: Torah Perspectives on Positive Psychology (New York: Shaar Press, 2014), pp. 101–125
Reprinted with permission of the authors

---

40 Krech, G. Exploring the link between gratitude and attention. To Do Institute (online).

Journey of Yourself

STAYING HONEST, HUMBLE, AND HAPPY

*Staying positive about life means
staying positive about ourselves.*

SELF-WORTH
NEGATIVE SELF-PERCEPTION

Exercise 2.1

Rosenberg Self-Esteem Scale

MORRIS ROSENBERG, *SOCIETY AND THE ADOLESCENT SELF-IMAGE* (PRINCETON, N.J.: PRINCETON UNIVERSITY PRESS, 1965)

Below is a list of statements dealing with your general feelings about yourself. Using the numbers 1–4, indicate how strongly you agree or disagree with each statement.

1..Strongly Disagree
2..Disagree
3...Agree
4..Strongly Agree

1	I feel that I'm a person of worth, at least on an equal plane with others	
2	I feel I have a number of good qualities.	
3	All in all, I am inclined to feel that I am a failure.	
4	I am able to do things as well as most other people.	
5	I feel I do not have much to be proud of, compared to most others.	

6	I take a positive attitude toward myself.	
7	On the whole, I am satisfied with myself.	
8	I wish I could have more respect for myself.	
9	I certainly feel useless at times.	
10	At times I think I am no good at all.	

To determine your score, first "reverse score" the ratings of 3, 5, 8, 9, and 10. For these items only, change 1 to 4, 2 to 3, 3 to 2, and 4 to 1. Then add up the ten ratings and calculate the sum. The highest self-esteem score that you can get is 40; the lowest is 10. People around the world score an average of 31 on this scale, and people in the U.S. score an average of 32.

Text 1

DR. ABRAHAM J. TWERSKI, *LET US MAKE MAN: SELF ESTEEM THROUGH JEWISHNESS* (NEW YORK: CIS PUBLISHERS, 1991), PP. 8–11

Although many people are aware that they have little self-confidence and that they harbor feelings of inadequacy, they believe these feelings are justified because they are convinced their inadequacies are real. *Quite often, this self-perception is incorrect,* and the low self-esteem and poor self-confidence are in reality unjustified. . . . Many people see themselves as less than what they are in reality, and they are fully convinced that their perceptions are absolutely correct. Others' opinions to the contrary and even concrete evidence of their excellence may have little or no impact. . . .

As I studied the negative self-image problem, I found that the most profound feelings of low self-esteem paradoxically occur most often in those who are in reality most gifted and competent. It appears that the person who develops a negative self-image sees himself as if he were looking through a trick lens which distorts the perception in such a manner that the person sees himself as the opposite of what he actually is.

RABBI ABRAHAM J. TWERSKI, M.D.
1930–

Psychiatrist and noted author. Rabbi Twerski is a scion of the Chernobyl Chasidic dynasty and a well-known expert in the field of substance abuse. He has authored more than 50 books on self-help and Judaism, and has served as a pioneer in heightening awareness of the dangers of addiction, spousal abuse, and low self-esteem. He served as medical director of the Gateway Rehabilitation Center in Pittsburgh and as associate professor of psychiatry at the University of Pittsburgh School of Medicine.

Text 2

NUMBERS 13:33 ⬚

וְשָׁם רָאִינוּ אֶת הַנְּפִילִים בְּנֵי עֲנָק מִן הַנְּפִלִים, וַנְּהִי בְעֵינֵינוּ
כַּחֲגָבִים וְכֵן הָיִינוּ בְּעֵינֵיהֶם.

There we saw giants of immense height. In our eyes, we seemed like grasshoppers, and we looked the same to them.

Question for Discussion

What causes people to harbor negative beliefs about themselves that are not grounded in reality?

PURPOSE
DIVINE IMAGE

Text 3
GENESIS 1:27–28

וַיִּבְרָא אֱלֹקִים אֶת הָאָדָם בְּצַלְמוֹ בְּצֶלֶם אֱלֹקִים בָּרָא אֹתוֹ, זָכָר
וּנְקֵבָה בָּרָא אֹתָם.
וַיְבָרֶךְ אֹתָם אֱלֹקִים וַיֹּאמֶר לָהֶם אֱלֹקִים פְּרוּ וּרְבוּ וּמִלְאוּ אֶת
הָאָרֶץ וְכִבְשֻׁהָ; וּרְדוּ בִּדְגַת הַיָּם וּבְעוֹף הַשָּׁמַיִם וּבְכָל חַיָּה
הָרֹמֶשֶׂת עַל הָאָרֶץ.

G-d created humankind in His image, in the image of G-d He created him; male and female He created them.

G-d blessed them and said to them, "Be fruitful and multiply, fill the earth and subdue it. Rule over the fish of the sea, the birds of the sky, and over all of the beasts that tread upon the earth."

THE INDIVIDUAL

Text 4

MISHNAH, SANHEDRIN 4:5 ⚇

לְפִיכָךְ נִבְרָא אָדָם יְחִידִי, לְלַמֶּדְךָ שֶׁכָּל הַמְאַבֵּד נֶפֶשׁ אַחַת מִיִּשְׂרָאֵל מַעֲלֶה עָלָיו הַכָּתוּב כְּאִלּוּ אִבֵּד עוֹלָם מָלֵא, וְכָל הַמְקַיֵּם נֶפֶשׁ אַחַת מִיִּשְׂרָאֵל מַעֲלֶה עָלָיו הַכָּתוּב כְּאִלּוּ קִיֵּם עוֹלָם מָלֵא . . .

וּלְהַגִּיד גְּדוּלָתוֹ שֶׁל הַקָּדוֹשׁ בָּרוּךְ הוּא, שֶׁאָדָם טוֹבֵעַ כַּמָּה מַטְבְּעוֹת בְּחוֹתָם אֶחָד וְכֻלָּן דּוֹמִין זֶה לָזֶה, וּמֶלֶךְ מַלְכֵי הַמְּלָכִים הַקָּדוֹשׁ בָּרוּךְ הוּא טָבַע כָּל אָדָם בְּחוֹתָמוֹ שֶׁל אָדָם הָרִאשׁוֹן וְאֵין אֶחָד מֵהֶן דּוֹמֶה לַחֲבֵרוֹ.

לְפִיכָךְ, כָּל אֶחָד וְאֶחָד חַיָּב לוֹמַר בִּשְׁבִילִי נִבְרָא הָעוֹלָם.

MISHNAH

The first authoritative work of Jewish law that was codified in writing. The Mishnah contains the oral traditions that were passed down from teacher to student; it supplements, clarifies, and systematizes the commandments of the Torah. Due to the continual persecution of the Jewish people, it became increasingly difficult to guarantee that these traditions would not be forgotten. Rabbi Yehudah Hanassi therefore redacted the Mishnah at the end of the 2nd century. It serves as the foundation for the Talmud.

Initially, only one human being was created. This is to teach us that one who destroys a single life is considered to have destroyed an entire world, and one who saves a single life is considered to have saved an entire world. . . .

It also communicates the greatness of G-d. For when a person mints many coins from the same mold, all the coins are alike; but G-d mints every person through the mold of the first human, and yet, no two people are alike.

Therefore, every person must say, "The world was created for me."

Text 5

RABBI SIMON JACOBSON, *TOWARD A MEANINGFUL LIFE*
(NEW YORK: WILLIAM MORROW, 2002), PP. 14–15

Birth is G-d saying you matter. . . .

Your birth was not an accident; G-d chooses each of us to fulfill a specific mission in this world, just as a composer arranges each musical note. Take away one note, and the entire composition is affected. Each person matters; each person is irreplaceable. . . .

Many people seem to feel that because *we* didn't *choose* to enter the world, our birth is a stroke of coincidence or serendipity. This couldn't be further from the truth. Birth is G-d's way of saying that He has invested His will and energy in creating you; G-d feels great joy when you are born, the greatest pleasure imaginable, for the moment of birth realizes His intention in wanting you.

RABBI SIMON JACOBSON

Author of the best-selling *Toward a Meaningful Life* (New York: William Morrow, 1995), which has been translated into 12 languages, and founder of the Meaningful Life Center, which seeks to bridge the secular and the spiritual. For over 14 years, Rabbi Jacobson headed a team of scholars responsible for publishing the public talks of Rabbi Menachem M. Schneerson, the Lubavitcher Rebbe. He is also the publisher of *The Algemeiner* (formerly *Der Algemeiner Journal*), a New York-based newspaper covering American and international Jewish and Israel-related news.

SELF-CONCEPT

Text 6

RABBI TSADOK HAKOHEN RABINOWITZ, *TSIDKAT HATSADIK* 154 📖

כְּשֵׁם שֶׁצָּרִיךְ אָדָם לְהַאֲמִין בְּהַשֵּׁם יִתְבָּרֵךְ, כָּךְ צָרִיךְ אַחַר כָּךְ
לְהַאֲמִין בְּעַצְמוֹ. רְצוֹנִי לוֹמַר, שֶׁיֵּשׁ לְהַשֵּׁם יִתְבָּרֵךְ עֵסֶק עִמּוֹ
וְשֶׁאֵינֶנּוּ פּוֹעֵל בָּטֵל . . . רַק צָרִיךְ לְהַאֲמִין כִּי נַפְשׁוֹ מִמְּקוֹר
הַחַיִּים יִתְבָּרֵךְ שְׁמוֹ, וְהַשֵּׁם יִתְבָּרֵךְ מִתְעַנֵּג וּמִשְׁתַּעֲשֵׁעַ בָּהּ
כְּשֶׁעוֹשָׂה רְצוֹנוֹ.

RABBI TSADOK HAKOHEN RABINOWITZ OF LUBLIN
1823–1900

Chasidic master and thinker. Rabbi Tsadok was born into a Lithuanian rabbinic family and later joined the Chasidic movement. He was a follower of the Chasidic leaders Rabbi Mordechai Yosef Leiner of Izbica and Rabbi Leibel Eiger. He succeeded Rabbi Eiger after his passing and became a rebbe in Lublin, Poland. He authored many works on Jewish law, Chasidism, kabbalah, and ethics, as well as scholarly essays on astronomy, geometry, and algebra.

Just as we must believe in G-d, so too, we must afterward believe in ourselves—that G-d cares about us, that we are not worthless laborers, . . . that we possess divine souls, and that G-d takes pleasure and joy when we fulfill His desire.

Question for Discussion

How might the aforementioned ideas help us deal with a low self-esteem that stems from comparing oneself to others?

KNOW THYSELF

Text 7

RABBI YOSEF YITSCHAK SCHNEERSOHN,
IGROT KODESH 7, P. 320 🎧

בְּמַעֲנֶה עַל כְּתָבוֹ; בְּהִתְאוֹנְנוּת עַל אֹדוֹת מַעֲמָדוֹ וּמַצָּבוֹ
הָרוּחָנִי, הִנֵּה בְּטַח קָרָאתָ אֶת הַשִּׂיחוֹת אֲשֶׁר מִתְּנָאֵי עֲבוֹדָה
מְסוּדֶּרֶת – שֶׁלֹּא לְהַכְבִּיד עַל עַצְמוֹ בְּטַעֲנוֹת וּתְבִיעוֹת בִּלְתִּי
מְיוּסָּדוֹת, כִּי הָרוֹצֶה לְתַקֵּן עַצְמוֹ הִנֵּה כְּשֵׁם שֶׁצָּרִיךְ לָדַעַת
אֶת חֶסְרוֹנוֹת עַצְמוֹ, כֵּן צָרִיךְ לָדַעַת מַעֲלַת עַצְמוֹ, כִּי בִּשְׁבִיל
עֲבוֹדָה צְרִיכִים שֶׁיִּהְיֶה אַ גוּטֶע שְׁטִימוּנג וְלֹא לְהַשְׁפִּיל עַצְמוֹ
תָּמִיד...

יֵשׁ לוֹ כַּמָּה עִנְיָנִים, הֵן מֵעִנְיָנֵי לִימוּד וְהֵן מֵעִנְיָנֵי הַנְהָגָה מַה
שֶּׁבְּעֶזְרַת הַשֵּׁם יִתְבָּרֵךְ יְכוֹלִים לְשַׂמֵּחַ אֶת לְבָבוֹ וְלָתֵת לוֹ כֹּחַ
וְעֹז לַעֲבֹד עֲבוֹדָתוֹ.

RABBI YOSEF YITSCHAK SCHNEERSOHN (RAYATS, FRIERDIKER REBBE, PREVIOUS REBBE) 1880–1950

Chasidic rebbe, prolific writer, and Jewish activist. Rabbi Yosef Yitschak, the sixth leader of the Chabad movement, actively promoted Jewish religious practice in Soviet Russia and was arrested for these activities. After his release from prison and exile, he settled in Warsaw, Poland, from where he fled Nazi occupation and arrived in New York in 1940. Settling in Brooklyn, Rabbi Schneersohn worked to revitalize American Jewish life. His son-in-law Rabbi Menachem Mendel Schneerson succeeded him as the leader of the Chabad movement.

In response to your letter with your complaints about your spiritual status.

I assume you read my talks in which I explained that a condition for orderly spiritual growth is to avoid burdening yourself with foundationless accusations and claims. If you desire to improve, then just as you need to know your shortcomings, so you must know your personal strengths. This is important, because spiritual growth hinges on a positive mood, not on constant self-degradation....

You have a number of things, both in terms of your studies as well as your actions, that should make you happy about yourself. Knowing these will give you the power to pursue spiritual growth.

Text 8

THE REBBE, RABBI MENACHEM MENDEL SCHNEERSON,
TORAT MENACHEM 5742:1, PP. 52–53

וְכַיָּדוּעַ פִּתְגָּם רַבּוֹתֵינוּ נְשִׂיאֵינוּ (לִיקּוּטֵי דִיבּוּרִים חֵלֶק ד',
תקפ"א, א):

"כְּשֵׁם שֶׁצְּרִיכִים לֵידַע אֶת הַחֶסְרוֹנוֹת, כְּמוֹ כֵן צְרִיכִים לֵידַע
מַעֲלוֹת עַצְמוֹ".

וּבָזֶה יֶשְׁנוֹ דִיוּק נִפְלָא: כַּאֲשֶׁר מְדוּבָּר אוֹדוֹת הַמַּעֲלוֹת, הַלָּשׁוֹן
הוּא מַעֲלוֹת עַצְמוֹ, וְאִילּוּ כַּאֲשֶׁר מְדוּבָּר אוֹדוֹת הַחֶסְרוֹנוֹת,
הַלָּשׁוֹן הוּא חֶסְרוֹנוֹת סְתָם וְלֹא חֶסְרוֹנוֹת עַצְמוֹ.

וְהַבִּיאוּר בָּזֶה עַל פִּי מַה שֶׁכָּתוּב בַּזֹהַר (ח"ג יג, ב): "וְנֶפֶשׁ כִּי
תֶחֱטָא (וַיִּקְרָא ד, ב)—תִּוְוהָא".

יְהוּדִי מִצַּד עַצְמוֹ אֵינוֹ שַׁיָּיךְ לְעִנְיָן שֶׁל חֵטְא כְּלָל. וְגַם כַּאֲשֶׁר
נִכְשַׁל בְּעִנְיָן שֶׁל חֵטְא חַס וְשָׁלוֹם, אֵין זֶה חִסָּרוֹן עַצְמוֹ אֶלָּא
זֶהוּ דָבָר שֶׁמִּחוּץ הֵימֶנּוּ שֶׁנִּדְבַּק אֵלָיו. זֹאת אוֹמֶרֶת: הֱיוֹת
שֶׁהוּא נִמְצָא בְּעוֹלָם הַזֶּה הַגַּשְׁמִי וְהַחוּמְרִי . . . יִתָּכֵן שֶׁנִּדְבַּק
אֶצְלוֹ מַשֶּׁהוּ מִגַּשְׁמִיּוּת וְחוּמְרִיּוּת הָעוֹלָם. וְלָכֵן אַף עַל פִּי
שֶׁזֶּהוּ חִסָּרוֹן, אֵין זֶה חִסָּרוֹן עַצְמוֹ, כִּי חִסָּרוֹן זֶה אֵינוֹ מִצַּד
עַצְמוֹ אֶלָּא מִצַּד מְצִיאוּת הָעוֹלָם שֶׁמִּסְבִיבוֹ.

RABBI MENACHEM MENDEL SCHNEERSON
1902–1994

The towering Jewish leader of the 20th century, known as "the Lubavitcher Rebbe," or simply as "the Rebbe." Born in southern Ukraine, the Rebbe escaped Nazi-occupied Europe, arriving in the U.S. in June 1941. The Rebbe inspired and guided the revival of traditional Judaism after the European devastation, impacting virtually every Jewish community the world over. The Rebbe often emphasized that the performance of just one additional good deed could usher in the era of Mashiach. The Rebbe's scholarly talks and writings have been printed in more than 200 volumes.

There is a well-known teaching of the rebbes of Chabad:

"Just as we need to know the defects, so too, we need to know our strengths."

The anomaly in this phrase is that it says "*our* strengths," but with regard to defects it merely says, "*the* defects," not "*our* defects." What is the reason for this?

Leviticus 4:2 states, "When a soul sins" [and discusses the process of rectification]. The *Zohar* (3:13b), however, phrases this as a question: "A soul sinned? Is that possible?"

> Meaning, the concept of sin is completely alien to our being. Even when we stumble, G-d forbid, it does not undermine who we are; rather, it is something outside of our nature that has latched on to us. We are residents of a material and mundane world. . . . It is therefore possible for something unholy to attach itself to us. Though it is a defect, in a sense, it is not *our* defect, but a defect imposed on us by our environment.

SELF-TRANSCENDENCE

Exercise 2.2

How do you define humility? Check all that apply.

	A low view of oneself
	Being modest about oneself when talking to others
	Refraining from flaunting
	A middle ground between low self-esteem and arrogance
	Other:

Text 9

RABBI SHALOM DOVBER SCHNEERSOHN,
SEFER HAMAAMARIM 5679, P. 91 (ⅱ)

דַּעֲנָוָה אֵינָהּ הַשִּׁפְלוּת מִצַּד פְּחִיתוּת הַנֶּפֶשׁ, שֶׁאֵינוֹ מוֹצֵא טוֹב בְּעַצְמוֹ, אוֹ שֶׁחַס וְשָׁלוֹם הוּא בְּדֶרֶךְ לֹא טוֹב.

כִּי אִם הַשִּׁפְלוּת דַּעֲנָוָה הוּא מִצַּד הֶעְדֵּר הָרֶגֶשׁ עַצְמוֹ, שֶׁאֵינוֹ מְחַשֵּׁב אֶת עַצְמוֹ לִמְצִיאוּת גַּם בְּכָל הַטּוֹב שֶׁלּוֹ. דְּעִם הֱיוֹתוֹ טוֹב וְיָשָׁר בַּתּוֹרָה וּמִצְוֹת וּבַעֲבוֹדָה בִּמְסִירוּת נֶפֶשׁ, אֵינוֹ בַּחֲשִׁיבוּת בְּעַצְמוֹ לִהְיוֹת בְּעֵינָיו בְּאֵיזֶה מַעֲלָה וּמַדְרֵגָא מִשּׁוּם זֶה. אֵין זֶה שֶׁאֵינוֹ יוֹדֵעַ מֵהַטּוֹב שֶׁלּוֹ, כִּי אִם יוֹדֵעַ הוּא שֶׁהוּא טוֹב וְיָשָׁר בְּכָל דָּבָר, וּמִכָּל מָקוֹם, אֵינוֹ מַחֲזִיק טִיבוּתָא לְנַפְשֵׁיהּ שֶׁהוּא בְּאֵיזֶה מַעֲלָה וּמַדְרֵגָא כו'. וְסִיבַּת הַדָּבָר הוּא מִפְּנֵי הַבִּטּוּל בְּעֶצֶם.

RABBI SHALOM DOVBER SCHNEERSOHN (RASHAB)

1860–1920

Chasidic rebbe. Rabbi Shalom Dovber became the 5th leader of the Chabad movement upon the passing of his father, Rabbi Shmuel Schneersohn. He established the Lubavitch network of *yeshivot* called Tomchei Temimim. He authored many volumes of Chasidic discourses and is renowned for his lucid and thorough explanations of kabbalistic concepts.

Humility is not synonymous with feelings of inferiority, or with not finding within yourself any good, or with thinking that you are on a bad path, G-d forbid.

To have humility means to not sense yourself.

Although you are good and on the correct path in matters of Torah and *mitzvot*, and although you are committed to serving G-d with great self-sacrifice, nevertheless, you do not self-aggrandize or think that you have reached some unique level. It is not that you do not know about your good; it's that you don't claim credit or think that you have earned special standing.

And this results from being completely unabsorbed in yourself.

Text 10

RABBI YOSEF YITSCHAK SCHNEERSOHN,
SEFER HAMAAMARIM 5701, P. 49 ⚇

וּכְמוֹ בְּמִי שֶׁמַּרְגִּישׁ בְּרֹאשׁוֹ אוֹ בְּאֶחָד מֵאֵבָרָיו, הִנֵּה הֶרְגֵּשׁ זֶה
עַצְמוֹ הוּא הוֹרָאָה עַל הַחֹלִי. דְּמִי שֶׁהוּא בָּרִיא אֵינוֹ מַרְגִּישׁ
אֶת אֵבָרָיו.

וְכֵן הוּא בְּרוּחָנִיּוּת, דְּמִי שֶׁהוּא מַרְגִּישׁ אֶת עַצְמוֹ, דְּזֶהוּ גַּסּוּת
הָרוּחַ וְגַאֲוָה, הֲרֵי הֶרְגֵּשׁ זֶה הוֹרָאָה עַל חֹלִי הַנֶּפֶשׁ. דְּמִי שֶׁהוּא
בָּרִיא בְּנַפְשׁוֹ הֲרֵי אֵינוֹ מַרְגִּישׁ אֶת עַצְמוֹ.

If you are feeling your head or one of your limbs, it indicates illness. Healthy people do not feel their limbs.

The same applies in the spiritual sense: if you are feeling your own existence, it indicates an illness of character, namely, arrogance. Those who are spiritually healthy do not feel themselves.

CONCLUSION

Text 11

VIKTOR FRANKL, *THE UNHEARD CRY FOR MEANING:*
PSYCHOTHERAPY AND HUMANISM (NEW YORK:
SIMON AND SCHUSTER, 1978), PP. 31–35

The will to meaning is not only a matter of faith but also a fact. Since I introduced the concept in 1949, it has been empirically corroborated and validated by several authors, using tests and statistics. . . . The will to meaning is not only a true manifestation of man's humanness, but also . . . a reliable criterion of mental health. . . .

I thereby understand the primordial anthropological fact that being human is being always directed, and pointing, to something or someone other than oneself: to a meaning to fulfill or another human being to encounter, a cause to serve or a person to love. Only to the extent that someone is living out this self-transcendence of human existence, is he truly human or does he become his true self. He becomes so, not by concerning himself with his self's actualization, but by forgetting himself and giving himself, overlooking himself and focusing outward.

Consider the eye, an analogy I am fond of invoking. When, apart from looking in a mirror, does the eye see anything of itself? An eye with a cataract may see something like a cloud, which is its cataract; an eye with glaucoma may see its glaucoma as a rainbow halo around the lights. A healthy eye sees nothing of itself—it is self-transcendent.

VIKTOR EMIL FRANKL
1905–1997

M.D., PhD, founder of logotherapy. Frankl was professor of neurology and psychiatry at the University of Vienna Medical School. During World War II, he spent 3 years in various concentration camps, including Theresienstadt, Auschwitz, and Dachau. Frankl was the founder of the psychotherapeutic school called logotherapy. Frankl authored 39 books, which have been published in 38 languages. His most famous book, *Man's Search for Meaning,* has sold over 9 million copies in the U.S. alone.

What is called self-actualization is, and must remain, the unintended effect of self-transcendence; it is ruinous and self-defeating to make it the target.

Exercise 2.3

1. Which idea from this lesson would be most helpful for you to enhance and reinforce a healthy self-concept?

2. In what way can I grow over the course of the next month in this regard?

3. What will be most difficult about doing so?

4. What will be the benefits of doing so?

Key Points

1. The way we perceive ourselves is crucial to our emotional well-being. A negative self-image or feeling dispensable can impede our happiness.

2. The Torah's Creation narrative conveys that the human being is created in the divine image, in order to partner with G-d to advance civilization and make the world a more G-dly place. Every individual is indispensable for this project, as each person has a specific task that only he or she can fulfill. Thus, birth is G-d saying you matter.

3. When we internalize the messages from the Torah about the human being, we emerge with a G-d-based, well-grounded perception of ourselves as important and indispensable. We are also empowered to cease comparing ourselves to others and their accomplishments.

4. When we find ourselves focusing on our flaws, we need to ensure that our assessment is accurate. This includes remembering that just as we need to know our shortcomings, so we must know our strengths. Indeed, we often need a mentor or good friend to help us gain a balanced self-concept. When engaged in an accurate assessment, we will surely find many merits and redeeming qualities that lead us to take a positive view of ourselves.

5. While we should not overlook our faults, we also should not define ourselves by them. Judaism empowers us to define ourselves (and others) exclusively by who we are: beings created in the divine image, who share an unbreakable bond with G-d, tasked with a specific mission that only we can execute.

6. True humility provides us with a self-concept that is conducive to happiness. Humility is not a distortion of the truth, it is not a negative self-image, and it does not ensue from our shortcomings and failures.

Humility means that our concept of self slips below the threshold of awareness, as we are completely focused on fulfilling life's calling. This insulates us from self-doubt and thus helps us cultivate a healthy self-concept.

7. Because we are purposeful beings, we find happiness when we are true to who we are—completely focused on our purpose.

APPENDIX
ARROGANCE

Text 12

MIDRASH, *BEREISHIT RABAH* 16:3

אוֹמְרִים לִפְרָת: לָמָה אֵין קוֹלְךָ הוֹלֵךְ? אָמַר לָהֶם: אֵינִי צָרִיךְ. מַעֲשַׂי מוֹדִיעִים אוֹתִי. אָדָם נוֹטֵעַ בִּי נְטִיעָה וְהִיא עוֹשָׂה לִשְׁלשִׁים יוֹם. זוֹרֵעַ בִּי יֶרֶק וְהִיא עוֹמֶדֶת לג׳ יָמִים.
אוֹמְרִים לְחִדֶּקֶל: לָמָה קוֹלְךָ הוֹלֵךְ?
אָמַר לָהֶם: הַלְוַאי נִשְׁמַע קוֹלִי וְנֵרָאֶה.

They say to the Euphrates River, "Why is your sound not audible?"

"My deeds make me known," it replied. "When a person plants a plant next to me, it matures in thirty days; when a person sows a vegetable next to me, it sprouts in three days."

They say to the Tigris River, "Why is your sound audible?"

"If only my voice would be heard so that I may be noticed," it answered.

BEREISHIT RABAH

An early rabbinic commentary on the Book of Genesis. This Midrash bears the name of Rabbi Oshiya Rabah (Rabbi Oshiya "the Great"), whose teaching opens this work. This Midrash provides textual exegeses and stories, expounds upon the biblical narrative, and develops and illustrates moral principles. Produced by the sages of the Talmud in the Land of Israel, its use of Aramaic closely resembles that of the Jerusalem Talmud. It was first printed in Constantinople in 1512 together with 4 other Midrashic works on the other 4 books of the Pentateuch.

MISGUIDED HUMILITY

Text 13

RABBI YISRAEL BAAL SHEM TOV, *KETER SHEM TOV* 145

שֵׁרוֹב עַנְוְתָנוּתוֹ שֶׁל הָאָדָם גּוֹרֵם שֶׁנִּתְרַחֵק מֵעֲבוֹדַת
הַשֵּׁם יִתְבָּרֵךְ. שֶׁמִּצַּד שִׁפְלוּתוֹ אֵינוֹ מַאֲמִין כִּי הָאָדָם
גּוֹרֵם עַל יְדֵי תְּפִלָּתוֹ וְתוֹרָתוֹ שֶׁפַע אֶל כָּל הָעוֹלָמוֹת, וְגַם
הַמַּלְאָכִים נִזּוֹנִין עַל יְדֵי תוֹרָתוֹ וּתְפִלָּתוֹ. שֶׁאִלּוּ הָיָה מַאֲמִין
זֶה כַּמָּה הָיָה עוֹבֵד ה' בְּשִׂמְחָה וּבְיִרְאָה מֵרוֹב כֹּל . . .
הָאָדָם רָאוּי לָשׂוּם לֵב וְלוֹמַר כִּי הוּא "סֻלָּם מֻצָּב אַרְצָה
וְרֹאשׁוֹ מַגִּיעַ הַשָּׁמָיְמָה" (בְּרֵאשִׁית כח, יב), וְכָל תְּנוּעוֹתָיו
וַעֲסָקָיו וְדִבּוּרוֹ וְהִלּוּכוֹ עוֹשֶׂה רוֹשֶׁם לְמַעְלָה.

RABBI YISRAEL BAAL SHEM TOV (BESHT)
1698–1760

Founder of the Chasidic movement. Born in Slutsk, Belarus, the Baal Shem Tov was orphaned as a child. He served as a teacher's assistant and clay digger before founding the Chasidic movement and revolutionizing the Jewish world with his emphasis on prayer, joy, and love for every Jew, regardless of his or her level of Torah knowledge.

Misguided humility distances a person from serving G-d. Our perceived lowliness leads us to disbelieve that our prayers and Torah study stimulate a flow of divine effluence to all the supernal worlds and that the angels are nourished by our Torah study and prayer. On the other hand, if we truly believe that our actions accomplish all this, how incredibly great would be the joy and reverence that accompany our service.…

We should be mindful that we are "a ladder that is stood upon earth whose head reaches the heavens" (Genesis 28:12). All our gestures, engagements, words, and movements have an effect on high.

SECOND DEFINITION OF HUMILITY

Text 14

RABBI SHALOM DOVBER SCHNEERSOHN,
SEFER HAMAAMARIM 5679, P. 92 🙂

כַּאֲשֶׁר מִתְבּוֹנֵן שֶׁכָּל הַטּוֹב שֶׁלוֹ אֵינוֹ מִצַּד עַצְמוֹ כִּי אִם בִּירוּשָׁה
לָנוּ מֵאֲבוֹתֵינוּ, וּכְמוֹ מַה שֶׁהוּא מַאֲמִין בַּה' וְדָבוּק בֶּאֱלֹקוּת
בִּדְבֵיקוּת אַהֲבָה וְיִרְאָה כוּ', הֲרֵי הָאֱמוּנָה שֶׁלוֹ אֵינוֹ מִשּׁוּם
הַהַכָּרָה שֶׁמַּכִּיר אֱלֹקוּת, רַק שֶׁהוּא לוֹ בִּירוּשָׁה מֵאַבְרָהָם אָבִינוּ
ע"ה, שֶׁהָיָה מַאֲמִין הָרִאשׁוֹן, וְהָיָה רֹאשׁ לְכָל הַמַּאֲמִינִים,
שֶׁאֶצְלוֹ הָיָה הָאֱמוּנָה בִּבְחִינַת הַכָּרָה, שֶׁהִכִּיר אֶת בּוֹרְאוֹ . . .
וְזֶהוּ שֶׁכָּתוּב (בְּמִדְבָּר יב, ג) "וְהָאִישׁ מֹשֶׁה עָנָיו מְאֹד מִכָּל
הָאָדָם", הֲגַם שֶׁיָּדַע אֶת הַטּוֹב שֶׁלוֹ וְשֶׁהוּא גָבוֹהַּ בְּמַעֲלָה מִכָּל
אָדָם, וּמִכָּל מָקוֹם הָיָה עָנָיו מִכָּל אָדָם, וְהוּא מִפְּנֵי שֶׁזֶּהוּ מַה
שֶׁנִּיתַּן לוֹ מִלְמַעְלָה . . . וְאִלּוּ הָיוּ אֵלּוּ הַכֹּחוֹת אֵצֶל אַחֵר, הָיָה
גַם כֵּן בְּמַדְרֵגָה זוֹ, וְאֶפְשָׁר הָיָה עוֹד מְגַלֶּה אֶת הַכֹּחוֹת יוֹתֵר.
וּמִשּׁוּם זֶה הָיָה עָנָיו מִכֹּל.

We should contemplate how all the good we possess is an inheritance from our ancestors. For example, our belief in G-d and our emotional connection to G-d have not resulted from our own recognition, but are a spiritual inheritance from our ancestor Abraham. He was the first believer, and he truly came to his belief through his own recognition. . . .

This is the meaning of the verse (Numbers 12:3), "Moses was exceedingly humble, more than any person on the face of the earth." Moses was cognizant of his own qualities and was aware that his lofty spiritual level was unparalleled; but he was still humble. He recognized that all of these qualities were given to him from Above. . . . He felt that if another person would be endowed with the same abilities and qualities as he, the other would have equaled his achievements—or perhaps even surpassed them. It was this that led Moses to be the humblest man of all.

FLOW

Text 15

MIHALY CSIKSZENTMIHALYI, *FLOW: THE PSYCHOLOGY OF OPTIMAL EXPERIENCE* (NEW YORK: HARPER & ROW, 1990), PP. 62–64

When an activity is thoroughly engrossing, there is not enough attention left over to allow a person to consider either the past or the future, or any other temporarily irrelevant stimuli.

One item that disappears from awareness deserves special attention, because in normal life we spend so much time thinking about it: our own self. . . .

In flow there is no room for self-scrutiny. . . . When a climber is making a difficult ascent, he is totally taken up in the mountaineering role. He is 100 percent a climber, or he would not survive. There is no way for anything or anybody to bring into question any other aspect of his self. . . .

The absence of the self from consciousness does not mean that a person in flow has given up the control of his psychic energy, or that she is unaware of what happens in her body or in her mind. In fact the opposite is usually true. . . . A violinist must be extremely aware of every movement of her fingers, as well as the sound entering her ears, and of the total form of the piece she is playing. . . .

Loss of self-consciousness does not involve a loss of self, and certainly not a loss of consciousness, but rather, only a loss of consciousness *of* the self. What slips below the threshold of awareness

MIHALY CSIKSZENTMIHALYI, PHD
1934–

Leading expert in positive psychology. Csikszentmihalyi is professor of psychology at Claremont Graduate University where he directs the Quality of Life Research Center. His research interests are in human strengths, such as optimism and creativity. He is the author of the seminal book *Flow: The Psychology of Optimal Experience*.

is the *concept* of self, the information we use to represent to ourselves who we are. And being able to forget temporarily who we are seems to be very enjoyable.

TETHERED TO THE MISSION

Text 16

THE REBBE, RABBI MENACHEM MENDEL SCHNEERSON,
TORAT MENACHEM 5712:1 (4), PP. 331–332 ⊕

> שֶׁכַּאֲשֶׁר הָאָדָם מִתְבּוֹנֵן שֶׁנִּיתְּנוּ לוֹ יָמִים קְצוּבִים, יָמִים יוּצָרוּ
> גו', לֹא פָּחוֹת וְלֹא יוֹתֵר, וּבְכָל יוֹם, בְּכָל שָׁעָה וּבְכָל רֶגַע צָרִיךְ
> לַעֲבוֹד עֲבוֹדָתוֹ לְמַלֵּא שְׁלִיחוּתוֹ בְּעָלְמָא דֵין, הֲרֵי הוּא טָרוּד
> בָּזֶה כָּל כַּךְ עַד שֶׁאֵין לוֹ פְּנַאי כְּלָל לַחְשׁוֹב אוֹדוֹת עִנְיָנִים שֶׁל
> מַדְרֵיגוֹת . . . וּמִזֶּה מוּבָן בְּמִכָּל שֶׁכֵּן וְקַל וָחוֹמֶר שֶׁלֹּא שַׁיָּיךְ
> אֶצְלוֹ רֶגֶשׁ שֶׁל שְׂבִיעוּת רָצוֹן . . . שֶׁבָּרֶגַע זֶה שֶׁאֵינוֹ עוֹבֵד
> עֲבוֹדָתוֹ, מוֹרֵד הוּא בְּמֶלֶךְ מַלְכֵי הַמְּלָכִים הַקָּבָּ"ה בְּכָךְ שֶׁאֵינוֹ
> מְמַלֵּא אֶת שְׁלִיחוּתוֹ . . . וֶוען מֶען פְרֶעגְט אִים וֶואס אִיז בָּא
> דִיר מִיטְן בְּאַרְצַךְ, זוֹעֵק הוּא (שְׁרֵייט עֶר אוֹיס) בְּמַר נַפְשׁוֹ: מַה
> לִי רָצוֹן, מַה לִי תַּעֲנוּג, מַה לִי אַהֲבָה, מַה לִי יִרְאָה (וָואס מִיר
> רָצוֹן, וָואס מִיר תַּעֲנוּג, וָואס מִיר אַהֲבָה, וָואס מִיר יִרְאָה),
> כֵּיצַד יָכוֹל לַחְשׁוֹב עַל עִנְיָנִים שֶׁל מַדְרֵיגוֹת בָּהּ בְּשָׁעָה שֶׁצָּרִיךְ
> לַעֲמוֹד עַל הַמִּשְׁמָר שֶׁלֹּא יַעֲבוֹר אֲפִילוּ רֶגַע אֶחָד בְּמַצָּב שֶׁל
> מְרִידָה בְּמַלְכוּת ח"ו מִצַּד הַחִסָּרוֹן בְּמִילוּי הַשְּׁלִיחוּת בְּרֶגַע זֶה.

When we contemplate that we have a limited number of days, and that on each day and during each moment, we must fulfill our mission, we will then be completely preoccupied with our mission to the extent that we will not have time to think about attaining levels. . . . Certainly, we will not take the time to feel satisfied about our accomplishments . . . because a sense of satisfaction means that we are not fulfilling our mission during that moment, and that is tantamount to rebelling against G-d. . . . Therefore, when you ask such people about their desires, they yell out bitterly, "What desire? What pleasure? What love? What awe? How can we think about such matters when we need to ensure that we don't miss out on even one second of our mission?"

ARROGANCE BLOCKS HAPPINESS

Text 17

RABBI SHALOM DOVBER SCHNEERSOHN,
SEFER HAMAAMARIM 5679, P. 92 (ii)

דְּשִׂמְחַת הָאָדָם הוּא בְּיוֹתֵר בְּמַתָּנָה, מִפְּנֵי שֶׁזֶּהוּ שֶׁלֹּא הִרְוִיחַ
וְאֵינוֹ מַגִּיעַ לוֹ, עַל כֵּן הוּא שָׂמֵחַ בָּזֶה.

אֲבָל כַּאֲשֶׁר בָּא עַל שְׂכָרוֹ הֲרֵי אֵינוֹ שַׁיָּךְ שִׂמְחָה כָּל כַּךְ, מֵאַחַר
שֶׁזֶּהוּ שֶׁהִרְוִיחַ בְּכֹחוֹ.

וְעַל כֵּן בְּהַרְגָּשַׁת עַצְמוֹ, הֲרֵי הוּא מְחַשֵּׁב אֶת הַטּוֹב וְהַיּוֹשֶׁר
שֶׁלּוֹ וְחוֹשֵׁב שֶׁמַּגִּיעַ לוֹ. מִמֵּילָא אֵין הַשִּׂמְחָה גְּדוֹלָה בָּזֶה.

מַה שֶּׁאֵין כֵּן בְּעָנָיו, הוּא שִׂמְחָה שְׁלֵמָה וְתָמִיד הוּא בְּשִׂמְחָה,
שֶׁהֲרֵי בְּהֶעְדֵּר הַרְגָּשַׁת עַצְמוֹ שֶׁאֵינוֹ מְחַשֵּׁב אֶת עַצְמוֹ, הֲרֵי
אֵינוֹ מַגִּיעַ לוֹ כְּלוּם, וְהוּא רַק בְּדֶרֶךְ מַתָּנָה, עַל כֵּן הוּא שָׂמֵחַ
מְאֹד בָּזֶה.

Our happiness is more pronounced when we receive a gift—something that we did not earn and don't deserve. When we work and get paid, we experience less happiness, because we earned what we received.

The result of this is that people who are overly self-aware, who take their goodness and properness very seriously, are prone to think that they deserve everything that they have. Consequently, their happiness from the things they have cannot be complete.

On the other hand, humble people experience constant and complete joy. They are not focused on themselves, so they don't assume that they deserve things. Everything they have is thus regarded as a gift and makes them very happy.

KINDNESS LEADS TO JOY

Text 18
SONJA LYUBOMIRSKY, *THE HOW OF HAPPINESS*
(NEW YORK: PENGUIN PRESS, 2008), PP. 130–131

There are multiple ways that kindness can make us happier. Surveys of volunteers, for example, show that volunteering is associated with diminished depressive symptoms and enhanced feelings of happiness, self-worth, mastery, and personal control—a "helper's high." . . .

Consider an unusual study that followed five women volunteers over a three-year period. These five women, all of whom had multiple sclerosis (MS), were chosen to act as peer supporters for sixty-seven other MS patients. They were trained in active and compassionate listening techniques and instructed to call each patient for fifteen minutes once a month. The results show that, over the three years, the peer supporters experienced increased satisfaction, self-efficacy, and feelings of mastery. They reported engaging in more social activities and enduring less depression.

SONJA LYUBOMIRSKY, PHD

Leading expert in positive psychology. Dr. Lyubomirsky is professor of psychology at the University of California, Riverside. Originally from Russia, she received her PhD in social/personality psychology from Stanford University. Her research on the possibility of permanently increasing happiness has been honored with various grants, including a million-dollar grant from the National Institute of Mental Health. She has authored *The How of Happiness* and, more recently, *The Myths of Happiness*.

ADDITIONAL READINGS

GOING LOW TO GET HIGH: THE LINK BETWEEN HUMILITY AND HAPPINESS

Excerpted from a Chasidic discourse by the fifth Rebbe of Chabad, Rabbi Shalom Dovber Schneersohn

"The humble shall increase their joy in G-d" (Isaiah 29:19). This verse suggests that there is some connection between humility and happiness; it is specifically the humble who rejoice in G-d.

This raises the question: Feeling humble implies a sense of inferiority to others, a low self-esteem, whereas happiness would seem to be associated with the opposing trait of pride and a feeling of self-importance. How, then, can humility be the vehicle for happiness?

The answer is that humility is neither synonymous with inferiority nor the product of a low self-esteem. Feeling humble is neither the result of a failure to find any positive qualities within ourselves, nor are feelings of humility on account of an inward-directed pessimism. Heaven forbid!

Rather, humility means not paying as much attention to ourselves and that we place less emphasis on our own existence. Despite all of their good qualities, humble people do not think of themselves as particularly special. Despite being virtuous and decent people, who uphold Torah and *mitzvot* even to the point of self-sacrifice, the humble do not self-aggrandize or think that they have reached some unique level. It is not that they are unaware of or in denial of

their goodness; they know that they are good and that they act properly; they simply do not claim credit for this achievement or think that it has earned them special standing.

The reason for this is that humble people are totally devoid of self-absorption [given their focus on G-d and their mission in life]. When people are unabsorbed in themselves, they don't make a fuss about themselves, or need anyone to celebrate them, because they have lost consciousness of the self. Therefore, there is nothing to prompt them to self-promote.

Additionally, those who are humble contemplate how the good that they have is not self-created, but comes as an inheritance from their ancestors. Take for example the fact that we believe in G-d and have an emotional connection to G-dliness. This is not the result of our own independent spiritual striving to recognize G-d or to achieve consciousness of the Divine; rather, it is an inborn trait inherited from our ancestor Abraham, the first believer. Abraham is the one who came to faith through recognizing G-d on his own, and he passed down this faith to his descendants. Likewise, the connection we have with G-d—the internal, concealed, divine love that we all possess—it, too, is an inheritance from our ancestors, as it says in *Tanya*.

Think of a child who inherits wealth from a parent. The child didn't work for it; the child merely takes that which was prepared by the parent. The same is true of faith and of our emotional connection to G-d: It is an inheritance. It is not by our own doing alone, but an inheritance from our ancestors.

All of this leads to humility: we don't self-aggrandize because whatever we have accomplished is not due to our own work alone.

RABBI SHALOM DOVBER SCHNEERSOHN (RASHAB)

1860–1920

Chasidic rebbe. Rabbi Shalom Dovber became the 5th leader of the Chabad movement upon the passing of his father, Rabbi Shmuel Schneersohn. He established the Lubavitch network of *yeshivot* called Tomchei Temimim. He authored many volumes of Chasidic discourses and is renowned for his lucid and thorough explanations of kabbalistic concepts.

This explains the verse (Numbers 12:3), "Moses was exceedingly humble, more than any person on the face of the earth." Moses was cognizant of his own qualities and was aware that his lofty spiritual level was unparalleled; yet he was still humble. He recognized that all of these qualities had been given to him from Above, as the verse (Exodus 2:2) describing the moment of Moses's birth says, "She saw that he was good," which is to say that his goodness was innate.

Moses knew that were others endowed with the same abilities and qualities as his, they would have equaled his achievements. In fact, they may have even surpassed them. This led Moses to be the humblest man of all.

It is this humility that is the vehicle for joy.

When people are focused on themselves, their joy cannot be complete. On the contrary, it is a cause for sadness. It is said that the snake is by nature constantly sad, because he descends from the snake in the Garden of Eden—the Primordial Serpent—who symbolizes the selfish inclination. This leads to sadness.

One might think that a stronger self-perception would mean that one also senses their own inner goodness more strongly, which should lead to more joy. Nevertheless, this joy is incomplete, and for two reasons:

First, focusing excessively on our positive qualities leads to a sense of entitlement, which causes our joy to be incomplete. After all, receiving a gift is more exciting than receiving a wage. We do not work for a gift, and so we do not deserve it, which is why receiving the gift is such a cause for joy. But when we work for a wage, we deserve it, so there is less reason to be glad upon receiving it. Therefore, when we are overly self-aware, when we take seriously our goodness and therefore think that we are entitled to everything we have—in this there is no great happiness.

Second, when we have a strong sense of ourselves, we never seem to have enough. As our sages have said, "When we have one hundred, we want to turn it into two hundred; when we have two hundred, we want to make of it four hundred, so that we die without ever having realized even half of our desires." Therefore, our joy will always be partial. In fact, we will experience sadness over not having what we think we deserve.

None of this is the case for the humble—they experience constant and complete joy. Because of their lack of self-consciousness, they don't self-aggrandize, and so they don't think they deserve anything. Everything that they have is a gift, and this makes them very happy. They always have enough. Therefore, their joy is complete.

When the humble don't get something, they are not saddened; they don't think in terms of being entitled to anything, so why should they be upset? More generally, their lack of self-perception leads them to feel that they are not missing anything and that all is fine. Therefore they don't get upset and can always be happy.

This is why it is said that Hillel was so very happy during the Simchat Beit Hasho'evah celebrations of Sukkot: it was because he was so very humble, and true humility leads to great joy.

Sefer Hamaamarim 5679, pp. 91–92

Job Opening: You!

WHAT AM I HERE FOR?

Living a holistic life inspired by the Torah means having a relationship with G-d in which our individual selves find expression.

CONFUSED SOULS

Text 1

RABBI YANKI TAUBER, *ONCE UPON A CHASSID*
(NEW YORK: KEHOT PUBLICATION SOCIETY, 1994), PP. 157–158

A wealthy businessman and his coachman arrived in a city one Friday afternoon. The rich man was settled at the best hotel in town, and the coachman went off to his humble lodgings.

Both washed and dressed for Shabbat, and then set out for the synagogue for the evening prayers. On his way to *shul*, the businessman came across a large wagon that had swerved off the road and was stuck in a ditch. Rushing to help a fellow in need, the businessman climbed down into the ditch and began pushing and pulling at the wagon together with its hapless driver. But for all his finesse at handling the most challenging of business deals, when it came to extracting a wagon and a team of horses from a muddy ditch, our businessman was hopelessly out of his depth. After struggling for an hour in the knee-deep mud, he succeeded only in ruining his best suit of Shabbat clothes, amassing a most impressive collection of cuts and bruises, and getting the wagon even more impossibly embedded in the mud. Finally, he dragged his limping body to the synagogue, arriving a scant minute before the start of Shabbat.

Meanwhile, the coachman arrived early to the synagogue and sat down to recite a few chapters of Psalms. At the synagogue he found a group

RABBI YANKI TAUBER
1965–

Chasidic scholar and author. A native of Brooklyn, N.Y., Rabbi Tauber is an internationally renowned author who specializes in adapting the teachings of the Lubavitcher Rebbe. He is a member of the JLI curriculum development team and has written numerous articles and books, including *Once Upon a Chassid* and *Beyond the Letter of the Law*.

of wandering paupers and, being blessed with a most generous nature, the coachman invited them all to share his Shabbat meal. When the synagogue sexton approached the poor and homeless to arrange meal placements for them with the town's householders—as is customary in Jewish communities—he received the same reply from them all: "Thank you, but I have already been invited for the Shabbat meal."

Unfortunately, however, the coachman's budget was hardly equal to his generous heart. It would be most difficult to believe that his dozen guests left his table with more than a shadow of a meal in their hungry stomachs.

Thus the coachman, with his twenty years of experience in pulling wagons out of mud holes, took it upon himself to feed a small army, while the wealthy businessman, whose Shabbat meal leftovers could easily have fed every hungry man within a ten-mile radius, floundered about in a ditch.

Rabbi Yosef Yitzchak of Lubavitch told this story, and explained its lesson: "Every soul is entrusted with a mission unique to her alone, and is granted the specific aptitudes, talents and resources necessary to excel in her ordained role. One must take care not to become one of those lost souls who wander haplessly through life, trying their hand at every field of endeavor except for what is truly and inherently their own.

TEN-POINT NARRATIVE

Text 2

RABBI YOSEF YITSCHAK SCHNEERSOHN,
IGROT KODESH 6, P. 295 (🎧)

תּוֹלְדוֹת אָדָם אִיז אַ סֵפֶר וֶועלְכֶען מֶען בֶּעדַארְף לֶערְנֶען,
אוּן דֶער סֵפֶר בֶּעדַארְף זַיין דֶער וֶועג-וֵוייזֶער אִין דֶעם
מֶענְטשֶׁענְס לֶעבֶּען.
תּוֹלְדוֹת אָדָם, דֶעם מֶענְשֶׁענְס גֶעבּוּרְט, מֵיינְט:
דֶעם תַּכְלִית פוּן דֶעם מֶענְשֶׁענְס גֶעבּוּרְטְס אוֹיף דֶער וֶועלְט.
בַּא וֶועמֶען מֶען וֶוערְט גֶעבָּארֶען.
אִין וֶועלְכֶען פְּלַאץ מֶען וֶוערְט גֶעבָּארֶען.
אִין וֶועלְכֶען זְמַן מֶען וֶוערְט גֶעבָּארֶען.
וָואסְעֶר הַדְרָכָה אוּן חִינוּךְ מֶען הָאט בַּאקוּמֶען.
אִין וָואס פַאר אַ סְבִיבָה מֶען אִיז אוֹיסְגֶעוָואקְסֶען.
וֶועלְכֶע כִּשְׁרוֹנוֹת מֶען הָאט.
וֶועלְכֶע מִדוֹת טִבְעִיוֹת מֶען הָאט.
וֶועלְכֶע אֵייגֶענְשַׁאפְטֶען אוּן נוֹיגוּנְגֶען מֶען הָאט.
וִוי אַזוֹי דִי הַשְׁגָחָה הָעֶלְיוֹנָה הָאט גֶעפִירְט דִי גַאנְצֶע צַייט
מִיט דֶעם מֶענְטשֶׁען בִּיז עֶר אִיז גֶעוָוארֶען זֶעלְבְּסְטְשְׁטֶענְדִיק
אוּן גֶענוּמֶען אַ שְׁטֶעלוּנְג אִין לֶעבֶּען.
פוּן דִי אַלֶע אוֹיבֶּענְדֶערְמָאנְטֶע צֶעהן זַאכֶען שְׁטֶעלְט זִיך
צוּזַאמֶען דֶער תּוֹלְדוֹת אָדָם אוּן דַאן אִיז דָאס אַ סֵפֶר וֶועלְכֶען
מֶען בֶּעדַארְף לֶערְנֶען אוּן אוֹיסְקְלַייבֶּען דִי דַרְכֵי הַחַיִים וִוי
דֶער מֶענְשׁ בֶּעדַארְף זִיך אוֹיפְפִיהְרֶען אִין אַלֶע זַיינֶע זַאכֶען,
הֵן בֵּין אָדָם לַמָקוֹם אוּן הֵן בֵּין אָדָם לַחֲבֵירוֹ.

**RABBI YOSEF
YITSCHAK SCHNEERSOHN
(RAYATS, FRIERDIKER REBBE,
PREVIOUS REBBE)**
1880–1950

Chasidic rebbe, prolific writer, and
Jewish activist. Rabbi Yosef Yitschak,
the sixth leader of the Chabad
movement, actively promoted Jewish
religious practice in Soviet Russia
and was arrested for these activities.
After his release from prison and exile,
he settled in Warsaw, Poland, from
where he fled Nazi occupation and
arrived in New York in 1940. Settling
in Brooklyn, Rabbi Schneersohn
worked to revitalize American Jewish
life. His son-in-law Rabbi Menachem
Mendel Schneerson succeeded him as
the leader of the Chabad movement.

The story of our lives is a book that requires study. This book ought to be the compass for how we go about life.

The story of our lives consists of:

1. The reason we were created

2. To whom we were born

3. The place of our birth

4. The time period of our birth

5. The type of education and guidance we received

6. The environment in which we grew up

7. Our talents

8. Our inborn emotional disposition

9. Our characteristics and inclinations

10. How divine providence guided us until the day we became independent and assumed a position in life.

These ten factors form the narratives of our individual lives and become a book that requires study. These factors are supposed to guide which pathways we choose and how we behave, whether in interpersonal relationships or our relationship with G-d.

Exercise 3.1

In what ways do these factors play a role in your personal mission, as you currently conceive it?

Parents	
Birth location	
Era of birth	
Education	
Environment in which you grew up	
Talents	
Notable experiences of childhood and adolescence	

PERSONALITY
THE *SEFIROT*

Text 3
TIKUNEI ZOHAR, INTRODUCTION ⊕

פָּתַח אֵלִיָּהוּ וְאָמַר:

רִבּוֹן עָלְמִין, דְּאַנְתְּ הוּא חָד וְלֹא בְּחֻשְׁבָּן, אַנְתְּ הוּא עִלָּאָה עַל
כָּל עִלָּאִין, סְתִימָא עַל כָּל סְתִימִין, לֵית מַחֲשָׁבָה תְּפִיסָא בָךְ
כְּלָל.

אַנְתְּ הוּא דְּאַפִּיקַת עֲשַׂר תִּקּוּנִין, וְקָרֵינָן לְהוֹן עֲשַׂר סְפִירָן,
לְאַנְהָגָא בְהוֹן עָלְמִין סְתִימִין דְּלָא אִתְגַּלְיָן, וְעָלְמִין דְּאִתְגַּלְיָן.

TIKUNEI ZOHAR

An appendix to the *Zohar*, the seminal work of kabbalah (Jewish mysticism). *Tikunei Zohar* consists mostly of seventy kabbalistic expositions on the opening verse of the Torah. It was first printed in Mantua in 1558.

Elijah opened [his discourse with a prayer]:

Master of the Worlds! You are One and transcend the *sefirot*. You are exalted above all the exalted ones, hidden from all the hidden ones; no thought can grasp You whatsoever.

You are the One Who brought forth ten "garments," which we call the ten *sefirot*, through which to direct concealed worlds and revealed worlds.

Figure 3.1

The Ten *Sefirot*

A. Intellectual Attributes

Chochmah	Wisdom/ Creativity	חָכְמָה
Binah	Understanding/ Discernment	בִּינָה
Daat	Knowledge/ Connection	דַּעַת

B. Emotional Attributes

Chesed	Kindness/Love	חֶסֶד
Gevurah	Strength/ Restraint	גְּבוּרָה
Tiferet	Beauty/ Harmony/ Compassion	תִּפְאֶרֶת
Netsach	Victory/ Endurance	נֶצַח
Hod	Splendor/ Humility	הוֹד
Yesod	Foundation/ Bonding	יְסוֹד
Malchut	Kingdom/ Influence	מַלְכוּת

THE *KOCHOT*

Chochmah

Exercise 3.2a

The following traits are dominant in *chochmah* souls. In the box next to each trait, rate yourself on a scale from 1–5.

5 = very dominant
4 = somewhat dominant
3 = neutral
2 = somewhat weak
1 = very weak

Creative	
Intuitive	
Original	
Spiritual	

Binah

Exercise 3.2b

The following traits are dominant in *binah* souls. In the box next to each trait, rate yourself on a scale from 1–5.

5 = very dominant
4 = somewhat dominant
3 = neutral
2 = somewhat weak
1 = very weak

Analytical	
Logical	
Organized	
Studious	

Daat

Exercise 3.2c

The following traits are dominant in *daat* souls. In the box next to each trait, rate yourself on a scale from 1–5.

5 = very dominant
4 = somewhat dominant
3 = neutral
2 = somewhat weak
1 = very weak

Decisive	
Emotionally Present	
Focused	
Forging Strong Connections	

Chesed

Exercise 3.2d

The following traits are dominant in *chesed* souls. In the box next to each trait, rate yourself on a scale from 1–5.

5 = very dominant
4 = somewhat dominant
3 = neutral
2 = somewhat weak
1 = very weak

Cheerful	
Extroverted	
Generous	
Kind	
Loving	
Optimistic	

Gevurah

Exercise 3.2e

The following traits are dominant in *gevurah* souls. In the box next to each trait, rate yourself on a scale from 1–5.

5 = very dominant
4 = somewhat dominant
3 = neutral
2 = somewhat weak
1 = very weak

Cautious	
Critical	
Disciplined	
Frugal	
Introverted	
Perfectionist	
Purist	

Tiferet

Exercise 3.2f

The following traits are dominant in *tiferet* souls. In the box next to each trait, rate yourself on a scale from 1–5.

5 = very dominant
4 = somewhat dominant
3 = neutral
2 = somewhat weak
1 = very weak

Balanced	
Compassionate	
Empathetic	
Listening	
Sensitive	

Netsach

Exercise 3.2g

The following traits are dominant in *netsach* souls. In the box next to each trait, rate yourself on a scale from 1–5.

5 = very dominant
4 = somewhat dominant
3 = neutral
2 = somewhat weak
1 = very weak

Bold	
Competitive	
Consistent	
Determined	
Gritty	
Thrives on Adversity	

Hod

Exercise 3.2h

The following traits are dominant in *hod* souls. In the box next to each trait, rate yourself on a scale from 1–5.

5 = very dominant
4 = somewhat dominant
3 = neutral
2 = somewhat weak
1 = very weak

Patient	
Accommodating	
Devoted	
Grateful	
Humble	

Yesod

Exercise 3.2i

The following traits are dominant in *yesod* souls. In the box next to each trait, rate yourself on a scale from 1–5.

5 = very dominant
4 = somewhat dominant
3 = neutral
2 = somewhat weak
1 = very weak

Selfless	
Altruistic	

Malchut

Exercise 3.2j

The following traits are dominant in *malchut* souls. In the box next to each trait, rate yourself on a scale from 1–5.

5 = very dominant
4 = somewhat dominant
3 = neutral
2 = somewhat weak
1 = very weak

Leader	
Communicator	
Expressive	
Receptive	
Implementer	

IMPLEMENTATION

Text 4

TALMUD, SHABBAT 118B ⚅

אָמַר לֵיהּ רַב יוֹסֵף לְרַב יוֹסֵף בְּרֵיהּ דְּרַבָּה: "אֲבוּךְ, בְּמַאי זָהִיר טְפֵי"?

Rav Yosef asked of Rav Yosef son of Rabah, "With which mitzvah was your father most careful?"

BABYLONIAN TALMUD

A literary work of monumental proportions that draws upon the legal, spiritual, intellectual, ethical, and historical traditions of Judaism. The 37 tractates of the Babylonian Talmud contain the teachings of the Jewish sages from the period after the destruction of the 2nd Temple through the 5th century CE. It has served as the primary vehicle for the transmission of the Oral Law and the education of Jews over the centuries; it is the entry point for all subsequent legal, ethical, and theological Jewish scholarship.

Text 5

THE REBBE, RABBI MENACHEM MENDEL SCHNEERSON,
SICHOT KODESH 5734:2, P. 98 ⚏

לְכָל אֶחָד וְאֶחָד עִנְיָנוֹ הוּא מַה שֶׁה' נוֹתֵן לוֹ כּוֹחוֹת בְּאוֹפֶן
עֲבוֹדָתוֹ, וְהוּא צָרִיךְ לַעֲבוֹד אֶת עֲבוֹדָתוֹ לְפִי הַכּוֹחוֹת וְהַחוּשִׁים
שֶׁה' נָתַן לוֹ – שֶׁזֶּה הַחֵלֶק שֶׁלּוֹ.

וְעַל דֶּרֶךְ אֶחָד שֶׁה' נָתַן לוֹ כֹּחַ בְּשֵׂכֶל, צָרִיךְ (הוּא) לְנַצֵּל אֶת
שִׂכְלוֹ לְלִימּוּד הַתּוֹרָה, וּבָזֶה צָרִיךְ לִהְיוֹת כָּל חַיּוּתוֹ. אָמְנָם הוּא
צָרִיךְ לְקַיֵּים מִצְווֹת וְכָל הָעִנְיָנִים שֶׁתּוֹבְעִים מִכָּל אֶחָד וְאֶחָד,
מִכָּל מָקוֹם, כֵּיוָן שֶׁיֵּשׁ לוֹ חוּשׁ בְּלִימּוּד הַתּוֹרָה, צָרִיךְ לִהְיוֹת לוֹ
בָּזֶה זָהִיר טְפֵי, כֵּיוָן שֶׁיֵּשׁ לוֹ חוּשׁ לָזֶה.

וְעַל דֶּרֶךְ זֶה מִי שֶׁיֵּשׁ לוֹ חוּשׁ בְּעִנְיָן שֶׁל הֶרְגֵּשׁ הַלֵּב, צָרִיךְ לְנַצֵּל
אֶת זֶה לְעִנְיָן שֶׁל אַהֲבַת יִשְׂרָאֵל, לְקָרֵב יְהוּדִי וּלְהַסְבִּיר לוֹ אֶת
הָעִנְיָן שֶׁל אַהֲבַת ה' וְאַהֲבַת הַתּוֹרָה. וְגַם מִמֶּנּוּ תּוֹבְעִים לִימּוּד
הַתּוֹרָה וְכָל הָעִנְיָנִים, אֶלָּא שֶׁעִיקַר חַיּוּתוֹ צָרִיךְ לִהְיוֹת בָּזֶה,
כֵּיוָן שֶׁיֵּשׁ לוֹ כּוֹחוֹת מְיוּחָדִים עַל זֶה.

וְעַל דֶּרֶךְ זֶה אֶחָד שֶׁהוּא בַּעַל פּוֹעֵל "אַ פְּרַאקְטִישֶׁער מֶענְטְשׁ",
שֶׁהוּא בַּעַל פּוֹעֵל, כְּשֶׁצָּרִיךְ לְהָקִים מוֹסָד, הוּא רָץ וְעוֹשֶׂה
אֶת כָּל הַמַּאֲמַצִּים שֶׁיּוּקַם הַמּוֹסָד הַזֶּה, אוֹ כְּשֶׁצָּרִיךְ לִרְאוֹת
שֶׁבַּמּוֹסָד לֹא יִהְיֶה מְדַי קַר וְלֹא מְדַי חַם, כְּדֵי שֶׁהַתַּלְמִידִים
יוּכְלוּ לִלְמוֹד מִתּוֹךְ הַרְחָבָה, אָז הוּא עוֹשֶׂה אֶת זֶה. וְעַל דֶּרֶךְ
זֶה כִּי תִרְאֶה עָרֹם וְכִסִּיתוֹ, וַעֲנִיִּים מְרוּדִים תָּבִיא בָיִת, וּכְמוֹ
כֵן אֶצְלוֹ גַּם כֵּן יֶשְׁנָם הָעִנְיָנִים שֶׁל לִימּוּד הַתּוֹרָה וְהֶרְגֵּשׁ הַלֵּב,
אֶלָּא הָעִיקָר עִנְיָנוֹ זֶה מַעֲשֶׂה זֶה בְּפוֹעַל.

**RABBI MENACHEM
MENDEL SCHNEERSON**
1902–1994

The towering Jewish leader of the 20th
century, known as "the Lubavitcher
Rebbe," or simply as "the Rebbe." Born
in southern Ukraine, the Rebbe escaped
Nazi-occupied Europe, arriving in
the U.S. in June 1941. The Rebbe
inspired and guided the revival of
traditional Judaism after the European
devastation, impacting virtually
every Jewish community the world
over. The Rebbe often emphasized
that the performance of just one
additional good deed could usher
in the era of Mashiach. The Rebbe's
scholarly talks and writings have been
printed in more than 200 volumes.

G-d gives a unique personality to each person.
We all must pursue our mission in accordance
with this personality, because it comprises our
portion in this world.

For example:

If you are more cerebral, utilize this trait for
the study of Torah. Surely, you will observe
the other *mitzvot* and commit yourself to the

mission shared by every Jew, but you will be extra particular and passionate about Torah study, because it comports with your personality.

If kindness is your personality, utilize this trait to love and care for others. This includes sharing the rich heritage of Judaism with Jews who never had the opportunity to learn about it. This doesn't mean that you won't study Torah or perform other *mitzvot*; it means that you ought to be particularly spirited about your caring for others, given the unique capacity you have for this.

If you are a pragmatic person who knows how to get things done, involve yourself in starting an organization and spare no effort to get it off the ground. Alternatively, an existing institution, a school, may have a particular challenge that is inhibiting student performance: Can you solve it? Perhaps you can alleviate the plight of the poor and homeless. Sure, you will also study Torah and develop emotional connections with others, but place extra focus on getting things done.

CONCLUSION

Text 6

MARTIN SELIGMAN, *FLOURISH: A VISIONARY NEW UNDERSTANDING OF HAPPINESS AND WELL-BEING* (NEW YORK: ATRIA, 2013), PP. 37–38

People who go to this link are invited to help us test new exercises. First they take depression and happiness tests. . . . Next, we randomly assign them to a single exercise. . . .

Two of the exercises—what-went-well and the signature strength exercise below—markedly lowered depression three months and six months later. These two exercises also substantially increased happiness through six months. . . .

The purpose of [the signature strengths] exercise is to encourage you to own your signature strengths by finding new and more frequent uses for them. . . .

After you have completed the test, perform the following exercise: this week I want you to create a designated time in your schedule when you will exercise one or more of your signature strengths in a new way, either at work or at home or in leisure—just make sure you create a clearly defined opportunity to use it.

MARTIN E. P. SELIGMAN, PHD
1942–

Noted psychologist and bestselling author. Seligman was president of the American Psychological Association in 1998, during which one of his presidential initiatives was the promotion of positive psychology as a field of scientific study. He is a leading authority in the fields of positive psychology, resilience, learned helplessness, depression, optimism, and pessimism. He has written more than 250 scholarly publications and 20 books, including *Flourish, Authentic Happiness*, and *Learned Optimism*.

Exercise 3.3

1. Consider an area of your personality (character, inclination, emotional disposition) that is important to you.

2. Consider how you can use this at least once per day, whether in performing a ritual mitzvah or in helping others.

Key Points

1. A number of personal factors point us toward our unique mission in life: our parents; our place of birth; the era of our birth; our education; the environment in which we grew up; our talents; our emotional makeup; our character and inclinations; and notable experiences of our childhood and adolescence.

2. These factors form "the book" of our life—a book that requires study, to learn from it how to behave, both in interpersonal relationships and our relationship with G-d.

3. Jewish mysticism teaches that G-d created the world through ten attributes. Every human soul is a microcosm of these ten attributes, but within each soul, one or two of these attributes are dominant, which gives us our personality. This, too, should guide us toward our mission in life.

4. Upon analyzing the different factors of our lives, we are empowered to use them as guides for how we make life's choices. This includes tapping into our background and personality to inform how we engage in various good deeds and which projects will become something into which we will pour extra investment.

5. When people find more ways to tap into and utilize their personality strengths, they substantially increase their happiness.

APPENDIX
GIVE IT ALL YOU'VE GOT

Text 7
TALMUD, KETUBOT 66B–67A 🎧

אָמַר לָה, בִּתִּי מִי אַתְּ? אָמְרָה לוֹ: בַּת נַקְדִּימוֹן בֶּן גּוּרְיוֹן אָנִי.
אָמַר לָה . . .

וְנַקְדִּימוֹן בֶּן גּוּרְיוֹן לֹא עָבַד צְדָקָה? וְהָתַנְיָא, אָמְרוּ עָלָיו עַל
נַקְדִּימוֹן בֶּן גּוּרְיוֹן כְּשֶׁהָיָה יוֹצֵא מִבֵּיתוֹ לְבֵית הַמִּדְרָשׁ כְּלֵי מֵילַת
הָיוּ מַצִּיעִין תַּחְתָּיו וּבָאִין עֲנִיִּים וּמְקַפְּלִין אוֹתָן מֵאַחֲרָיו . . .
כִּדְבָעֵי לֵיהּ לְמֶיעֱבַד לֹא עָבַד. כִּדְאָמְרֵי אֵינְשֵׁי, לְפוּם גַּמְלָא
שִׁיחֲנָא.

Rabbi Yochanan ben Zakai met the daughter of Nakdimon ben Gurion. . . . [In their conversation, she told him that her father had not been charitable.] . . .

But didn't Nakdimon ben Gurion give charity? Indeed, a *beraita* states that people would say about Nakdimon ben Gurion that when he would leave his home to go to the study hall, his attendants would spread fine woolen garments underneath him for him to walk on, and he would allow the poor to follow him and take the expensive garments for themselves. . . .

Although Nakdimon gave much charity, he did not give enough in proportion to his wealth. As the saying goes, "The burden is set according to the strength of the camel."

WORKING ON WEAKNESS

Questions for Discussion

1. What is a possible blind spot of a person with a *chochmah*-oriented soul?

2. What is a possible blind spot of a person with a *chesed*-oriented soul?

Text 8a

TALMUD, SHABBAT 31A

שׁוּב מַעֲשֶׂה בְּנָכְרִי אֶחָד שֶׁבָּא לִפְנֵי שַׁמַאי. אָמַר לוֹ, "גַּיְירֵנִי עַל מְנָת שֶׁתְּלַמְדֵנִי כָּל הַתּוֹרָה כּוּלָהּ כְּשֶׁאֲנִי עוֹמֵד עַל רֶגֶל אַחַת". דְּחָפוֹ בְּאַמַּת הַבִּנְיָן שֶׁבְּיָדוֹ.

בָּא לִפְנֵי הִלֵּל, גַּיְירֵיהּ. אָמַר לוֹ, "דַּעֲלָךְ סְנִי לְחַבְרָךְ לֹא תַּעֲבֵיד. זוֹ הִיא כָּל הַתּוֹרָה כּוּלָהּ וְאִידָךְ פֵּירוּשָׁהּ הוּא, זִיל גְּמוֹר".

A man once came before Shamai and said to him, "I would like to convert, on the condition that you teach me the whole Torah while I stand on one foot." Shamai chased him away with the builder's measuring tool that was in his hand.

The prospective convert went to Hillel, who converted him and said, "What is hateful to you, do not do to your fellow. That is the whole Torah, the rest is commentary; go and learn it."

Text 8b

ETHICS OF THE FATHERS 1:15 ⊞

שַׁמַּאי אוֹמֵר: "עֲשֵׂה תוֹרָתְךָ קֶבַע, אֱמוֹר מְעַט וַעֲשֵׂה הַרְבֵּה,
וֶהֱוֵי מְקַבֵּל אֶת כָּל הָאָדָם בְּסֵבֶר פָּנִים יָפוֹת".

Shamai would say, "Make your Torah study a permanent fixture of your life. Say little and do much. And receive every human being with a pleasant countenance."

ETHICS OF THE FATHERS
(*PIRKEI AVOT*)

A 6-chapter work on Jewish ethics that is studied widely by Jewish communities, especially during the summer. The first 5 chapters are from the Mishnah, tractate Avot. Avot differs from the rest of the Mishnah in that it does not focus on legal subjects; it is a collection of the sages' wisdom on topics related to character development, ethics, healthy living, piety, and the study of Torah.

ADDITIONAL READINGS

SOUL DNA

By Rabbi Levi Potash

THE QUESTION AND SEARCH

It was one specific meeting that changed everything. I was raising funds for my Chabad center, and met with Sam,[1] a well-to-do doctor in my community, to ask for his help.

I showed up to this meeting one fine Tuesday, at lunchtime, and I sat there in his mahogany adorned office, sharing a coffee and sandwich.

"So," he asked me, "how many of your siblings are rabbis?"

"Well," I said, "I have seven siblings. Four of them are rabbis, or married to rabbis. One is a teacher, and two of my siblings are in business."

"Oh," he said, as a look of consternation crossed over his face, "I thought *all* of you, in your community, *had* to become rabbis!" He said it with a tone of expectation, almost as if, had I answered yes to his question it would unburden him of some unknown misery.

I sensed his sadness and guessed the question was coming from somewhere deeper. I leaned forward and asked him, "How did you become a doctor?"

"Aagh," he sighed, "when I was in high school, my father called me in to his study and said, 'You are going to become an accountant.' When I adamantly refused, my father said, 'All right then, you will become a doctor!'"

He confided in me that he hates his job and will be stuck with it until "the day I die. It's funny, because in junior high school I always thought that I should become a movie producer," he finished.

I was stunned by this secret that Sam shared with me.

This and other things got me curious to investigate the best ways to make career choices—which leads to a much broader and fundamental question: "What is my mission in life, and how can I find it?" Thus began my ongoing search in Torah and Jewish writings for an answer. Perhaps Chasidic teachings could shed some light on the topic.

Here is a taste of some of the things that I discovered.

YOU ARE SUPPOSED TO BE YOU

There is an anecdote from the great Chasidic master, Reb Zushe of Anipoli:[2]

One day Reb Zushe was seen crying in his bed. When asked by his students for an explanation for his sadness, this was his reply: "When I come to Heaven and they ask me, 'Why weren't you like Abraham our forefather?' I will answer: 'Because I wasn't Abraham.' If they inquire: 'Why didn't you match the greatness of Moses?' I can answer that I wasn't Moses. Even if they try to compare me to my brother, Reb Elimelech, I can still say that I wasn't Elimelech. However, if they ask me why I wasn't the way Zushe needed to be . . . to that I have no answer."

We weren't sent down here to this world to live someone else's life. If that were the case, we wouldn't need to be sent here in the first place. G-d has the other person's life already! We all have our own specific mission, and we should live our own life, to the best of our ability.

This highlights a teaching from Ben Azai in Pirkei Avos that states: *"Ein loch adam she'ein*

RABBI LEVI POTASH

Rabbi Potash directs the Chabad center in Redwood City, CA and is a popular lecturer on the practical application of kabbalah.

---

1 Some of the details of this true story have been changed, to protect this person's privacy.
2 http://www.chabad.org/blogs/blog_cdo/aid/708696/jewish/I-Dont-Want-to-be-ME.htm

lo sho'oh—There is no person who doesn't have his time."[3] In the context of this discussion, this would mean that Hashem gives each of us unique circumstances and resources with which to do good in the world, and it is our job to try and fulfill that mission.

Unfortunately, sometimes our souls get lost and wander around trying to fulfill someone else's mission.

LOST SOULS

They tell a story about lost souls...

Once there was a fellow who came to town on a Friday. He was traveling by horse and cart through the muddy roads, and his horse got stuck in the mud. Trapped, lonely, and hungry, the traveler called out for help. A wealthy person was walking by and heard his cry for help. Though he did not have any experience working with horses, he rolled up his sleeves and got to work. After two hours, the helpful wealthy man had ripped his jacket and soiled his pants, and the horse—exhausted from shlepping and shlepping—died on the spot. With just minutes to Shabbos, the wealthy man and the traveler both went rushing to the bathhouse to wash up.

Shabbos eve at the synagogue, the traveler was welcomed by a very friendly though destitute member of the shul, a wagon driver by occupation, and he was invited back to the wagon driver's home to share the Shabbos dinner. The poor wagon driver was only able to muster together some challah and sardines, so unfortunately the weary traveler went to bed hungry that night.

These two people, the wealthy man and the wagon driver, were kind and well-meaning individuals and yet they are known as "lost souls." The wealthy man could have served this visitor a feast fit for a king and yet he dirtied himself struggling to free the horse from the mud—something he did not know how to do. And the wagon driver, who could have easily rescued the horse from the mud, shared his last few crumbs

of bread with the visitor, who remained hungry nonetheless.

Had these two acted nobly? Sure. Did they push themselves beyond their capabilities? Absolutely. But they weren't making the best use of their resources.

As is true with life circumstances and resources, so it is true with our personality, talents, and temperament.

The Talmud says "*Kesheim shein partzfeihem shavim kach ein daatom shaveh*—Just as their faces aren't the same, so too are their opinions not the same."[4] We each have different perspectives and opinions, as well as a different personality and temperament. By gaining clarity as to our unique personality and temperament, we are able to focus our energies on making an impactful difference in the world, getting the most bang for our buck—not just trying to do good with little effect because so much energy is wasted on projects that we are not good at.

But how do we get to know our own personality and temperament?

SEFIROT AND IDENTITY

The Kabbalah is replete with references to the ten *sefirot*. These are manifestations of Hashem's light and energy that He used to create and interact with the world. As such, the entire universe is a reflection of these ten spiritual powers. We, human beings with the unique quality of being created in the image of G-d,[5] are a human reflection of these ten powers, which makeup our identity and personality.

The Tikunei Zohar[6] states (and it is cited in the *Tanya*[7]) that there are ten types of Jews, based on the ten *sefirot*. This implies that different people are influenced by one or more of the ten *sefirot*. In the introduction of the *Tanya*,[8] Rabbi Shne'ur Zalman of Liadi references the concept that the differing root-source of our soul affects our opinions and ways of thinking.

---

3 Chapter 4, Mishna 3.

4 Tosefta, Berochos, chapter 6.
5 Bereishit, chapter 1:26–27.
6 http://hebrewbooks.org/pdfpager.aspx?req=20445&st=&pgnum=20
7 See *Tanya*, p. 20a.
8 Ibid., p. 3b.

The Previous Lubavitcher Rebbe, Rabbi Yosef Yitschak Schneersohn, discusses this concept in a Chasidic discourse:[9]

> Souls are called lights. As it states, "The soul of man is G-d's light" (Proverbs 20:27). In the *menorah* there were seven lights, which are the seven levels[10] in serving G-d. One person serves through love and another through fear, and so on with all the levels; each person, according to the source of his soul in the supernal *midot* of *chesed, gevurah, tiferet, netsach, hod, yesod,* and *malchut* of *atsilut*. For example, our forefathers . . . Abraham would welcome guests and share kindness. He is called Abraham who loves me: the source of his soul is *chesed*; and Isaac: his source was *gevurah* (fear/awe) . . .

WHAT ARE THE TEN?

Here is a list of the ten *sefirot*, and a word or two of definition:

Chochmah, (lit., wisdom): spirituality, creativity
Binah (lit., understanding): logic, analyzer
Daat (lit., knowledge): focus, decisions, planning
Chesed (lit., kindness): love, kindness
Gevurah (lit., strength): fear, protection
Tiferet (lit., beauty): pity, caring
Netsach (lit., eternity): dominating, winning
Hod (lit., splendor): accepting, supporting
Yesod (lit., foundation): passion, communication
Malchut (lit., kingship): action, results

We are each made up of all of these ten. But if you are honest with yourself you will realize that you gravitate toward one or more of these traits and temperaments. And more importantly, there are some of these categories that you dislike and maybe even detest.

There are dominant soul powers and there are recessive soul powers. We each have all of the ten soul powers but some of them are more dominant than others. And we are more comfortable expressing ourselves through some of them more than through others.

In some ways we can compare these ten soul powers to genetics and DNA. We all share the same basic genes and DNA structure, yet we are all so different. Some are tall, and others are short. Some have a large nose; others a small one. We are physically strong or weak; we need to sleep nine hours each night or make do with six—our DNA may be the same, but we are all so different.

Although the research in this area is still advancing, it's safe to assume that these differences are a result of our genes. Although we often share similar genes with others, we each have dominant genes and recessive genes. Although you may have a recessive gene for blue eyes, if your dominant gene is for brown eyes, you will end up with brown eyes. That blue-eyes gene is still there, hidden away. It won't necessarily affect you, but you can potentially transfer it on to your children.

Similarly, we all have the ten soul powers—our soul DNA, if you will. And like DNA, some are dominant and some are recessive; some of our soul powers we tend to express and others we don't. But they are all there.

Or perhaps, imagine the ten soul powers as rooms in your house. There are many rooms, each decorated differently and each serving a distinct purpose. While you prefer to spend more time in one or two particular rooms, this doesn't in any way preclude you from entering the other rooms. You can enter them, you can even spend time in them, but you won't be as comfortable as in your preferred rooms.

So it is with the ten soul powers. We each have all ten, however some are preferred over the others.

BENEFITS OF THE SYSTEM

After familiarizing oneself with these concepts and getting a better grasp of our one's personality traits and temperament, there is great value that this can bring to one's relationships, professional life, and religious life.

---

9 *Sefer Hamaamarim,* 5692, p. 226.

10 This is referring to the seven emotional/instinctive levels of the *sefirot*: *chesed, gevurah, tiferet, netsach, hod, yesod,* and *malchut*. When the number ten is used, it is referring to these seven plus the three mental faculties: *chochmah, binah,* and *daat*

RELATIONSHIPS

We all talk about how opposites attract. And we all know the stereotypes about how men do things this way and woman do things that way . . . But what happens when the model doesn't fit your relationship?

They say that women are talkative and men don't like to talk. But what happens when the husband is talkative and the woman is reserved? A couple can use this ten-*sefirot* model to better understand their uniqueness and how their spouse is unique in different ways. They can then better appreciate their differences as well as their unique qualities.

When appreciating how one's spouse is different and the specific ways in which his or her traits complement one's own, a married couple can then work better as a team to build a loving and balanced home and raise a new generation of stable and healthy children who appreciate each other's differences.

CAREER: SOME EXAMPLES

Do you like to analyze? Is that one of your identifying traits? If you seek to work in a job or career that requires a lot of thinking and analyzing, you will enjoy your work more. If you work in a job that requires a lot of doing as opposed to thinking, you may be very unhappy.

Does your job require a lot of decision-making and planning? If you score low in *daat*—focus and decisions—you will be frustrated.[11] Do you score high in *chesed*—loving-kindness? You want to ensure that you have a lot of interaction with people in your work. Solitary work is not for you.

RELIGION

Do you "get" G-d? Do you love G-d? Do you even have a relationship? Or is G-d too abstract? When we better understand our own personality and temperament, we can better relate to Hashem, because G-d has all of the character traits of all of the temperaments in the most perfect way.

If someone is accepting and supportive, and considers that an admirable trait; think about

how accepting, patient and supportive G-d is. Hashem is described as humble and patient, waiting for the person to repent on their own. Now, you will have an easy way to appreciate and relate to G-d. If you are generous and loving, think about all the things that G-d gives to the world and its inhabitants. How generous G-d is: just read the first blessing of the grace after meals.

If you are an intellectual, think about how much of a genius G-d is to create the universe with all of its intricate laws of nature. This can be gleaned from studying kabbalah, and even from scientific exploration. If you are all about the bottom line and getting things done, just think about how G-d pulled off the biggest building project in history: the very creation of the physical universe.

These are just some examples. But whatever traits you possess and admire, you will be able to find them expressed by G-d in an even better way. By focusing on those aspects of G-d's so-called "personality," you will have a natural affinity to (this aspect of) the divine.

CAN WE CHANGE OUR PERSONALITY?

Now of course one can make changes and adjustments in one's personality and character through hard work and *avodah* (prayer). One of the foundational principles of Chabad Chasidism is that we can and should make changes in our personality. But it is very helpful to get to know who we are when we are starting out, so that we know what is what. Just as it is very helpful for a business consultant to assess all aspects of a business to know what is working and what isn't, so too we should know who we are, in order to know what needs work and what doesn't.

Similar to DNA, we have dominant and recessive *midot*; however, unlike DNA,[12] we can change (at least some of) them. Just like the preferred rooms in our house, we can always

---

11 See *Sefer Halikutim, Erech Daat*, p. 299.

12 Although, the latest in DNA research is showing that some changes can possibly be made to the DNA—depending on the environment and other factors. For example, see: http://www.scientificamerican.com/article/changing-our-dna-through-mind-control/

choose to spend more time in a different room; so too we can always choose to spend more time developing a different *midah*.

At the same time, there are parts of our personality that we can't change. It would therefore be most productive, and the best use of our time and energy, to accept them and incorporate this reality into our mission, so that we don't spend our life trying to whisk water into cream.

Working on changing our personality and challenging ourselves to do things we don't naturally like to do is important. We should focus on personal growth, and there is great satisfaction when we make a breakthrough. However, when it comes to making a difference in this world—when it comes to making this earth a better place—the more we work in harmony with our natural talents, temperament, and interests, the more people we will be able to impact and the more good we will be able to achieve in this world, making it into a more G-dly place.

So I challenge you to discover *your unique* temperament, strengths, and talents. Use them in your own unique way to serve G-d, and make this world a better place.

For if *you* don't live ***your*** life, *who will?*

Reprinted with permission of the author

Journey from Oy to Yay!

OVERCOMING STRESS THROUGH POSITIVITY

....

We learn how to cultivate optimism and trust from the inspiring example of King David. The benefits are borne out by contemporary research.

INTRODUCTION

Exercise 4.1

Over the past two weeks, how often have you experienced the following?

1. Not being able to stop or control worrying

Not at all	Several days	Over half the days	Nearly every day

2. Worrying too much about different things

Not at all	Several days	Over half the days	Nearly every day

3. Having trouble relaxing

Not at all	Several days	Over half the days	Nearly every day

4. Feeling afraid as if something awful might happen

Not at all	Several days	Over half the days	Nearly every day

Question for Discussion

What strategies have you found effective in managing your worries?

FEND WITH FRIENDS

Text 1a
PROVERBS 12:25 ⚀

> דְּאָגָה בְלֶב אִישׁ יַשְׁחֶנָּה.

A worry in a person's heart—cast it away.

Text 1b
TALMUD, YOMA 75A ⚀

> רַבִּי אַמִי וְרַבִּי אַסִי - חַד אָמַר: יַשְׁחֶנָּה מִדַּעְתּוֹ. וְחַד אָמַר:
> יְשִׂיחֶנָּה לַאֲחֵרִים.

Rabbi Ami and Rabbi Asi [interpreted this verse]. One said, "Cast it from the mind." The other said, "Speak about it with others."

BABYLONIAN TALMUD

A literary work of monumental proportions that draws upon the legal, spiritual, intellectual, ethical, and historical traditions of Judaism. The 37 tractates of the Babylonian Talmud contain the teachings of the Jewish sages from the period after the destruction of the 2nd Temple through the 5th century CE. It has served as the primary vehicle for the transmission of the Oral Law and the education of Jews over the centuries; it is the entry point for all subsequent legal, ethical, and theological Jewish scholarship.

Question for Discussion

Why does it often help to discuss a worrisome matter with a friend?

Text 1c

RABBI YOSEF YITSCHAK SCHNEERSOHN,
CITED IN *HAYOM YOM*, 25 SIVAN 🕮

וּפֵירֵשׁ הַצֶּמַח צֶדֶק: "לַאֲחֵרִים" רַק בְּגוּף, אֲבָל מְאוּחָדִים אִתּוֹ
עִמּוֹ, שֶׁמַּרְגִּישִׁים אֶת עִנְיָנוֹ.

The third rebbe of Chabad explained: They are "others" only in the bodily sense. However, they are completely united with you, for they empathize with you.

RABBI YOSEF YITSCHAK SCHNEERSOHN
(RAYATS, FRIERDIKER REBBE, PREVIOUS REBBE)
1880–1950

Chasidic rebbe, prolific writer, and Jewish activist. Rabbi Yosef Yitschak, the sixth leader of the Chabad movement, actively promoted Jewish religious practice in Soviet Russia and was arrested for these activities. After his release from prison and exile, he settled in Warsaw, Poland, from where he fled Nazi occupation and arrived in New York in 1940. Settling in Brooklyn, Rabbi Schneersohn worked to revitalize American Jewish life. His son-in-law Rabbi Menachem Mendel Schneerson succeeded him as the leader of the Chabad movement.

MIND CONTROL

Text 2a

RABBI MENACHEM MENDEL OF LUBAVITCH, *IGROT KODESH*, P. 19

עַל דְּבַר מְבוּקָשׁוֹ נִידוֹן הַמּוֹרֶךְ לֵב כוּ׳, הֲגַם עַל חִנָּם מַמָּשׁ, לֹא מָנַעְתִּי מִלִּכְתּוֹב בָּזֶה אֲשֶׁר עִם לְבָבִי.

Regarding your questions concerning fears, etc. Although they are over naught, I have not refrained from answering by sharing what's on my heart.

RABBI MENACHEM MENDEL OF LUBAVITCH (*TSEMACH TSEDEK*)
1789–1866

Chasidic rebbe and noted author. The *Tsemach Tsedek* was the third leader of the Chabad Chasidic movement and a noted authority on Jewish law. His numerous works include halachic responsa, Chasidic discourses, and kabbalistic writings. Active in the communal affairs of Russian Jewry, he worked to alleviate the plight of the cantonists, Jewish children kidnapped to serve in the Czar's army. He passed away in Lubavitch, leaving seven sons and two daughters.

Text 2b

RABBI MENACHEM MENDEL OF LUBAVITCH, IBID., PP. 19–20 ⓘ

וַדַּאי שֶׁיֵּשׁ לְבַקֵּשׁ מֵה' עַל שִׂמְחַת הַנֶּפֶשׁ, כְּמַאֲמַר: "שַׂמֵּחַ נֶפֶשׁ
עַבְדֶּךָ" וְכֵן "וְהָסֵר מִמֶּנּוּ יָגוֹן וַאֲנָחָה כו'".
עִם כָּל זֶה יֵשׁ גַּם כֵּן פַּחַד שֶׁהָאָדָם גּוֹרֵם לְעַצְמוֹ, וְהַבְּחִירָה
וּרְשׁוּת נְתוּנָה לוֹ לִמְנוֹעַ עַצְמוֹ מִמֶּנּוּ.

It is certain that you should ask G-d for joy, as it is written, "Cause the soul of your servant to rejoice" (Psalms 86:4). Similarly, we say in our prayers, "Remove gloom and lamenting from us." Nevertheless, there are also fears that people trigger themselves, and the choice and authority is given to them to withhold themselves from them.

Figure 4.1

First Three Soul Attributes

Chochmah	Wisdom/Creativity	חָכְמָה
Binah	Understanding/Discernment	בִּינָה
Daat	Knowledge/Connection	דַּעַת

Text 2c

RABBI MENACHEM MENDEL OF LUBAVITCH, IBID., P. 20 ⏸️

דְּיֵשׁ לְכָל אָדָם ג׳ לְבוּשֵׁי הַנֶּפֶשׁ, מַחֲשָׁבָה דִּבּוּר וּמַעֲשֶׂה, וְהֵם עִיקָר בְּהַנְהָגַת הָאָדָם, וּבָהֶם הַבְּחִירָה וּרְשׁוּת נְתוּנָה לַחֲשׁוֹב וּלְדַבֵּר וְלַעֲשׂוֹת כִּרְצוֹנוֹ בְּמוֹחוֹ. וְאַף אִם מְפַחֵד בְּלִבּוֹ, יוּכַל לְסַלֵּק הַמַּחֲשָׁבָה, דִּבּוּר, וּמַעֲשֶׂה. וְהָעִיקָר שֶׁלֹּא לַחֲשׁוֹב וּלְדַבֵּר מִזֶּה כְּלָל, אֶלָּא לְצַד הַהִיפוּךְ . . . וּמִיַּד שֶׁלֹּא יַחֲשׁוֹב בָּזֶה כְּלָל, מִמֵּילָא יִתְבַּטֵּל גַּם הַפַּחַד שֶׁבַּלֵּב. וְעַל כָּל פָּנִים, מִיַּד יִהְיֶה הַפַּחַד כְּאִילוּ הוּא יָשֵׁן וְאֵינוֹ נִרְגָּשׁ בַּגּוּף. וּבְמֶשֶׁךְ יָמִים אֲחָדִים יִתְבַּטֵּל לְגַמְרֵי עַד שֶׁלֹּא יִפּוֹל בְּמוֹחוֹ כְּלָל . . .

וְהַטַּעַם לָזֶה שֶׁעַל יְדֵי סִילּוּק הַמַּחֲשָׁבָה יִתְבַּטֵּל הַפַּחַד הוּא לְפִי שֶׁכָּל הַמִּדוֹת קִיּוּמָן מֵהַדַּעַת . . . עַל יְדֵי אֶמְצָעוּת הַמַּחֲשָׁבָה. וְלָכֵן עַל יְדֵי סִילּוּק הַמַּחֲשָׁבָה הֲרֵי זֶה מִמֵּילָא הִיסַח הַדַּעַת מֵהַמִּדָּה, וְאָז אֵין הַמִּדָּה מִתְעוֹרֶרֶת . . .

וְהִנֵּה רָאוּי לְמַעֲלָתוֹ לִלְמוֹד אֶת עַצְמוֹ מִכָּל מָרָה שְׁחוֹרָה, שֶׁיֵּשׁ לָאָדָם לְסַלֵּק הַפַּחַד מִלִּבּוֹ, אַף בְּמָקוֹם שֶׁיֵּשׁ מִמַּה לִיפַחֵד, כְּמוֹ שֶׁכָּתַבְתִּי. וְכָל שֶׁכֵּן בַּנִּדּוֹן דְּמַעֲלָתוֹ, שֶׁבָּרוּךְ הַשֵּׁם אֵין לוֹ מִמַּה לִיפַחֵד כְּלָל וּכְלָל, בֵּין בִּבְרִיאוּת הַגּוּף וּבֵין בְּמָמוֹנוֹ.

Each person has three soul-garments—thought, speech, and action—that comprise the primary components of human behavior. The choice and power is granted to us to think, speak, and act according to our desire.

Even if you are emotionally afraid, you are able to remove your thought, speech, and action from that emotion. . . . Immediately upon letting go of the thought, the fear will dissolve on its own. At the very least, the fear will become dormant and will not be felt in your body. And over the course of a few days, it will completely dissipate, to the point that it will not come up in your mind at all. . . .

Removing your thought from the fear will lead to the fear's dissipation because emotions come from the faculty of *daat* . . . by means of thought. Therefore, by removing your thought, *daat* is automatically removed from the emotion and it will not awaken. . . .

It is appropriate for you to train yourself away from all melancholy. You can remove the fear from your heart, even when there is something legitimate to fear; all the more so in your case, in which, thank G-d, you have nothing to fear at all, whether in matters of your health or finances, etc.

Text 3

FYODOR DOSTOEVSKY, *WINTER NOTES ON SUMMER IMPRESSIONS*
(EVANSTON, IL.: NORTHWESTERN UNIVERSITY PRESS, 1988), P. 49

Try to pose for yourself this task: not to think of a polar bear, and you will see that the cursed thing will come to mind every minute.

FYODOR DOSTOEVSKY
1821–1881

Russian novelist, essayist, journalist, and philosopher. Dostoevsky's literary works explore human psychology in the context of the troubled political, social, and spiritual atmosphere of 19th-century Russia. He began writing in his 20s, and his first novel, *Poor Folk*, was published in 1846 when he was 25. His major works include *Crime and Punishment* (1866), *The Idiot* (1869), and *The Brothers Karamazov* (1880).

Text 4

RABBI MENACHEM MENDEL OF LUBAVITCH, IBID., P. 21 ⚇

אַךְ עִיקַר הֶיסַח הַדַּעַת וְהַמַחֲשָׁבָה הוּא עַל יְדֵי שֶׁיִּשְׁמוֹר
מַחֲשַׁבְתּוֹ לְהַלְבִּישָׁה בְּעִנְיָנִים אֲחֵרִים, דְּהַיְינוּ אֲפִילוּ בְּעִנְיָנִים
דְּהַאי עָלְמָא הַנִּצְרָכִים וּמְשַׂמְּחִים, וּבְתוֹרַת ה' הַמְשַׂמְּחִים לֵב
דְּבַר יוֹם בְּיוֹם בִּקְבִיעוּת עִתִּים לַתּוֹרָה, וּבִפְרָט עִם עוֹד אֶחָד.

The primary method of removing negative thoughts from your mind is by directing your mind toward other matters. This can be worldly things, if they are necessary and make you happy, and G-d's Torah—which delights the heart—by establishing fixed times for daily study, particularly with another.

IN G-D WE TRUST
MY SHEPHERD

Text 5

PSALMS 23 🎧

מִזְמוֹר לְדָוִד, ה׳ רֹעִי לֹא אֶחְסָר.

בִּנְאוֹת דֶּשֶׁא יַרְבִּיצֵנִי, עַל מֵי מְנֻחוֹת יְנַהֲלֵנִי.

נַפְשִׁי יְשׁוֹבֵב, יַנְחֵנִי בְמַעְגְּלֵי צֶדֶק לְמַעַן שְׁמוֹ.

גַּם כִּי אֵלֵךְ בְּגֵיא צַלְמָוֶת לֹא אִירָא רָע כִּי אַתָּה עִמָּדִי, שִׁבְטְךָ וּמִשְׁעַנְתֶּךָ הֵמָּה יְנַחֲמֻנִי.

תַּעֲרֹךְ לְפָנַי שֻׁלְחָן נֶגֶד צֹרְרָי, דִּשַּׁנְתָּ בַשֶּׁמֶן רֹאשִׁי כּוֹסִי רְוָיָה.

אַךְ טוֹב וָחֶסֶד יִרְדְּפוּנִי כָּל יְמֵי חַיָּי, וְשַׁבְתִּי בְּבֵית ה׳ לְאֹרֶךְ יָמִים.

A song of David. G-d is my shepherd; I shall not want.

He causes me to lie down in green pastures; He leads me beside still waters.

He restores my soul; He leads me in paths of righteousness, bringing honor to His name.

Even when I walk in the valley of darkness, I will fear no evil, for You are with me; Your rod and Your staff—they comfort me.

You prepare a feast for me in the presence of my adversaries; You anointed my head with oil; my cup overflows.

May only goodness and kindness pursue me all the days of my life, and I will dwell in the house of G-d for my entire life.

Text 6

RABBI BACHYA IBN PAKUDAH, *CHOVOT HALEVAVOT,*
INTRODUCTION TO *SHAAR HABITACHON* ⚏

אַךְ תּוֹעֲלוֹת הַבִּטָּחוֹן בָּעוֹלָם, מֵהֶן - מְנוּחַת הַלֵּב מִן הַדְּאָגוֹת
הָעוֹלָמִיּוֹת . . . וְהוּא בְּהַשְׁקֵט וּבְבִטְחָה וּבְשַׁלְוָה בָּעוֹלָם הַזֶּה,
כְּמוֹ שֶׁכָּתוּב (יִרְמְיָה יז, ז): "בָּרוּךְ הַגֶּבֶר אֲשֶׁר יִבְטַח בַּה' וְהָיָה
ה' מִבְטַחוֹ".

The benefits of trust in G-d include tranquility of the heart in the face of worldly worries. . . . The one who has trust finds quiet, security, and serenity within this world. As it is written, "Blessed are those who trust in G-d; G-d will be their reassurance" (Jeremiah 17:7).

RABBI BACHYA IBN PAKUDAH
11TH CENTURY

Moral philosopher and author. Ibn Pakudah lived in Muslim Spain, but little else is known about his life. *Chovot Halevavot (Duties of the Heart),* his major work, was intended to be a guide for attaining spiritual perfection. Originally written in Judeo-Arabic and published in 1080, it was later translated into Hebrew and published in 1161 by Judah ibn Tibbon, a scion of the famous family of translators. Ibn Pakudah had a strong influence on Jewish pietistic literature.

Exercise 4.2a

Think of someone you trust. Think of what makes them trustworthy in your eyes. Think of them as G-d's messenger, being sent to help you in your life. Think of their presence in your life as a gift from G-d and try to feel that G-d loves you.

Exercise 4.2b

Think of something that you value very dearly in your life (e.g., your hands, your sense of sight, a family member). Think of it as a gift from G-d and try to feel that G-d gave it to you as an act of great love and care. Muster up your appreciation and thank G-d verbally.

Exercise 4.2c

Think of a stressful time when things turned out better than you expected. Think of how you felt before the situation was resolved. Think about G-d's involvement in the situation and what may have occurred had a random force been in control instead. Think of the outcome as a gift from G-d and try to feel G-d's love for you.

Exercise 4.2d

Try to feel trust in G-d the next time you do a basic life activity (e.g., get food from the fridge, turn on/off a light switch, or stand up from your chair).

Text 7

DAVID H. ROSMARIN, ET AL., "A RANDOMIZED
CONTROLLED EVALUATION OF A SPIRITUALLY INTEGRATED
TREATMENT FOR SUBCLINICAL ANXIETY IN THE JEWISH
COMMUNITY, DELIVERED VIA THE INTERNET," *JOURNAL
OF ANXIETY DISORDERS* 24 (2010), PP. 806–807

Participants in the SIT [Spiritually-Integrated Treatment] group reported significant reductions [in] stress, worry, depression, and intolerance to uncertainty.... Symptom improvement was clinically significant; at pre-treatment, participants in the SIT group reported near-clinical levels of stress and worry...and at post-treatment and 6–8-week follow-up, reported levels were in the normal range.... The SIT group reported greater treatment gains ... compared to WLC [Wait List Condition] participants. Surprisingly, PMR [Progressive Muscle Relaxation] and WLC participants did not differ on most outcomes....

It is also interesting that Orthodox affiliation was not a predictor of treatment outcomes in the SIT group.... SIT is likely not appropriate for all Jewish individuals. Nevertheless, this surprising finding suggests that interest in SITs among Jews extends beyond the Orthodox community.

DAVID H. ROSMARIN, PHD

Psychologist. Rosmarin is an instructor in the department of psychiatry at Harvard Medical School and director of the Center for Anxiety in Manhattan. He received his PhD in clinical psychology from Bowling Green State University and has written 30 peer-reviewed publications. His research examines the relevance of spiritual and religious issues to psychopathology and its treatment.

VALLEY OF DARKNESS

Text 8a
PSALMS 37:23 ⓘ

מֵה' מִצְעֲדֵי גֶבֶר כּוֹנָנוּ.

G-d establishes the steps of man.

Text 8b

RABBI LEVI YITSCHAK OF BERDITCHEV,
CITED IN *PITGAMIN KADISHIN*, P. 16 ⊞

יֵדַע הָאָדָם בִּידִיעָה בְּרוּרָה וְצַלוּלָה, שֶׁכָּל נְסִיעוֹת וַהֲלִיכוֹת
הָאָדָם לְאֵיזֶה מְקוֹמוֹת, הַכֹּל לֹא בְּמִקְרֶה הוּא חָלִילָה, רַק
מֵאֵת ה' הָיְתָה זֹאת, וּבְהַשְׁגָּחָה פְּרָטִית. וְכַוָּנַת הַבּוֹרֵא בָּרוּךְ
הוּא בָּזֶה, שֶׁיֵּשׁ לוֹ לְאָדָם הַלָּזֶה שׁוּם חֵלֶק מַה לְתַקֵּן שָׁמָּה
בַּמָּקוֹם הַלָּזֶה, הֵן בְּכֹחַ תּוֹרָה וּתְפִלָּה, וְהֵן בְּכֹחַ אֲכִילָה וּשְׁתִיָּה
וְשֵׁינָה לְשֵׁם שָׁמַיִם, וְהֵן בִּשְׁאָר עֲבוֹדוֹת לְשֵׁם שָׁמַיִם . . .
וּכְמוֹ שֶׁאָמַר הַבַּעַל שֵׁם טוֹב זְכוּתוֹ יָגֵן עָלֵינוּ: "מֵה' מִצְעֲדֵי גֶבֶר
כּוֹנָנוּ" (תְּהִלִּים לז, כג), דְּהַיְנוּ שֶׁהַשֵּׁם יִתְבָּרֵךְ עוֹשֶׂה לְהָאָדָם
חֵשֶׁק לֵילֵךְ וְלִנְסוֹעַ לְאֵיזֶה מָקוֹם, וְכַוָּנָתוֹ יִתְבָּרֵךְ הוּא . . .
שֶׁיַּעֲשֶׂה שָׁם הָאָדָם הַלָּזֶה אֵיזֶה עוֹבְדָא מֵעֲבוֹדָתוֹ יִתְבָּרֵךְ, כְּדֵי
שֶׁיְּתַקֵּן שָׁם הָאָדָם אֵיזֶה תִּקּוּן הַצָּרִיךְ לוֹ, כַּנִּזְכָּר לְעֵיל.
וְעַל כֵּן חַיָּב הָאָדָם לִרְאוֹת אֶת עַצְמוֹ בִּהְיוֹתוֹ בָּא אֶל אֵיזֶה
מָקוֹם לִיתֵּן אֶל לִבּוֹ מַה זֶה וְעַל מַה זֶה הֱבִיא אוֹתוֹ הַשֵּׁם יִתְבָּרֵךְ
לְכַאן, וַדַּאי לֹא לְחִנָּם הוּא.

RABBI LEVI YITSCHAK OF BERDITCHEV
1740–1809

Chasidic rebbe. Rabbi Levi Yitschak was one of the foremost disciples of the Magid of Mezeritch and later went on to serve as rabbi in Berditchev, Ukraine. His Chasidic commentary on the Torah, *Kedushat Levi*, is a classic that is popular to this day. He is known in Jewish history and folklore for his all-encompassing love, compassion, and advocacy on behalf of the Jewish people.

We should clearly recognize that our travels to different places are not random, G-d forbid, but specifically directed by G-d. G-d's intention is that a particular person has a specific "portion" to rectify in a particular place, whether through Torah study and prayer, or through eating, drinking, and sleeping for the sake of Heaven, or through another means of serving G-d. . . .

The Baal Shem Tov, of righteous memory, explained the verse "G-d establishes the steps of man" to mean that G-d imparts the desire to a person to travel to a specific place with G-d's intention being that the person should engage there in a particular divine service . . . thereby rectifying what this person must rectify.

Therefore, when we come to a particular place, we must take this to heart and ask ourselves, "Why am I here? For what purpose did G-d bring me here? It is certainly not for naught."

Text 9

THE REBBE, RABBI MENACHEM MENDEL SCHNEERSON,
LIKUTEI SICHOT 23, P. 468 (FEBRUARY 19, 1979) 🎧

לְפֶלֶא הָכִי גָדוֹל שֶׁלְאַחֲרֵי שֶׁמְּדַבְּרִים וּבַאֲרִיכוּת וְכַמָּה וְכַמָּה
פְּעָמִים עַל דְּבַר תּוֹרַת הַבַּעַל שֵׁם טוֹב (שֶׁבְּכָל דָּבָר, הוֹרָאָה
בַּעֲבוֹדַת הַשֵּׁם) וְגַם הֵן בְּעַצְמָן בְּוַדַּאי נוֹאֲמוֹת עַל דָּבָר זֶה,
כְּשֶׁקָּרָה לָהֶן עִנְיָן שֶׁכַּוָּנָתוֹ בְּרוּרָה - מְחַפְּשׂוֹת בֵּיאוּרִים מְשׁוּנִים
בְּתַכְלִית (שֶׁאוּלֵי זֶה לְצַעֲרֵן חַס וְשָׁלוֹם, אֵיךְ תַּחֲזֹרְנָה לְבֵיתָן
וְכוּ') מִלְבַד הַפֵּירוּשׁ הַפָּשׁוּט:

אֶפְשָׁר הָיָה לְפַרְסֵם הַתּוֹרָה וּמִצְווֹת יוֹתֵר, יוֹתֵר מִשֶּׁנַּעֲשָׂה בְּעֵת
הַקָאנְוֶוענִשֶׁאן, וּמְזַכִּין אוֹתָן עַל יְדֵי שֶׁלֶג הַיּוֹרֵד מִן הַשָּׁמַיִם,
לְהַשְׁלִים הַנַּ"ל עַל יְדֵי שׁוּפִי (שֶׁלֹּא כְּרָגִיל) (עַל דֶּרֶךְ הַשֶּׁלֶג)
סְטָארְם בְּיַהֲדוּת וְכוּ' – בָּעִיר, בִּשְׂדֵה הַתְּעוּפָה, בְּמִכְתְּבֵי-עֵת
וְכַיּוֹצֵא בָזֶה וְכוּ'.

**RABBI MENACHEM
MENDEL SCHNEERSON**
1902–1994

The towering Jewish leader of the 20th century, known as "the Lubavitcher Rebbe," or simply as "the Rebbe." Born in southern Ukraine, the Rebbe escaped Nazi-occupied Europe, arriving in the U.S. in June 1941. The Rebbe inspired and guided the revival of traditional Judaism after the European devastation, impacting virtually every Jewish community the world over. The Rebbe often emphasized that the performance of just one additional good deed could usher in the era of Mashiach. The Rebbe's scholarly talks and writings have been printed in more than 200 volumes.

The Baal Shem Tov's teaching that every occurrence contains a directive in serving G-d is a topic that has been spoken of and discussed at length many, many times; I am sure that you, too, have given speeches on this topic. Yet, now, when an incident has happened to you (i.e., your being delayed in Detroit by the N.Y. snowstorm) whose occurrence has a clear meaning and purpose, you seek to attach to the incident most distorted interpretations (e.g., "Perhaps the delay is designed to distress us," G-d forbid, or "How are we going to return home?" etc.)—anything but the simple and obvious interpretation.

The simple and obvious reason for the delay is: It is possible to disseminate Torah and *mitzvos* to a far greater degree than was accomplished during the Convention. You are therefore being granted the merit—through the snow which descends from heaven—of completing the above task with an extraordinary abundance and storm intensity of Judaism, similar to the extraordinary abundance of the snowstorm.

Your efforts in completing the Convention's task of disseminating Torah and *mitzvot* should be extended to the city, the airport, publicity in the newspapers, etc.

Exercise 4.3

Think for a moment about a recent hassle:

1. What did I need out of life at that moment?
2. What was needed of me at that moment?

CONCLUSION

Exercise 4.4

1. Which of the ideas in this lesson resonated most with you?
2. Which of the concepts would be the most difficult for you to implement? Why?

Key Points

1. We are not hostages of our emotions. We can do more than wait out negative emotions.

2. The Talmud presents two approaches for dealing with worrisome thoughts. One approach is to talk over your worries with another person. Another approach is to cast away worrisome thoughts.

3. In most situations, we can govern our emotional lives by controlling our thoughts. Nevertheless, it is often counterproductive to try to stop thinking of something. To cast away a thought, the mind must become absorbed in something else that is relevant and engaging.

4. The basic principles of Jewish monotheistic belief teach us that G-d is benevolent, omnipotent, and caring. This forms the basis of *bitachon*, or trust. We can relax because we are in good hands. "In G-d we trust" helps us cultivate optimism about the future.

5. In one study, believing (but not necessarily religious) Jews, with elevated but subclinical levels of stress and worry, engaged in reflection on the topic of *bitachon* each day for two weeks. They reported significant reductions in stress, worry, depression, and intolerance to uncertainty.

6. One common hindrance to *bitachon* is the feeling that there is no precedent upon which to base this trust. When we stop taking the blessings in our life *for* granted, but *as* granted, we rapidly find robust precedent upon which to build our *bitachon*.

7. Our trust in G-d need not ignore the possibility of future hardship. Rather, "Even when I walk in the valley of darkness, I will fear no evil, for You are with me." While we will likely never understand why G-d allows troubles to occur, we can trust that G-d will

be with us—guiding us, supporting us, encouraging us. Knowing this helps us remain calm.

8. The places we go are not random, but directed by G-d toward a specific purpose. When we come to a particular place, we should ask ourselves, "For what purpose did G-d bring me here?" This applies just the same for the events of our lives, including those that normally cause us frustration and sadness.

9. Trusting that there is a purpose in every experience—and being determined to discover it and implement it—enables us to remain calm and unafraid when considering the dark moments that may materialize in the future.

10. If we plumb within, we will discover a Divine spark that has passionate faith and unwavering trust in G-d. Bringing trust to our conscious minds is not creating something new but revealing that which is always there.

APPENDIX
I AM WITH YOU

Text 10a
MIDRASH, *SHEMOT RABAH* 2:5

מַה הַתְּאוֹמִים הַלָּלוּ, אִם חָשַׁשׁ אֶחָד בְּרֹאשׁוֹ חֲבֵירוֹ מַרְגִּישׁ, כֵּן אָמַר הַקָּדוֹשׁ בָּרוּךְ הוּא כִּבְיָכוֹל (תְּהִלִּים צא, טו) "עִמּוֹ אָנֹכִי בְצָרָה" . . .

אָמַר לוֹ הַקָּדוֹשׁ בָּרוּךְ הוּא לְמֹשֶׁה: אִי אַתָּה מַרְגִּישׁ שֶׁאֲנִי שָׁרוּי בְּצַעַר כְּשֵׁם שֶׁיִּשְׂרָאֵל שְׁרוּיִם בְּצַעַר? הֱוֵי יוֹדֵעַ מִמָּקוֹם שֶׁאֲנִי מְדַבֵּר עִמְּךָ - מִתּוֹךְ הַקּוֹצִים. כִּבְיָכוֹל אֲנִי שׁוּתָּף בְּצַעֲרָן.

SHEMOT RABAH

An early rabbinic commentary on the Book of Exodus. "Midrash" is the designation of a particular genre of rabbinic literature usually forming a running commentary on specific books of the Bible. *Shemot Rabah*, written mostly in Hebrew, provides textual exegeses, expounds upon the biblical narrative, and develops and illustrates moral principles. It was first printed in Constantinople in 1512 together with 4 other Midrashic works on the other 4 books of the Pentateuch.

In conjoined twins, if one of them feels pain in the head, the other feels it too. Likewise, G-d says, "I am with him in distress" (Psalms 91:15)." . . .

G-d said to Moses, "Don't you realize that I'm in pain just as the Jewish people are in pain? Note the place from where I am talking to you—from the thorns." This is as if to say, "I am a partner to their pain."

Text 10b

SIFREI, BEHAALOTECHA 84 ⊕

כָּל זְמַן שֶׁיִשְׂרָאֵל מְשׁוּעְבָּדִים, כִּבְיָכוֹל שְׁכִינָה מִשְׁתַּעְבֶּדֶת
עִמָּהֶם, שֶׁנֶּאֱמַר . . . "בְּכָל צָרָתָם לוֹ צָר" (יְשַׁעְיָה סג, ט). אֵין
לִי אֶלָּא צָרַת צִבּוּר, צָרַת יָחִיד מְנַיִן? תַּלְמוּד לוֹמַר . . . "עִמּוֹ
אָנֹכִי בְצָרָה".

Whenever we are enslaved, the G-dly presence is, so to speak, enslaved with us, as it says . . . "Whenever they have pain, He has pain" (Isaiah 63:9). From this we only know that the G-dly presence suffers with the suffering of the masses; how do we know that this applies when individuals suffer as well? The verse therefore says, ". . . I am with *him* in distress" (Psalms 91:15).

SIFREI

An early rabbinic Midrash on the biblical books of Numbers and Deuteronomy. *Sifrei* focuses mostly on matters of law, as opposed to narratives and moral principles. According to Maimonides, this halachic Midrash was authored by Rav, a 3rd-century Babylonian Talmudic sage.

PURPOSE INSTEAD OF FRUSTRATION

Text 11

RABBI YOSEF YITSCHAK SCHNEERSOHN,
SEFER HASICHOT 5702, PP. 84–85 📖

אַז ר' הלל פלעגט אַרויספאָרן אין וועג, פלעגט ער
מיטנעמען . . . זיין תלמיד ר' שָׁלוֹם הומענער . . . פאַרנאַכט־
צו, זיינען זיי אָנגעקומען אין אַ אַכסניא אין מאַלאָראָסיא. ר'
שָׁלוֹם האָט זיך געשטעלט דאַווענען מעריב און האָט מאַריך
געווען אין דאַווענען ביז עס איז געוואָרן טאָג. איז ווי קען
מען זיך דאָס לייגן שלאָפן? האָט ר' שָׁלוֹם זיך גלייך מכין
געווען צום דאַווענען בערך אַ שָׁעָה אָדער מעהר, און האָט
זיך געשטעלט דאַווענען שַׁחֲרִית, און האָט אַזוי געדאַווענט
אַ גאַנצען טאָג. ביז אַז ער איז צוגעקומען צו קְרִיאַת שְׁמַע,
שְׁמַע יִשְׂרָאֵל הוי' אֱלֹקֵינו וְגו' איז שוין געווען מִנְחָה צייט.
דער בַּעַל האַכסניא, אַ דאָרפס־מאַן, איז געקומען דאַווענען
מִנְחָה. ערשט ער דערזעהט ווי ר' שָׁלוֹם האַלט ערשט אין
מיטן דאַווענען שַׁחֲרִית. רופט ער זיך אָפ: "וואָס איז דאָס מיט
דעם אידן? נעכטן האָט ער אָפגעדאַווענט אַ גאַנצע נאַכט
מעריב ביז טאָג, און היינט אַ גאַנצען טאָג אַז ער דאַווענט.
בא מיר איז אַנדערש. איך קען גלייך זאָגן שְׁמַע יִשְׂרָאֵל און
ער איז אַזוי פיל מאַריך. עס איז גאָר פשוט, בײַ איהם איז אַ
פראָסטע קאָפ!"
ר' שָׁלוֹם האָט שוין געהאַט געענדיגט דעם דאַווענען און האָט
זיך צוגעהערט וואָס דער דאָרפסמאַן זאָגט.
האָט נאָכדעם געזאָגט ר' הלל, אַז דרײַ יאָהר חַסִידוּת וואָס
ר' שָׁלוֹם האָט בײַ אים געלערנט האָט ניט געפּוֹעֶל'ט אַזוי
פיעל ווי די וווערטער פון דעם דאָרפס־מאַן האָט מען געפּוֹעֶל'ט.

When Reb Hillel used to travel, he would take along . . . his student, Reb Shalom Huminer. . . . One evening, they came to an inn in the Ukraine. Reb Shalom began the evening prayer and spent such a long time meditating and praying that morning came. So how can one lie down to sleep? So Reb Shalom set to prepare himself for the morning prayers, taking an hour or more. He then recited the morning prayers, and this took the entire day. By the time he came to the *Shema*, it was already time for the afternoon prayer.

The innkeeper, a simple villager, came to recite the afternoon prayer and saw that Reb Shalom was still in middle of his morning prayers. He cried out, "What is it with this Jew? Last night, he spent the whole night praying, and now he has prayed the whole day! I'm different. I can just say, 'Shema Yisrael,' unlike this man who takes so long. There is only one way to understand this: obviously, this man is a simpleton!"

Reb Shalom had already completed his prayers and heard what the villager had said.

Reb Hillel said afterward, "Three years of studying the teachings of Chasidism with Reb Shalom did not have as much of an effect on him [in terms of self-improvement] as these words of the simple villager."

Text 12

RABBI YOSEF YITSCHAK SCHNEERSOHN,
SEFER HASICHOT 5708, P. 235 ⚏

הָרַב גֶּרְשׁוֹן דוֹב אִיז אַיינְמָאל גֶעקוּמֶען אִין לִיוּבַּאוִויטְשׁ אוּן
הָאט גֶעוָוארְט אִין פָּאדֶער-צִימֶער פוּן דֶעם יְחִידוּת-חֶדֶר
שֶׁל הוֹד כ"ק אַדמוּ"ר הרה"ק אוֹיף אַרַיינְצוּגַיין אוֹיף יְחִידוּת.
דֶערְוַוייל הָאט עֶר זִיךְ אַוַוועקְגֶעשְׁטֶעלְט לֶעבְּן דֶעם אָרְט וואוּ
מֶען פְלֶעגְט אוֹיפְהַיינְגֶען דִי אוֹיבֶּערְשְׁטֶע קְלַיידֶער אוּן הָאט
זִיךְ פַארְטְרַאכְט. מֶענְדְּל דֶער מְשָׁרֵת, נִיט וִויסֶענְדִיק וֶוער
דָאס אִיז אוּן זֶעהֶענְדִיק אַז עֶר שְׁטַייט לֶעבְּן דִי קְלַיידֶער הָאט
חוֹשֵׁד גֶעוֶוען אַז עֶר וִויל עֶפֶּעס צוּנֶעמֶען. הָאט עֶר גֶענוּמֶען
ר' גֶּרְשׁוֹן דוֹב'ן אוּן הָאט עֶם צוּגֶעפִירְט צוּ דֶער אַרוֹיסְגַאנְג-
טִיר. הָר' גֶּרְשׁוֹן דוֹב בָּכָה וְאָמַר . . . "פוּן דֶעם רֶבִּינְס פָּאדֶער-
צִימֶער טְרַייבְּט מֶען מִיךְ אַרוֹיס".

Reb Gershon Dov once came to Lubavitch and was waiting in the antechamber for his private audience with the rebbe, Rabbi Shalom Dovber. As he waited, lost in thought, he stood near the place where the Rebbe's family would hang their overcoats. The attendant, Mendel, not knowing who this was, and seeing that he was standing near the coats, was suspicious that he wanted to steal something. He grabbed Reb Gershon Dov and escorted him out.

Reb Gershon Dov wept and said . . . "I've been driven out from the Rebbe's antechamber. [Evidently, I'm not ready for *yechidut.*]"

ADDITIONAL READINGS

PATIENCE

Rabbi Raphael Pelcovitz
David Pelcovitz, PhD

This chapter will focus on patience facing the daily "hassles" of life as well as patience in the face of long-term challenge. Patience is a trait that is often called for in our daily life. Maintaining one's composure can make the difference between a flourishing or tension-filled marriage, one's ability to parent effectively, and one's effectiveness in getting along with difficult personalities in the workplace.

On a more mundane level, the inevitable frustrations that routinely confront us often challenge our ability to remain calm. A recent poll[1] found that 86 percent of American consumers are put on hold every time they place a call to a business establishment. The time spent on hold by more than half of the respondents added up to thirteen hours a year. That this process tries one's equanimity is documented

RABBI RAPHAEL PELCOVITZ

Rabbi emeritus, author, and teacher. Rabbi Pelcovitz served as the pulpit rabbi and community leader of Congregation Kneseth Israel (the White Shul) in Far Rockaway, New York, for more than 50 years. He authored a number of books in which he presents ideas from Jewish thought in a compelling and comprehensible way. He also co-authored 2 books with his son, Dr. David Pelcovitz.

DAVID PELCOVITZ, PHD

Psychologist, teacher, and author. Dr. Pelcovitz, who received his PhD from the University of Pennsylvania, has published and lectured extensively on a variety of topics related to education, parenting, and mental health. He is currently the Straus Professor of Psychology and Education at the Azrieli Graduate School, Yeshiva University. His books include *Balanced Parenting* and *Life in the Balance*, both written in collaboration with his father, Rabbi Raphael Pelcovitz.

by the pollsters' finding that 58 percent report that they find the experience of being placed on hold "very frustrating." Developing the capacity for patience can transform the internal experience of being placed on hold, stuck in traffic, or waiting in a long line from one of annoyance and frustration to an opportunity to relax, and welcome the rare opportunity for "downtime."

The far-reaching benefits of patience have been documented in an array of research studies that find higher levels of happiness and more effective overall coping skills in individuals who are patient.[2] In a similar vein, studies have found that minor daily hassles, such as encountering heavy traffic or missing a train, are even more stressful than dealing with major life crises such as a chronic illness or financial difficulties. In one of the first studies that documented this counterintuitive finding, psychologist Allen Kanner and his colleagues[3] found that difficulty dealing with minor daily hassles, such as losing things or feeling time pressure at work, was a better predictor of psychological difficulties than was facing major life events. Similar findings were noted by Dr. Anita DeLongis and colleagues[4] who found that the repeated "minor" annoyances of everyday life were better predictors of health problems, such as headaches or

1 *Time Magazine*, (January 24th, 2013) Business and Money Section, Poll completed by Talk to Text Message Service.
2 Schnitker, S.A., & Emmons, R.A. (2007). Patience as a virtue: Religious and psychological perspectives. *Research in the Social Scientific Study of Religion*, 18, 177–207.
3 Kanner, A., Coyne, J. & Schaefer, C. (1981). Comparison of two modes of stress measurement: Daily hassles and uplifts versus major life events. *Journal of Behavioral Medicine*, 4, 1–39.
4 Delongis, A. Coyne, J. & Dakof, G. (1982). Relationship of daily hassles, uplifts, and major life events to health status. *Health Psychology*, 1, 119–136.

backaches, than more serious major life events. Here too, whether hassles are viewed as a burden or met with patience determines whether life's inevitable minor annoyances will make us ill and unhappy or be faced with equanimity.

JEWISH PERSPECTIVES ON PATIENCE

One of the Thirteen Attributes of Mercy taught to Moshe as the formula for seeking Divine forgiveness is *Erech Apayim*, slow to anger, or patience. We are commanded to "walk in G-d's ways," including nurturing this all-important trait of patience in the face of provocation. The central significance of patience in Jewish life is highlighted by the very first guideline to ethical living recorded in Ethics of the Fathers—the admonition given by the Men of the Great Assembly, the 120 Elders who lived at the beginning of the Second Temple Era:

> *"Be deliberate (mesunim) in judgment."*[5]

This admonition to judges, to show *mesinus*, patience, and caution while they "deliberate" a case, ensures a careful consideration of both sides of an argument in a manner that fairly analyzes all of the evidence. *Mesinus* means taking the time to investigate thoroughly, and allows for compromise as well.

Recent research has documented how essential careful deliberation is to the process of truly understanding interpersonal difficulties. Referring to recent brain research on the need for focus, patience, and "slowness" in being able to truly understand the complexity of interpersonal conflict, Daniel Goleman, the renowned expert on emotional intelligence and social-emotional learning, writes the following:

"While volunteers listened to tales of people subjected to *physical* pain, brain scans revealed that their own brain centers for experiencing such pain lit up instantly. But if the story was about *psychological* suffering, it took relatively longer to activate the higher brain centers involved in empathic concern and compassion. As the research team put it, 'It takes time to tell the psychological and moral dimension of a situation. . . . Where we focus matters: our emotional empathy grows stronger if we attend to the intensity of the pain and lessens as we look away.'"[6]

* * *

Another facet of patience—*savlanus*—is often used in situations where patience is required over the long term. The word *savlanus* is based on the root "saval" which also means to suffer, or to shoulder a burden. *Saval* is the Hebrew word as well for a porter: an individual who carries luggage. The inner psychological meaning of "carrying luggage" depends on one's perspective. One can view the suitcase as an efficient way of organizing one's belongings while traveling or as "baggage"—a source of suffering, a burden that weighs one down.

A classic example of this is contained in the following beautiful passage from Isaiah, which is recited at the end of the daily *Aleinu* prayer:

> *"Even when you grow old, I will be the same. When your hair turns gray, I will still carry you (esbol). I made you, I will bear you. I will carry (esbol) you, and I will rescue you."*[7]

Here the word *esbol* refers to the concept of *savlanus*: G-d's being there to patiently carry us even in our most advanced years. This is patience over the very long term. It refers to the ability to maintain equanimity even in the face of chronic stress, such as what we face in confronting the inevitable challenges of old age. As Angela Duckworth, a psychologist whose work will be discussed in the next chapter, says in her description of "grit," this refers to the marathon, not the sprint—the ability to maintain one's composure over the long term. As the *Mussar* masters point out, by emulating G-d's infinite patience in "carrying" us in spite of our imperfections and frailties, we, who are commanded to guide our lives by walking in G-d's ways, should internalize the value of patience both in the short term (*mesinus*) and the long term (*savlanus*). . . .

---

5 *Ethics of the Fathers (Pirkei Avos)* 1:1.

6 Goleman, D. (2013). *Focus*, New York: HarperCollins, p. 107.
7 *Isaiah* 46:4.

TORAH PERSPECTIVES ON GROWING FROM CHALLENGE[8]

Developing increased patience with challenges posed by life's setbacks by appreciating their growth-inducing potential is echoed throughout the Torah. The Ramban, in a discussion of Hashem's "testing" Avraham, teaches us a valuable lesson in the Jewish perspective of tribulations:

> "And Hashem tested Avraham": Hashem tests a person to bring out his or her potential, so that the individual who is tested can earn the reward that comes from a good action rather than that of a good heart alone. . . . All tests that we encounter in the Torah are for the benefit of the individual who is tested.[9]

This view of the growth potential that is actualized by engaging in the struggles presented by life's ordeals is further elucidated in a *midrash* on this same verse that teaches us about the common etymology of the words *nisayon* (ordeal) and *nes* (miracle or banner) as follows:

> "And Hashem tested Avraham"[10] it is written, "You gave those who fear You a banner (nes) to raise on high, in order to be adorned"[11] nisayon (test) after nisayon, i.e., growth after growth, in order to raise them up in the world.[12]

In a particularly eloquent description of this process we find the following passage in the *Orchos Tzaddikim*:

> Troubles are for the long-term benefit of the individual. As it says: "Rejoice not against me, my enemy; for when I fall, I will get up; when I sit in darkness, Hashem is a light to me."[13] Our Rabbis, of blessed memory, taught us, "If I had not fallen, I would not have picked myself up. If I did not sit in darkness, I would not have seen the light."[14]

A final thought on developing a patient attitude when dealing with the challenge of having others remain angry with us after we have wronged them and our efforts at apologizing fall on deaf ears. Reflecting a view that a certain amount of suffering in life is inevitable and even beneficial, the *Tomer Devorah*—the 16th-century work of Rabbi Moshe Cordovero—explains that having others angry at us, because of real or perceived offenses committed by us against them, should be viewed as a blessing. To be "scorned, shamed, or cursed" is viewed as a desirable form of purification, far better than suffering through illness or poverty. As Rabbi Cordovero writes:

> "A person should actually desire these forms of suffering and say to himself. . . . 'It is far better for me to be afflicted with being shamed and scorned by other people, which do not remove my power or weakness.' Thus, when insults are meted out to him, he will rejoice in them, and contrary to the typical reaction, he will desire them . . . and make a balm for his heart."[15]

INSTILLING PATIENCE IN CHILDREN

The widely respected research of Dr. Carol Dweck, a Stanford University psychologist, further informs approaches to life's frustrations in a manner that fosters patience and continued effort at self-improvement. Dr. Dweck found, that when faced with challenge, parents and teachers tend to foster one of two mindsets in teaching children how to respond to demanding situations. A fixed mindset is one in which children are taught to believe that whatever talent, abilities, and intelligence they have are innate qualities that exist regardless of how much hard work they put into the task at hand. In contrast, parents and teachers who foster a growth mindset engender a belief in the child that success is about effort and persisting in working hard even

8 Based on Pelcovitz, D. (2002). Helping children, adolescents, as well as adults, to cope with loss and terror: Jewish and psychological perspectives. New York State Project Liberty.
9 *Ramban, Genesis* 22:1.
10 Genesis 22:1.
11 Psalms 60:6.
12 Midrash Rabbah, 55:1.
13 Micah 7:8.
14 *The Ways of the Righteous (Orchos Tzaddikim) Shaar HaTeshuvah*, Gate 26.
15 *Tomer Devorah* (2005). Translated by Fink, D. & Finkelman, S. Jerusalem, Israel: Tomer Publications, page 40.

in the face of the toughest challenges. A growth mindset is what parents should strive for since children are often energized by challenge, as they demonstrate high levels of patience and the belief that with enough hard work they are up to confronting even the most daunting challenges.

The study that is most often cited as documenting this effect involved fifth-grade students being asked to complete a set of puzzles that were not too challenging for their age.[16] Half the children were told that their performance reflected being "smart," while half were told, "You must have worked hard." When the children were subsequently offered another set of puzzles to complete, 90 percent of the children praised for their effort chose more difficult puzzles. In contrast, most of the children who were told that their intelligence was the reason for their strong performance on the easy set of puzzles chose the less challenging set of puzzles. They avoided challenge to protect themselves from the embarrassment of making mistakes, thereby showing the researchers that they weren't as smart as the researchers thought.

One of the final stages of the study involved giving both groups of children puzzles that were so far beyond their age level and ability that it was virtually impossible for them to correctly assemble them. Again, the two groups approached the task in a totally different manner. Those fifth-graders previously praised for their hard work seemed energized by the challenge. Even though they were unable to successfully assemble the puzzles they persisted longer, showing much higher levels of patience than their peers who were praised for being intelligent. Indeed, the group praised for their "brilliance" gave up much more easily, manifesting high levels of impatience and frustration. In the concluding study, the children who had just faced the frustrating, undoable task were again given the simple puzzles, and the power of the type of praise was now most pronounced. Those children praised for working hard did 30 percent better than the first time they encountered the puzzles, while those praised for being smart

showed a 20 percent decrease in their puzzle-assembling performance....

GENERAL INTERVENTIONS TO IMPROVE PATIENCE

Patience is thought to manifest itself primarily in three arenas:[17]
1. INTERPERSONAL PATIENCE—This type of patience is evident when our interactions with others often result in frustration. For example, showing patience when teaching someone who is not grasping a basic concept that you find to be self-evident, or dealing with an oppositional child without losing one's cool.
2. PATIENCE IN THE FACE OF MAJOR STRESSFUL LIFE EVENTS—Level of patience demonstrated when facing tough times, such as serious illness, financial crisis, or serious marital conflict.
3. DAILY HASSLES—Patience evidenced in the face of life's minor annoyances, such as long lines at the check-out counter, or being stuck behind a slow driver.

RECOMMENDATIONS FOR FOSTERING PATIENCE

The following strategies have been proven to be effective in trying to improve frustration tolerance while increasing one's ability to remain calm in the face of provocation, regardless which of these three arenas are operative:
1. AWARENESS OF TRIGGERS—A first step in increasing one's level of patience is learning how to become more self-aware about what situations or events might be most likely to trigger an angry, impatient response. Specific triggers will differ from person to person. Some might become particularly impatient when faced with individuals whose critical nature reminds them of a family member who they didn't get along with during their childhood. Another might find that situations that are beyond their control, such as a major traffic jam or an unusually long wait at a doctor's office, is particularly exasperating.

16 Mueller, C. & Dweck, C. (1998). Praise for intelligence can undermine children's motivation and performance. *Journal of Personality and Social Psychology*, 75, 33–52.

17 Schnitker, S. (2012). An examination of patience and well-being. *The Journal of Positive Psychology*, 7, 263–280.

Systematically tracking one's individual pattern of causes and triggers is a crucial first step. Rabbi Yechiel Perr, of Yeshiva of Far Rockaway, calls nipping impatience in the bud, "opening the space between the match and the fuse."[18] This is similar to Viktor Frankl's description, mentioned earlier in this book, of the space between stimulus and response as the source of our growth. When we become more aware of precipitants of impatience, we are better equipped to occupy the space between the trigger and the fuse of impatience with calming strategies.

2. AFFECT REGULATION AND MINDFULNESS—The ability to regulate emotions such as anger and impatience is based on a number of skills that can, with practice, be learned. A cornerstone of developing the key skills of affect regulation is learning how to be mindful. Mindfulness means moment-to-moment, nonjudgmental awareness that involves developing the ability to learn how to pay attention in a focused manner that avoids "mindlessly" being pulled into anger and impatience. Developing the skill of observing, describing, and fully participating in the moment without judging one's self, others, or the situation is a skill that can be gradually developed.

3. DEVELOPING PATIENCE IN OUR APPROACH TO LEARNING—In *Harvard Magazine,*[19] Professor Jennifer Roberts persuasively argues that the increased pressures and tempo of daily life engendered by technology and the accompanying expectations of constant accessibility and instant responses directly impacts our level of patience. She proposes that one of the antidotes is to develop in ourselves and our children the lost art of paying careful attention to the pace and tempo of learning experiences. In a fascinating essay, she describes an assignment she gives her students that is typically met with resistance and disbelief. The Harvard undergraduates who take her art history class are asked to spend three uninterrupted hours in a museum looking at a single painting while taking notes about what they see. In an age where multitasking often competes with deeper levels of thinking, this assignment provides an experience that helps students better appreciate the difference between *looking* at something and truly *seeing* it. Roberts uses her own experience, spending three hours studying the John Singleton Copley painting *Boy with a Flying Squirrel.* She explains: "It took me 21 minutes before I registered the fact that the fingers holding the chain exactly span the diameter of the water glass beneath them. It took a good 45 minutes before I realized that the seemingly random folds and wrinkles in the background curtain are actually perfect copies of the shapes of the boy's ear and eye—as if Copley had imagined those sensory organs distributing or imprinting themselves on the surface behind him." Roberts concludes that teaching patience, by helping students slow down, focus deeply, and mindfully nurture their ability to develop the skill for deeper attention and thought is a crucial skill for today's students.

In a recent talk I (DP) gave to parents of yeshivah students in Chicago, the audience was surveyed about what they considered to be the greatest challenge to their ability to educate their children in a manner that fostered a meaningful connection to Judaism. The number one challenge chosen by parents was that their children were growing up in a world that lacked "stillness"; i.e., their children's spiritual connections were being hampered by a pervasive state of distraction caused by continuous connection to the world of texting, social media and multitasking. The Baal Shem Tov was said to interpret the phrase *"v'avaditem m'heirah"* in the daily prayer of *"Shema"* as, "get rid of the feeling of being hurried in your life."

Roberts argues that the cognitive and emotional changes brought on by the digital revolution require educators to teach patience as a core social-emotional skill necessary for in-depth learning. If recent research in neuroscience documents that brains of digital natives are being rewired in a manner that can lead to

---

18 Morinis, A. (2007). *Everyday Holiness,* Boston, MA.: Trumpeter Press, p. 58.
19 Roberts, J. (2013). The power of patience. *Harvard Magazine,* 40–41.

shallow rather than deep thinking, then parents and teachers need to develop a set of tools that include what Roberts describes as "the deliberate engagement of delay."

Some specific strategies for bringing such an approach to the classroom, which, in turn, might also inform our pacing was described by Bauerline[20] who recommends that teachers carve out time in their day for children to read with an unbroken and unbothered focus, similar to that described by Roberts. This approach includes setting aside a time for "slow reading" following these recommendations:

   a Promote a willingness to pause and probe while helping the student develop enough patience to ponder a single sentence for a few minutes: "to insert a hesitant question before moving on."

   b Develop the capacity for uninterrupted thinking. If one pauses in the middle of deep reading to check texts or e-mail they "lose their place in the argument."

   c Foster receptivity to deep thinking—provide space to understand and reflect before agreeing or arguing.

4. FOSTERING A SENSE OF EMPATHY AND PERSPECTIVE-TAKING—It is easier to be patient when we are able to see things through the eyes of those who are provoking us. When difficult people at home or work upset us, empathy for the underlying causes of their behavior can be very calming. Having an attitude of curiosity about why a family member who is being difficult is acting in a certain manner can lead to improved frustration tolerance. For example, in the case of parenting, reminding yourself that your child's irritability may be related to stress in school or on the playground can lead to greater understanding and lower levels of emotionalism. In general, an impatient response to the provocations of others is almost guaranteed to fuel more resistance and difficult behavior from the other party. When one deals with interpersonal provocations with criticism or yelling, a vicious cycle can be created that will try even the most patient

individual's ability to remain calm. When one reflects back calmness and empathy in a manner that allows the person who is the source of your impatience to feel understood, a de-escalation of the mutual tensions will feed a far less upsetting interaction.

Psychologist Dr. John Krug beautifully illustrates this concept with the following story:

Imagine yourself on a crowded elevator in midtown Manhattan at the height of rush hour. You're going up to the 50th floor, but you become increasingly irritated as the man behind you, in his impatience to get off at his floor, is crowding your personal space by jamming into your back. You find yourself increasingly upset and decide that you are going to give him a piece of your mind when he finally gets off the elevator. When the elevator reaches his floor and he makes his way to get off, you see that this man is blind. What you thought was an inconsiderate individual, rudely jockeying for a good position to quickly leave the elevator, was, in fact, a blind man with a cane trying to steady himself to meet the challenge of keeping his balance.

What effect does the knowledge that this man is blind have on your feelings of impatience? Your righteous indignation gives way to empathy. Your anger and sense of irritation yields to guilt about unfair judgment. Developing the ability to view situations through the eyes of others is often one of the most effective ingredients nourishing the ability to be patient.

CONCLUSION

Developing the ability to remain patient in face of life's inevitable stress is a skill that can have major impact on one's relationships, health, and overall happiness. By working on changing one's perspective when faced either with the "little" annoyances of daily routine as well as when struggling to cope with more major life events, an individual can transform his life into one where frustration can serve as a source of growth rather than as a source of conflict.

Life in the Balance: Torah Perspectives on Positive Psychology (New York: Shaar Press, 2014), pp. 177–199
Reprinted with permission of the authors

20 Bauerline, M. (2011), Too dumb for complex texts? *Educational Leadership*, 68, 28–32.

Judging Ourselves? Yes!

PERFECTLY HAPPY BEING IMPERFECT

How can I ever be at peace if I've made serious mistakes in my life or if I'm upset about my character shortcomings?

INTRODUCTION

Exercise 5.1

From the following list, identify one trait that does not pose a challenge for you. Then select one that does.

Selfishness	Crassness
Jealousy	Cynicism
Greed	Dishonesty
Pettiness	Disloyalty
Laziness	Disorganization
Anger	Extravagance
Arrogance	Flakiness
Timidity	Intrusiveness
Stinginess	Frivolity
Fickleness	Pessimism
Insensitivity	

2

22

INNER CONFLICT
TWO SOULS

Exercise 5.2

Try to give an honest "yes" or "no" response to each of the following statements. Answer each question on its own, without regard to its consistency with the other answers.

	YES	NO
I am a selfish person.		
I'm not a selfish person.		
There are times I really only care about my own existence and well-being.		
I know that it's not just about me—that there are things that are greater and more important than my own existence.		
I would never knowingly do something to hurt another person.		
I know that I've hurt others in pursuit of my own goals.		
I sometimes feel glad when someone else fails.		
I don't want to rejoice over someone else's troubles.		
When I really want something, I find it very difficult to resist it, even when I know that it is harmful to my moral and spiritual well-being.		
I am careful to weigh short-term gains against the long-term harm they might bring.		

Text 1a

RABBI SHNE'UR ZALMAN OF LIADI, *TANYA*, CH. 1

דִלְכָל אִישׁ יִשְׂרָאֵל, אֶחָד צַדִּיק וְאֶחָד רָשָׁע, יֵשׁ שְׁתֵּי נְשָׁמוֹת, וּכְדִכְתִיב: "וּנְשָׁמוֹת אֲנִי עָשִׂיתִי" (יְשַׁעְיָהוּ נז, טז), שֶׁהֵן שְׁתֵּי נְפָשׁוֹת.

נֶפֶשׁ אַחַת מִצַּד הַקְלִיפָּה וְסִטְרָא אַחֲרָא . . . וּמִמֶּנָּה בָּאוֹת כָּל הַמִּדּוֹת רָעוֹת . . .

וְגַם מִדּוֹת טוֹבוֹת . . . כְּמוֹ רַחֲמָנוּת וּגְמִילוּת חֲסָדִים, בָּאוֹת מִמֶּנָּה.

Each of us, whether righteous or wicked, has two souls, as it is written, "I have created souls" (Isaiah 57:16).

One soul originates in unholiness . . . and all negative character traits stem from it. . . . This soul is also the source of positive traits . . . such as mercy and benevolence.

RABBI SHNE'UR ZALMAN OF LIADI (ALTER REBBE)
1745–1812

Chasidic rebbe, halachic authority, and founder of the Chabad movement. The Alter Rebbe was born in Liozna, Belarus, and was among the principal students of the Magid of Mezeritch. His numerous works include the *Tanya*, an early classic containing the fundamentals of Chabad Chasidism; and *Shulchan Aruch HaRav*, an expanded and reworked code of Jewish law.

Text 1b

RABBI SHNE'UR ZALMAN OF LIADI, *TANYA*, CH. 2

וְנֶפֶשׁ הַשֵּׁנִית בְּיִשְׂרָאֵל הִיא חֵלֶק אֱלוֹ-הַ מִמַּעַל מַמָּשׁ.

Our second soul is a part of G-d above, literally.

Text 2

RABBI SHNE'UR ZALMAN OF LIADI, *TANYA*, CH. 9 ⚅

וּכְמוֹ שְׁנֵי מְלָכִים נִלְחָמִים עַל עִיר אַחַת, שֶׁכָּל אֶחָד רוֹצֶה
לְכָבְשָׁהּ וְלִמְלוֹךְ עָלֶיהָ, דְּהַיְנוּ לְהַנְהִיג יוֹשְׁבֶיהָ כִּרְצוֹנוֹ וְשֶׁיִּהְיוּ
סָרִים לְמִשְׁמַעְתּוֹ בְּכָל אֲשֶׁר יִגְזוֹר עֲלֵיהֶם.

כָּךְ שְׁתֵּי הַנְּפָשׁוֹת, הָאֱלֹקִית וְהַחִיּוּנִית הַבַּהֲמִית שֶׁמֵּהַקְּלִיפָּה,
נִלְחָמוֹת זוֹ עִם זוֹ עַל הַגּוּף וְכָל אֲבָרָיו. שֶׁהָאֱלֹקִית, חֶפְצָהּ
וּרְצוֹנָהּ שֶׁתִּהְיֶה הִיא לְבַדָּהּ הַמּוֹשֶׁלֶת עָלָיו וּמַנְהִיגָתוֹ, וְכָל
הָאֲבָרִים יִהְיוּ סָרִים לְמִשְׁמַעְתָּהּ וּבְטֵלִים אֶצְלָהּ לְגַמְרֵי
וּמֶרְכָּבָה אֵלֶיהָ . . .

אַךְ נֶפֶשׁ הַבַּהֲמִית שֶׁמֵּהַקְּלִיפָּה רְצוֹנָהּ לְהֵפֶךְ מַמָּשׁ, לְטוֹבַת
הָאָדָם שֶׁיִּתְגַּבֵּר עָלֶיהָ וִינַצְּחֶנָּה, כִּמְשַׁל הַזּוֹנָה שֶׁבַּזֹּהַר הַקָּדוֹשׁ.

Imagine two kings locked in battle, each desperate to gain control over the same city, so that all its inhabitants will obey his every decree.

That same battle rages within each of us, between our two souls. Our divine soul longs to be the sole ruler of our body and its functions, directing all of our limbs to serve as a vehicle for her. . . .

Its rival, the animalistic soul, desires the exact opposite.

Nevertheless, the desires of the animalistic soul are ultimately for our benefit, for when we overcome them, we emerge more spiritually empowered.

TSADIK AND *BEINONI*

Text 3
TALMUD, YOMA 38B 👥

רָאָה הַקָּדוֹשׁ בָּרוּךְ הוּא שֶׁצַדִיקִים מוּעָטִין, עָמַד וּשְׁתָלָן בְּכָל
דוֹר וָדוֹר.

G-d saw that the righteous are few in number, so He planted them in every generation.

BABYLONIAN TALMUD

A literary work of monumental proportions that draws upon the legal, spiritual, intellectual, ethical, and historical traditions of Judaism. The 37 tractates of the Babylonian Talmud contain the teachings of the Jewish sages from the period after the destruction of the 2nd Temple through the 5th century CE. It has served as the primary vehicle for the transmission of the Oral Law and the education of Jews over the centuries; it is the entry point for all subsequent legal, ethical, and theological Jewish scholarship.

Text 4

RABBI SHNE'UR ZALMAN OF LIADI, *TANYA*, CH. 14 🙂

> וְהִנֵּה, מִדַּת הַבֵּינוֹנִי הִיא מִדַּת כָּל אָדָם, וְאַחֲרֶיהָ כָּל אָדָם
> יִמְשׁוֹךְ. שֶׁכָּל אָדָם יָכוֹל לִהְיוֹת בֵּינוֹנִי בְּכָל עֵת וּבְכָל שָׁעָה.
> כִּי הַבֵּינוֹנִי אֵינוֹ מוֹאֵס בָּרַע, שֶׁזֶּהוּ דָּבָר הַמָּסוּר לַלֵּב . . . אֶלָּא
> "סוּר מֵרָע וַעֲשֵׂה טוֹב" (תְּהִלִּים לד, טו), דְּהַיְינוּ בְּפוֹעַל מַמָּשׁ
> בְּמַעֲשֵׂה דִּבּוּר וּמַחֲשָׁבָה, שֶׁבָּהֶם הַבְּחִירָה וְהַיְכוֹלֶת וְהָרְשׁוּת
> נְתוּנָה לְכָל אָדָם לַעֲשׂוֹת וּלְדַבֵּר וְלַחֲשׁוֹב גַּם מַה שֶׁהוּא נֶגֶד
> תַּאֲוַת לִבּוֹ וְהָפְכָה מַמָּשׁ.

The status of *beinoni* is [attainable] for all people; achieving this status ought to be every person's goal. At any time, any person can be a *beinoni*, because the *beinoni* does not have an aversion for the unholy, which is a feeling that we cannot necessarily control. . . . Rather, the *beinoni's* task is only to "turn away from evil and do good" (Psalms 34:15) in actual practice—in deed, speech, and thought. In these areas, the choice, ability, and freedom are given to every person to act, speak, and think in ways that are contrary to the desire of the heart and even diametrically opposed to it.

EMBRACING THE STRUGGLE
EXPECTATIONS

Exercise 5.3

Realistically, to which degree are the following
scenarios likely to frustrate you?

1 = very frustrated

2 = somewhat frustrated

3 = not at all frustrated

SCENARIO	YES
Your car breaks down and you need to hire a cab.	1 2 3
You can't afford the car of your choice.	1 2 3
You can't afford the luxury car of your choice.	1 2 3
You can't afford a private jet.	1 2 3
You haven't yet sprouted wings.	1 2 3

Text 5

RABBI SHNE'UR ZALMAN OF LIADI, *TANYA*, CH. 27

וְאַדְּרַבָּה, הָעַצְבוּת הִיא מִגַּסוּת הָרוּחַ, שֶׁאֵינוֹ מַכִּיר מְקוֹמוֹ,
וְעַל כֵּן יֵרַע לְבָבוֹ עַל שֶׁאֵינוֹ בְּמַדְרֵגַת צַדִּיק, שֶׁלַּצַּדִּיקִים בְּוַדַּאי
אֵין נוֹפְלִים לָהֶם הִרְהוּרֵי שְׁטוּת כָּאֵלּוּ.

כִּי אִלּוּ הָיָה מַכִּיר מְקוֹמוֹ, שֶׁהוּא רָחוֹק מְאֹד מִמַּדְרֵגַת צַדִּיק,
וְהַלְוַאי הָיָה בֵּינוֹנִי וְלֹא רָשָׁע כָּל יָמָיו אֲפִלּוּ שָׁעָה אַחַת, הֲרֵי
זֹאת הִיא מִדַּת הַבֵּינוֹנִים וַעֲבוֹדָתָם, לִכְבֹּשׁ הַיֵּצֶר.

To the contrary! Despondency [over your spiritual struggles] stems from an inflated self-assessment, from not recognizing your place. This delusion leads you to feel badly that you are not on the level of the perfect person, who is certainly not bothered by such foolish thoughts.

Know your place. You are very far from the level of the perfect person. Rather, you should aspire to always be a *beinoni* and never for a moment to fail [in thought, speech, and action]. This, after all, is the lot of the *beinoni* and their task in life: to [struggle against and] subdue their negative impulses.

APPRECIATING WHAT'S EXPECTED

Text 6

RABBI SHNE'UR ZALMAN OF LIADI, *TANYA*, CH. 36

וְהִנֵּה תַּכְלִית הִשְׁתַּלְשְׁלוּת הָעוֹלָמוֹת וִירִידָתָם מִמַּדְרֵגָה
לְמַדְרֵגָה אֵינוֹ בִּשְׁבִיל עוֹלָמוֹת הָעֶלְיוֹנִים . . . אֶלָּא הַתַּכְלִית
הוּא עוֹלָם הַזֶּה הַתַּחְתּוֹן. שֶׁכָּךְ עָלָה בִּרְצוֹנוֹ יִתְבָּרֵךְ, לִהְיוֹת
נַחַת רוּחַ לְפָנָיו יִתְבָּרֵךְ כַּד אִתְכַּפְיָא סִטְרָא אַחֲרָא וְאִתְהַפֵּךְ
חֲשׁוֹכָא לִנְהוֹרָא.

The purpose of the evolution of the worlds, and their descent from level to level, is not for the sake of the higher worlds. . . . Rather, the purpose is this lowly world. For so it arose in G-d's desire: that He should derive satisfaction when the negativity of this world is vanquished and its darkness is transformed into light.

Text 7

RABBI SHNE'UR ZALMAN OF LIADI, *TANYA*, CH. 27 ⊕

וְלָכֵן אַל יִפּוֹל לֵב אָדָם עָלָיו, וְלֹא יֵרַע לְבָבוֹ מְאֹד גַּם אִם יִהְיֶה
כֵּן כָּל יָמָיו בְּמִלְחָמָה זוֹ, כִּי אוּלַי לְכָךְ נִבְרָא, וְזֹאת עֲבוֹדָתוֹ -
לְאַכְפְיָא לְסִטְרָא אַחֲרָא תָּמִיד . . .
וּשְׁנֵי מִינֵי נַחַת רוּחַ לְפָנָיו יִתְבָּרֵךְ לְמַעְלָה:
אֶחָד, מִבִּטוּל הַסִּטְרָא אַחֲרָא לְגַמְרֵי וְאִתְהַפְּכָא מְמִרִירוּ
לְמִתְקָא וּמֵחֲשׁוֹכָא לִנְהוֹרָא עַל יְדֵי הַצַּדִּיקִים.
וְהַשֵּׁנִית, כַּד אִתְכַּפְיָא הַסִּטְרָא אַחֲרָא בְּעוֹדָהּ בְּתָקְפָּהּ
וּגְבוּרָתָהּ . . . עַל יְדֵי הַבֵּינוֹנִים.

Do not feel distressed or exceedingly troubled even if you are engaged in this conflict all your life, for perhaps this is the reason why you were created and this is your calling—to constantly subdue unholiness. . . .

There are two kinds of enjoyment for G-d:

One is from the complete annihilation of unholiness. This is accomplished by perfect people, who transform [their internal] bitterness to sweetness and darkness to light.

The second is from the subduing of unholiness while it is at the apex of its strength . . . through the effort of the strugglers.

YOUR PORTION IN THE WORLD

Text 8

RABBI AHARON OF KARLIN, CITED IN
KENESET YISRAEL, LIKUTIM, P. 145 ⊞

RABBI AHARON OF KARLIN
1736–1772

Chasidic rebbe. Rabbi Aharon was a
disciple of Rabbi Dov Ber of Mezeritch.
He was known as Rabbi Aharon the
Great, and was one of the pioneers of
Chasidism in Lithuania. He is known
for his ecstatic and unrestrained fervor
during his prayers and for his caring
for the needy. He is the composer of
the Shabbat hymn "Kah echsof."

וואָס איז דער עצם ענין פון עצבות? עצבות איז טײַטש "עס
קומט מיר", "עס פעהלט מיר", הן בגשמיות הן ברוחניות,
איז דאָך אַלץ זיך. וואָס עפּעס "מיר פעלט"? אַבֿיא אין דעם
הימעל זאָל ניט פעלין!

אבֿרהם אבֿינו זאָל זיך וועלין מיט מיר בײַטן וועל איך ניט
וועלן. וואָס אבֿרהם אבֿינו אַ צדיק מיט מדרגות, אין איך
בין אַ פּראָסטער מענטש. אין אַז איך וועל מיר ביטין
מיט אבֿרהם אבֿינו, ער וועט זיַין אַ פּראָסטער מענטש,
אין איך וועל וועארין אַ בעל מדריגה. אבער אין הימעל
וועט גאָר ניט צו קימען. נאהר מיר, וואָס איך וועל וועארין אַ
בעל מדריגה. איז דאָס ווידער מיר אין זיך!

What is the essence of despondency? Despondency means, "I deserve this," "I am missing
that"—whether it is a material lack, or a spiritual
lack, it's all about me.

Why should I be concerned over what I lack?
I should be concerned that nothing is lacking for G-d!

If our patriarch Abraham would wish to change
places with me, I would refuse. Abraham is a
tsadik, with very lofty spiritual attainments,
and I'm a plain person. If I changed places with
Abraham, then he would be a plain person and I
would be a lofty person. G-d would get nothing
out of this exchange. The only one who would

gain is me, in that I would achieve loftiness. But that would only be about me and myself!

Text 9

RABBI SIMCHAH BUNIM OF PESHISCHA,
CITED IN *IMREI EMET*, MIKETS 5696 (🎧)

שֶׁכָּל אֶחָד מִיִשְׂרָאֵל יֵשׁ לוֹ חֲבִילָה מִמַּה שֶׁעוֹבֵר עָלָיו, וּלְעָתִיד יִתְעָרְבוּ כָּל הַחֲבִילוֹת, וְכָל אֶחָד יַכִּיר חֲבִילָתוֹ וְיִרְצֶה בָּהּ.

Every one of us has a "bundle" that contains everything we experience in the course of our lives. In the World to Come, all of the bundles will be mixed together. And yet, every person will recognize their own "bundle" and want only it.

RABBI SIMCHAH BUNIM BONHART OF PESHISCHA
1765–1827

Chasidic rebbe. Rabbi Simchah Bunim spent many years in business and pharmaceutics, but later became one of the prominent disciples and then succeeded Rabbi Yaakov Yitschak of Peshischa, known as "The Holy *Yid* of Peshischa." Many of his teachings were transmitted orally, some of which have been collected in *Kol Simchah*.

DISTRESS OVER WRONGDOING
TESHUVAH

Text 10
TALMUD, YOMA 86B

גְּדוֹלָה תְּשׁוּבָה שֶׁזְּדוֹנוֹת נַעֲשׂוֹת לוֹ כִּשְׁגָגוֹת . . .
גְּדוֹלָה תְּשׁוּבָה שֶׁזְּדוֹנוֹת נַעֲשׂוֹת לוֹ כִּזְכָיוֹת.

Great is *teshuvah,* as it transforms a person's deliberate sins into errors. . . .

Great is *teshuvah,* as it transforms a person's deliberate sins into virtues.

Text 11

THE REBBE, RABBI MENACHEM MENDEL
SCHNEERSON, *LIKUTEI SICHOT* 14, P. 355

אֲפִילוּ אוֹיב מֶען אִיז אַמָאל אִיבֶּערְגֶעפַאלֶן אוּן מֶען הָאט
גֶעטָאן אַ עִנְיָן פַארְקֶערְט פוּן דֶעם וָואס דֶער אוֹיבֶּערְשְׁטֶער
הָאט גֶעהֵייסֶען, אָבֶּער בְּשַׁעַת מֶען בַּאטְרַאכְט זִיך אוּן מֶען
קוּמְט צוּ דֶער הַכָּרָה אַז נִיט קוּקֶענְדִיק אַז עֶר אִיז אַמָאל
אִיבֶּערְגֶעפַאלֶן אוּן גֶעטָאן פַארְקֶערְט פוּן דֶעם צִיווּי הַשֵׁם,
פוּנְדֶעסְטוֶועגֶען הָאט אִים דֶער אוֹיבֶּערְשְׁטֶער גֶעגֶעבֶּען
דִי מֶעגְלִיכְקֵייט צוּ תְּשׁוּבָה טָאן וָואס דוּרְך דֶעם וֶוערְט עֶר
רָצוּי צוּם אוֹיבֶּערְשְׁטֶן אַזוֹי וִוי קוֹדֶם הַחֵטְא, בִּיז אַז נַעֲשָׂה
לוֹ כִּזְכֻיּוֹת, אַזוֹי וִוי עֶר וָואלְט גֶעטָאן אַ מִצְוָה, יֶעמוֹלְט אִיז
צוּזַאמֶען מִיטְן מְרִירוּת גֶעפִיל וָואס סְ'אִיז פַארַאן בְּשַׁעַת
הַתְּשׁוּבָה, צוּזַאמֶען מִיט דֶעם אִיז פַארַאן דִי גְרֶעסְטֶע שִׂמְחָה
פוּן דֶעם וָואס עֶר טוּהְט תְּשׁוּבָה אוּן וֶוערְט בַּאוִויליִקְט צוּם
אוֹיבֶּערְשְׁטֶן.

Even those who have failed and behaved in a manner that is contrary to G-d's commandments have the ability to be joyous. When they contemplate and clearly recognize that in spite of their wrongdoings G-d provides the option of *teshuvah* (return)—a process that allows them to regain favored status and even to transform past mistakes into positives—then, concurrent with the bitterness and remorse of *teshuvah*, they will also experience tremendous joy. After all, they have returned, and their previously fractured relationship with G-d has been completely restored!

RABBI MENACHEM MENDEL SCHNEERSON

1902–1994

The towering Jewish leader of the 20th century, known as "the Lubavitcher Rebbe," or simply as "the Rebbe." Born in southern Ukraine, the Rebbe escaped Nazi-occupied Europe, arriving in the U.S. in June 1941. The Rebbe inspired and guided the revival of traditional Judaism after the European devastation, impacting virtually every Jewish community the world over. The Rebbe often emphasized that the performance of just one additional good deed could usher in the era of Mashiach. The Rebbe's scholarly talks and writings have been printed in more than 200 volumes.

DESPAIR VS. REMORSE

Figure 5.1

Despair vs. Remorse

1. Despair is passive, while remorse is active. Remorse is something you initiate, while despair is something that befalls you.

2. Despair has no goal, while remorse is goal-oriented. Remorse is a vehicle for achieving self-transformation.

3. Despair is a bottomless pit, while remorse has *boundaries*. Remorse is contained within a certain time frame in order to achieve a specific goal.

Text 12

RABBI SHNE'UR ZALMAN OF LIADI, *TANYA*, CH. 26 ㉖

וְהִנֵּה, בֵּין שֶׁנָּפְלָה לוֹ הָעַצְבוּת בִּשְׁעַת עֲבוֹדָה בְּתַלְמוּד תּוֹרָה אוֹ בִּתְפִלָּה, וּבֵין שֶׁנָּפְלָה לוֹ שֶׁלֹּא בִּשְׁעַת עֲבוֹדָה, זֹאת יָשִׂים אֶל לִבּוֹ, כִּי אֵין הַזְּמַן גְּרָמָא כָּעֵת לְעַצְבוּת אֲמִתִּית, אֲפִלּוּ לְדַאֲגַת עֲווֹנוֹת חֲמוּרִים חַס וְשָׁלוֹם.

רַק לָזֹאת צָרִיךְ קְבִיעוּת עִתִּים וּשְׁעַת הַכּוֹשֶׁר בְּיִשּׁוּב הַדַּעַת, לְהִתְבּוֹנֵן בִּגְדוּלַת ה' אֲשֶׁר חָטָא לוֹ, כְּדֵי שֶׁעַל יְדֵי זֶה יִהְיֶה לִבּוֹ נִשְׁבָּר בֶּאֱמֶת בִּמְרִירוּת אֲמִתִּית.

וּכְמְבוֹאָר עֵת זוֹ בְּמָקוֹם אַחֵר. וְשָׁם נִתְבָּאֵר גַּם כֵּן, כִּי מִיָּד אַחַר שֶׁנִּשְׁבַּר לִבּוֹ בְּעִתִּים קְבוּעִים הָהֵם, אֲזַי יָסִיר הָעֶצֶב מִלִּבּוֹ לְגַמְרֵי, וְיַאֲמִין אֱמוּנָה שְׁלֵימָה כִּי ה' הֶעֱבִיר חַטָּאתוֹ וְרַב לִסְלוֹחַ.

Whenever sadness happens upon us, whether we are involved in the service of G-d or in some other matter, we must realize that now is an inappropriate time for genuine remorse, even over egregious misdeeds, G-d forbid.

For genuine remorse, we need designated times when we have calmness of mind. During those appropriate times, we should reflect upon the greatness of G-d against Whom we have sinned, and thereby cause our hearts to be truly broken and genuinely embittered.

Elsewhere it is clarified precisely when this time should be. It is also explained there that once our hearts have been broken during these designated times, we should completely dismiss the sorrow and believe with a perfect faith that G-d, in His abundant forgiveness, has removed our sin.

CONCLUSION

Exercise 5.4

Keep a daily tally of the victories you score in the internal conflict between your "G-dly self" and your "animal self." Each time you are faced with any of the choices listed below (feel free to add additional challenges), and you react with a G-dly response rather than an animalistic response, note your victory on the chart. Remember, you're only marking your victories, not your defeats. (Dwelling on your defeats is counterproductive—this will only drag you down.)

Count your victories at the end of each day, and take a moment to experience the fulfillment and happiness that comes from engaging in your calling in life.

	VICTORY
Anger vs. forgiveness	
Greed vs. generosity	
Impulse vs. mindfulness	
Arrogance vs. humility	
Other:	

Key Points

1. We are, by nature, conflicted beings. There is a constant struggle within our minds and hearts between our self-centered animalistic self and our altruistic G-dly self.

2. Perfect people do exist. Endowed with lofty souls, such people are extremely rare. They are holy, selfless, flawless, and have vanquished their negative impulses and character flaws. The majority of people, however, struggle their entire lives against their character flaws and negative impulses.

3. Frustration over our internal struggles is a result of an unreasonable expectation of perfection. We need to come to terms with who we are and always will be, and understand that struggling is our mission in life.

4. Common wisdom attributes value to struggling over an aspect of our personality if it leads to an enduring change. From the Jewish perspective, there's value in the struggle even absent any personal attainment. When we struggle against and suppress our internal unholy instincts, we suppress the forces of unholiness and unleash a tremendous amount of divine light into this world.

5. Our engagement in this struggle—and the small daily victories we score—is at the heart of our calling in life. G-d derives exquisite *nachas* from the extraordinary work of the struggler. Our flaws are not impediments. They are gifts; they make us valuable and cosmically relevant.

6. We are supposed to feel genuine remorse over actual wrongdoing. Yet the opportunity to do *teshuvah* after a transgression—to restore our relationship with G-d and recast wrongdoing as a positive power—is reason for great joy. We can experience this joy even as we experience remorse.

7. The remorse that we experience during *teshuvah* is not an instance of losing control over our emotions and falling into debilitating sadness. We *initiate* remorseful thoughts on our own, and we do it *for a specific purpose*—to do *teshuvah* and to achieve joy—and only at *appropriate times*.

ADDITIONAL READINGS

CHANGE

Rabbi Raphael Pelcovitz
David Pelcovitz, Phd

Anyone who has tried to master a negative aspect of his/her personality or behavior has experienced the difficulty and complexity of attaining enduring change. Surveys find that by February most New Year's resolutions have given way to relapse, and every Rosh Hashanah we are once again faced with a long list of actions and traits that we once again seek to change. Research in positive psychology, bolstered by the insights of our Rabbis on the process of repentance (*teshuvah*), can help provide a greater understanding of the nature of this process, as well as some solutions to achieve more effective enduring modification of behavior. The process of change is more a spiral than a straight line. For example, in the case of addictions, multiple attempts at change is the norm. Studies have found that the average smoker spirals back into

RABBI RAPHAEL PELCOVITZ

Rabbi emeritus, author, and teacher. Rabbi Pelcovitz served as the pulpit rabbi and community leader of Congregation Kneseth Israel (the White Shul) in Far Rockaway, New York, for more than 50 years. He authored a number of books in which he presents ideas from Jewish thought in a compelling and comprehensible way. He also co-authored 2 books with his son, Dr. David Pelcovitz.

DAVID PELCOVITZ, PHD

Psychologist, teacher, and author. Dr. Pelcovitz, who received his PhD from the University of Pennsylvania, has published and lectured extensively on a variety of topics related to education, parenting, and mental health. He is currently the Straus Professor of Psychology and Education at the Azrieli Graduate School, Yeshiva University. His books include *Balanced Parenting* and *Life in the Balance*, both written in collaboration with his father, Rabbi Raphael Pelcovitz.

relapse three to four times before his cessation of smoking becomes an enduring change. This chapter will address the stages of change filtered through the dual prism of Jewish writings on repentance and research on the psychology of change.

STAGES OF CHANGE: JEWISH PERSPECTIVES ON REPENTANCE

In Jewish thought one of the most widely used models for change are the stages of repentance (*teshuvah*) described by the Rambam (Maimonides).[1] This multistep process consists of:

1. **ABANDONING SIN**—This involves concrete behavioral change marked by overtly stopping the behavior that needs to be changed. This stage is a cornerstone of some of the most effective therapeutic programs that help people change destructive behavior. For example, 12-step programs such as Alcoholics Anonymous place initial emphasis on overt behavioral change without requiring an initial process of internal change. While common belief may cause one to question whether behavioral change can last when not supported by deep insight into the underlying motivation, the Rambam's conceptualization posits that behavior alone can eventually lead to a more internal change process.

2. **REGRET FOR WHAT ONE HAS DONE**—This step refers to the inner emotional state of contrition that many researchers on the psychology of change consider to be an important component of the change process.

3. **AN INTERNAL RESOLVE**—and commitment never to repeat the wrongdoing.

---

1 Rambam, *Hilchos Teshuvah* Chapter 2.

4. **A VERBALIZED CONFESSION**—describing the nature of the sin that was committed.

In the 13th century, Rabbeinu Yonah, one of the great Talmudic teachers of his time, described more comprehensively the various stages of *teshuvah,* some of which overlap those of the Rambam while adding other dimensions of the change process. In *Shaarei Teshuvah*[2] (*The Gates of Repentance,* one of the most often read ethical treatises), he describes the following steps necessary for repentance:

1. Acknowledging the sin

2. Abandoning the sin

3. Worrying about the future consequences of the sin

4. Acting in a way opposite to that of the sin

5. Understanding the seriousness of the sin

6. Avoiding certain behaviors as a means of building a fence that helps prevent commission of sins

7. Verbal confession of the sin

8. Prayer for forgiveness

9. Making reparations to the offended party

10. Remembering the sin for the rest of one's life

11. Refraining from committing the same sin if the opportunity presents itself again

12. Teaching others not to make the same mistakes

Recognizing how difficult enduring change is, this comprehensive approach to repentance adds a variety of both emotional and behavioral actions that can serve to lessen the chances of relapse.

SECULAR PERSPECTIVES ON REPENTANCE

One of the most widely used models to help facilitate our understanding of the change process is a "stage theory of change" proposed by psychologist James Prochaska and his colleagues. In a series of books and carefully implemented research studies, Prochaska discovered a number of stages that individuals go through as they gradually come to a decision to **truly** change their actions.[3] While some of the processes described by Prochaska align nicely with the Rambam's and Rabbeinu Yonah's models of change, however, Prochaska's model places much greater emphasis on the internal process that precedes translating change into action. As noted earlier, this model is contrary to the Jewish model which is anchored in the premise that overt behavioral change will lead to internalization. There remains much to benefit from his analysis, however.

The five stages described by Prochaska and his colleagues are:

1. **PRECONTEMPLATION**—This stage is characterized by individuals who have little or no recognition that they have a problem that needs to be solved. Filtered through the prism of Rabbeinu Yonah's writings on the change process, such individuals have not yet reached the level of recognition that they are sinning. If an individual in this stage is forced by a parent, spouse, or friend into counseling, the prognosis for sustained improvement is grim. While they may show evidence of temporary change when the pressure of friends, family, therapist, or employer is intense, whatever changes are made under such pressure often are not sustained. As soon as the demands of the concerned others are removed, regression to the problematic behavior is likely. A clue that an individual is in the stage of precontemplation is denial and resistance when efforts are made to get them to change. Precontemplators often become experts at displacing the blame for their difficulties on others, or responding with angry countercharges that they are being persecuted, nagged, or misunderstood.

2. **CONTEMPLATION**—Contemplators have reached the stage of recognizing that their behavior needs to be changed.

2 Yonah ben Avraham of Gerona, *Shaarei Teshuvah: The Gates of Repentance.* Translated by: Shraga Silverstein (1971). Jerusalem, Israel: Feldheim.

3 Prochaska, J., Norcross, J. & Diclemente, C. (1994). *Changing for Good.* New York: Harpers Collins.

Using Rabbeinu Yonah's conceptualization of change, they have arrived at the stage of *"hakaras ha'cheit"*—recognition of sin, but are not yet ready to translate this recognition into action. Such individuals might say that they are thinking about changing, or considering working on themselves, but have not yet shown an ability to convert their thinking to the concrete world of action. Many individuals stay "stuck" in this stage for long periods of time. While in the contemplation stage, an internal cost-benefit analysis is often taking place. This internal struggle is typically marked by seesawing between the attraction of the pleasures of the problematic behavior on one hand, and a growing recognition of the emotional, behavioral, interpersonal, and spiritual damage caused by continuing to engage in the behavior, on the other hand.

A famous story is often used by psychologists to illustrate the heart of the contemplation process:

> *A man traveling in a foreign city was lost, so he stopped a stranger to ask for directions. The stranger was a patient man, who took the time to meticulously give the tourist detailed directions. He was confused when, after thanking him, the tourist walked in the opposite direction. The man started yelling at the visitor, pointing him, again, in the right direction. The visitor answered, "I know I'm going in the wrong direction, I'm just not ready to go there yet."*

This is the essence of contemplation: knowing where one has to go, recognizing what the road map is for getting there, but not yet having reached a place where one has the emotional energy and conviction that would propel one toward external change.

3. **PREPARATION**—Prochaska defines the preparation stage as characterizing individuals who are on the immediate threshold of implementing change. They are ready to take concrete action next month and often have experimented with actual minor behavioral changes. For example, a cigarette smoker might delay the first cigarette of the day or might already be smoking fewer cigarettes than was typical before arriving at this stage in the change process.

4. **ACTION**—As the description regarding the preliminary stages of change makes clear, much work often goes into the change process *before* action is actually taken. When consistent action is taken, a true commitment to change one's behavior and environment is clear to others in the changing individual's life. This stage of change corresponds to the Rambam's first stage, and Rabbeinu Yonah's second stage.

5. **MAINTENANCE**—Maintaining change permanently is very difficult work. As we are reminded every Yom Kippur, it is human nature to relapse into old habits. This stage involves working to prevent relapse, while gains made during the action stage are consolidated and internalized as a more permanent pattern of behavior.

SUPERFICIAL VS. ENDURING CHANGE

Another helpful way of conceptualizing change is Bateson's "first order change" versus "second order change."[4] First order change is the kind of superficial change against which Maimonides cautions. This type of change is easily reversed and is characterized by *doing* something differently rather than by *being* different. Typically, the process involves doing more or less of a certain behavior in a manner that doesn't require new learning, emotional commitment, or a qualitative change in who the person really is. In contrast, second order change involves the *teshuvah* process described by the Rambam. One views one's old behavior in a qualitatively different manner; the learning of new patterns is involved, and a total relapse to the old way of acting is far less likely than is the case in first order change. This type of change is more likely to involve the Maimonidean concept of *"teshuvah gemurah."* This is total repentance, which is characterized by being challenged by exactly the same situation that led to the problematic behavior in the past. Such enduring

---

4 Bateson, G. (1979). *Mind and Nature: A Necessary Unity.* New York: Dutton.

change is distinguished by being faced with identical temptations in an identical setting and yet not succumbing to old patterns. This type of second order change proves that one is a qualitatively different person than in the past. Reverting to old patterns is unthinkable.

Life in the Balance: Torah Perspectives on Positive Psychology (New York: Shaar Press, 2014), pp. 229–235

Reprinted with permission of the authors

SPIRITUAL WARRIOR

Jay Litvin

Frankly, I loathe being called a religious person. It sounds so boring.

I'm reminded of a person who once told me how much he envied me. "Life for you is so simple," he said. "Your religion tells you what to do and what not to do, and gives you all the answers."

Boy, I wish.

But, in truth, this is what the word "religion" conjures up: something kind of old and staid, perhaps even a bit crusty. Something calm and peaceful, barely alive and never in motion.

And so, I reject the title of "religious person." I'm just a guy who looks like a religious person.

So then, what am I?

Well, in truth, life feels more to me like a battleground than a prayer service, and my inner reality is more that of a warrior than a pious person.

So, if I have to label myself anything (which I vigorously avoid doing), I would have to call myself a "spiritual warrior." And here's what that means for me.

A warrior is one who enters the battlefield with a healthy dose of fear and a larger dose of love. He fights for a principle, or for his country, or for his king, and his love for these outweighs the fear he feels for his own safety. He requires courage and skill, for he risks his very life.

A warrior loves the battlefield; it is here that he is most alive. He must at all times act with

---

JAY LITVIN

1944–2004

Born in Chicago, Litvin moved to Israel in 1993 to serve as medical liaison for Chabad's Children of Chernobyl program, and took a leading role in airlifting children from the areas contaminated by the Chernobyl nuclear disaster. He also founded and directed Chabad's Terror Victims Project in Israel. He was a frequent contributor to the Jewish website Chabad.org.

his full awareness and ability; even the slightest lapse will cause his downfall.

The battlefield brings forth from the warrior capabilities and potentials that he didn't even know existed within himself. And so, as he fights, he is in a constant state of self-discovery.

The true warrior longs for the battlefield, for the rest of life seems in comparison like a place where he is able to actualize only a small part of who he is. So he craves the challenge and the encounter. He loves living on the edge. It is here that he is the most of who he is, and where he discovers that he is in fact more than who he thinks he is.

Living as a Jew and a chassid is this experience. It is an encounter with the Almighty and with myself. It is the place of self-discovery and challenge. It requires the bravery of facing who I am and who I am not. It takes a willingness to see the potential of who I can be, and face the smallness of who I have allowed myself to be.

When I am living Jewishly, I am living at the edge. I am in a no-man's land where each encounter, each moment, presents an opportunity to learn, to act, to refine and to transform. Sometimes, like King Arthur, I am battling dragons within and without; sometimes I am challenged by beasts that threaten to devour me with their anger and fear; sometimes I am fighting for my own sanity, attempting to reconcile the tactual world with a world which can neither be seen, heard nor touched.

As a spiritual warrior, when I am blessed to be living smack in the middle of the battlefield I am fully alive, wrestling at the edge of who I am. It matters not whether I am in prayer, giving my child a bath, or sitting at my computer. The battlefield includes my personal relationships, my inner desires, my overdrawn bank account, and my constant lack of sleep. It embraces my marriage and employment. My frustration, patience, envy, lust and greed. It is a state of mind, a willingness to find G-d in all places and to meet Him fully, allowing Him to penetrate into the deepest recesses of who I am and to dispel all the images of who I think I am.

Each time, and there are many such times, that I confront the imperative of what I must do with the reluctance of what I want to do; each time that I must transform thoughts and attitudes formed through years of life and conditioning into holy thoughts and holy attitudes, I am on the battlefield. Whether it's giving charity from the few pennies left in the coffer, or taking on an additional responsibility, or offering to help a friend—or not even a friend—when I can barely stay awake, I am on the battlefield. When tragedy strikes my family, G-d forbid, and I must discover a way to be both genuine with my grief and yet remain cognizant of the good I know that G-d gives to the world, I am being a spiritual warrior.

As a spiritual warrior, I discover my faith when I am at the limits of my faith. I find my love of G-d when I am angry with G-d. I find my trust in the Protector of the world when I am at my most frightened. And I find my obedience to the Almighty when I feel the most rebellious.

I am a spiritual warrior when I fully feel my despair, and find the hope to go on. When I feel betrayed, yet discover my trust. When I reach higher than I should, then fail and fall, only to discover that I have landed at a station higher than the one from which I reached.

On this battlefield called Yiddishkeit, I am stretched to the limit only to find that my limit is nowhere near what I thought it was. I am alive and growing, moving, in process. Scared and exhilarated. Craving victory, and having not the slightest idea of what it means.

To me, all the rest, as Rabbi Schneur Zalman of Liadi says in his *Tanya*, is conceit. To be despondent over the fact that I am constantly in the midst of a struggle is to pretend that I am something more than who I really am. It is to pretend that I am a *tzaddik*, one of the righteous few who have vanquished the negative within themselves, when in fact I can aspire, at my best moments, only to the level of *beinoni*, the spiritual warrior in the battlefield of life.

The *Tanya* tells us to rejoice when we are challenged within or without, because this is our task: to enter the battlefield. We are, it seems to me, like soldiers who have trained endlessly for battle, and shout in joy when the moment finally arrives to test their abilities and find the real stuff of which they are made.

And this is the spiritual warrior's challenge: to find the stuff of which he is made, whether it is to his liking or not, and bring himself fully into the struggle with himself and his encounter with G-d.

I find this battle terrifying, because I have no idea where it will lead. It forces me to open myself to G-d and allow Him into the innermost, most intimate confines of myself. It forces me to confront the plaguing question: if I truly let G-d in, what will He do to me once He is there? Who will I be? What will the world have become? And what is my place and purpose within it?

Religious? Me? Hardly. A Torah life is no place for a religious person. Religion is much too safe for such a journey into the unknown, into a meeting place with G-d. Only a warrior can embrace such a task. Only a chassid of the Rebbe can hope to possess such courage.

Reprinted with permission of *The Judaism Website, Chabad.org*

Joining Others = Yields

INVESTING IN HEALTHY RELATIONSHIPS

. . . .

Both social science and personal experience show that loneliness, disconnection, and division are stubborn realities of life. How can we arrest this disconcerting drift apart?

HAPPINESS AND RELATIONSHIPS
JUDAIC SOURCES

Exercise 6.1

Take a moment to think of a close and trusting relationship in your life. What would be lacking if this relationship weren't so close and trusting?

Text 1

ECCLESIASTES 4:9-12 ⚏

טוֹבִים הַשְּׁנַיִם מִן הָאֶחָד, אֲשֶׁר יֵשׁ לָהֶם שָׂכָר טוֹב בַּעֲמָלָם. כִּי אִם יִפֹּלוּ הָאֶחָד יָקִים אֶת חֲבֵרוֹ, וְאִילוֹ הָאֶחָד שֶׁיִּפּוֹל וְאֵין שֵׁנִי לַהֲקִימוֹ.

גַּם אִם יִשְׁכְּבוּ שְׁנַיִם וְחַם לָהֶם, וּלְאֶחָד אֵיךְ יֵחָם.

וְאִם יִתְקְפוֹ הָאֶחָד הַשְּׁנַיִם יַעַמְדוּ נֶגְדּוֹ, וְהַחוּט הַמְשֻׁלָּשׁ לֹא בִמְהֵרָה יִנָּתֵק.

Two are better than one, since they have good reward for their toil. For if they fall, one will lift the other; but woe to those who fall and have no second one to lift them up.

Moreover, if two lie down, they will have warmth, but how will one have warmth?

If attacked by someone, the two will stand against the attacker; and a three-stranded cord will not quickly be broken.

Text 2

MAIMONIDES, *GUIDE FOR THE PERPLEXED* 2:40 ⊕

הָאָדָם מְדִינִי בְּטָבַע, וְשִׁטְבְעוֹ שֶׁיְּהֵא בְּתוֹךְ חֲבוּרָה, וְאֵינוֹ כִּשְׁאָר בַּעֲלֵי חַיִּים אֲשֶׁר אֵין לוֹ הֶכְרֵחַ לִהְיוֹת בַּחֲבוּרָה.

The human being is naturally social. The nature of the human being is to be part of a community—unlike the life forms that need not be part of a collective.

RABBI MOSHE BEN MAIMON (MAIMONIDES, RAMBAM)
1135–1204

Halachist, philosopher, author, and physician. Maimonides was born in Córdoba, Spain. After the conquest of Córdoba by the Almohads, he fled Spain and eventually settled in Cairo, Egypt. There, he became the leader of the Jewish community and served as court physician to the vizier of Egypt. He is most noted for authoring the *Mishneh Torah*, an encyclopedic arrangement of Jewish law; and for his philosophical work, *Guide for the Perplexed*. His rulings on Jewish law are integral to the formation of halachic consensus.

Figure 6.1

The Four Kingdoms

Silent (Inanimate)	דוֹמֵם
Vegetative (Vegetable)	צוֹמֵחַ
Animate (Animal)	חַי
Articulate (Human)	מְדַבֵּר

MODERN RESEARCH

Text 3

ED DIENER AND ROBERT BISWAS-DIENER, *HAPPINESS:
UNLOCKING THE MYSTERIES OF PSYCHOLOGICAL WEALTH*
(MALDEN, MASS.: BLACKWELL PUBLISHING, 2011), PP. 50–52

Relationships are themselves a crucial part of psychological wealth, without which you cannot be truly rich. Simply put, we need others to flourish. Indeed, the results of research on social relationships and happiness are clear on this point: healthy social contact is essential for happiness. Family relationships and close friendships are important to happiness. . . . In fact, the links between happiness and social contact are so strong that many psychologists think that humans are genetically wired to need one another. . . .

In one study, for example, we collected mood data from people using the experience sampling method (ESM). Throughout the day, we signaled the research participants with random alarms, after which they would complete a short mood survey and indicate the type of situation they were in: Were they alone, or with other people?

Initially, we suspected that introverts would be happier when they were alone and that extroverts would be happier when they were in a social setting. . . . Flying in the face of our prediction, both extroverts and introverts had more positive emotions when they were with other people. That's right: even introverts who have the reputation for being social wallflowers enjoyed themselves more when they were in social

ED DIENER, PHD
1946–

Psychologist and professor. Dr. Diener is a leading researcher in positive psychology who coined the expression "subjective well-being," or SWB, as the aspect of happiness that can be empirically measured. Noted for his research on happiness, he has earned the nickname "Dr. Happiness."

ROBERT BISWAS-DIENER, PHD
1972–

Positive psychologist. Biswas-Diener is the son of Ed Diener and is an instructor at Portland State University. Biswas-Diener's research focuses on income and happiness, culture and happiness, and positive psychology. Biswas-Diener's research has led him to many nations, including India, Greenland, Israel, Kenya, and Spain, and he has been called the "Indiana Jones of positive psychology." He sits on the editorial boards of the *Journal of Happiness Studies* and the *Journal of Positive Psychology*.

settings. Although it's true that extroverts spent a bit more time with other people, both groups showed more pleasant moods when they were engaged in social contact. Indeed, the introverts get as much boost from being with people as did extroverts. . . .

It's certainly not true that we would like to surround ourselves with other people all the time, but when we do, we tend to feel good.

Text 4

SONJA LYUBOMIRSKY, *THE MYTHS OF HAPPINESS*
(NEW YORK: PENGUIN BOOKS, 2014), P. 63

Most of the time, social support won't make a problem disappear, but it can go a long way in helping us address the problem, mitigate it and lighten our emotional reaction to it.

In a clever study that supports this claim, researchers recruited volunteers who happened to be passing the base of a hill and were either alone or with a friend. Incredibly, those who were accompanied by a friend—especially a friend they were close to and knew a long time—judged the hill to be *less steep* than those who were alone.

Serving as a metaphor for the challenges of life . . . companions and confidants can make us feel that our problems and stresses are less steep as well.

SONJA LYUBOMIRSKY, PHD

Leading expert in positive psychology. Dr. Lyubomirsky is professor of psychology at the University of California, Riverside. Originally from Russia, she received her PhD in social/personality psychology from Stanford University. Her research on the possibility of permanently increasing happiness has been honored with various grants, including a million-dollar grant from the National Institute of Mental Health. She has authored *The How of Happiness* and, more recently, *The Myths of Happiness*.

CONTEMPORARY CONCERN

Text 5
"LONELINESS IS A SERIOUS PUBLIC-HEALTH PROBLEM,"
THE ECONOMIST, SEPTEMBER 1, 2018

The Economist and the Kaiser Family Foundation (KFF), an American non-profit group focused on health, surveyed nationally representative samples of people in three rich countries. The study found that 9% of adults in Japan, 22% in America and 23% in Britain always or often feel lonely, or lack companionship, or else feel left out or isolated.

The findings complement academic research which uses standardised questionnaires to measure loneliness. One drawn up at the University of California, Los Angeles (UCLA), has 20 statements, such as "I have nobody to talk to," and "I find myself waiting for people to call or write." Responses are marked based on the extent to which people agree. Respondents with tallies above a threshold are classed as lonely. A study published in 2010 using this scale estimated that 35% of Americans over 45 were lonely.... In 2013 Britain's Office for National Statistics (ONS), by dint of asking a simple question, classed 25% of people aged 52 or over as "sometimes lonely" with an extra 9% "often lonely."

Questions for Discussion

1. What are the causes leading people to feel isolated?

2. What can people who feel isolated do to overcome this? And how can others help?

LESSON GOAL

Exercise 6.2

ED DIENER AND ROBERT BISWAS-DIENER, *HAPPINESS:*
UNLOCKING THE MYSTERIES OF PSYCHOLOGICAL WEALTH
(MALDEN, MASS.: BLACKWELL PUBLISHING, 2011), PP. 65–66

Answer yes or no to each of the statements:

1. I give lots of compliments and positive remarks to others.

2. I have someone to whom I can tell my most intimate thoughts and feelings.

3. I rarely or never feel lonely.

4. I am careful about making negative remarks to others.

5. I get along well with my co-workers.

6. I can relax and be myself when I am with friends.

7. I mostly trust my family and friends.

8. There are people I very much love and care about.

9. There are people I could call in the middle of the night if I have an emergency.

10. I have fun when I am with other people.

Exercise 6.3

List some of the character traits that are helpful for friendships and relationships. Then list some of the traits that hinder friendships and relationships.

Traits that help	Traits that hinder

CYNICISM

Text 6
TALMUD, BERACHOT 58A

הוּא הָיָה אוֹמֵר:

אוֹרֵחַ טוֹב מַהוּ אוֹמֵר? כַּמָּה טְרָחוֹת טָרַח בַּעַל הַבַּיִת בִּשְׁבִילִי! כַּמָּה בָּשָׂר הֵבִיא לְפָנַי! כַּמָּה יַיִן הֵבִיא לְפָנַי! כַּמָּה גְלוּסְקָאוֹת הֵבִיא לְפָנַי! וְכָל מַה שֶּׁטָּרַח לֹא טָרַח אֶלָּא בִּשְׁבִילִי! אֲבָל אוֹרֵחַ רַע מַהוּ אוֹמֵר? מַה טּוֹרַח טָרַח בַּעַל הַבַּיִת זֶה? פַּת אַחַת אָכַלְתִּי, חֲתִיכָה אַחַת אָכַלְתִּי, כּוֹס אֶחָד שָׁתִיתִי. כָּל טוֹרַח שֶׁטָּרַח בַּעַל הַבַּיִת זֶה לֹא טָרַח אֶלָּא בִּשְׁבִיל אִשְׁתּוֹ וּבָנָיו ...

עַל אוֹרֵחַ רַע כְּתִיב, "לָכֵן יְרָאוּהוּ אֲנָשִׁים" (אִיּוֹב לז, כד).

BABYLONIAN TALMUD

A literary work of monumental proportions that draws upon the legal, spiritual, intellectual, ethical, and historical traditions of Judaism. The 37 tractates of the Babylonian Talmud contain the teachings of the Jewish sages from the period after the destruction of the 2nd Temple through the 5th century CE. It has served as the primary vehicle for the transmission of the Oral Law and the education of Jews over the centuries; it is the entry point for all subsequent legal, ethical, and theological Jewish scholarship.

Ben Zoma used to say:

What does a good guest say?

"How much trouble the host took for my sake! How much meat he brought before me! How much wine he brought before me! How many fine rolls he brought before me! And all the trouble that the host took was only for my sake!"

What does a bad guest say?

"What trouble did this host take? I ate one piece of bread. I ate one slice. I drank one cup. Any trouble that this host took was only for his wife and children." . . .

With regard to a bad guest, it is written, "People therefore fear him" (Job 37:24).

Exercise 6.4

1. Identify someone who did something nice for you recently.

2. Imagine what your sense of gratitude would look like if you believed this person was motivated to help you purely out of love. Imagine as well what your gratitude would look like if this person went through a lot of trouble to help you.

3. Consider whether you have already expressed gratitude to this person in a way that corresponds to these thoughts.

4. If not, reach out to this person this week and express gratitude (in speech or deed) in accordance with these thoughts.

DISAGREEMENT

Text 7

RABBI MENACHEM MENDEL MORGENSTERN,
EMET VE'EMUNAH (JERUSALEM, 2005), NO. 629, P. 488 ⊕

בְּתַנְחוּמָא פָּרָשַׁת פִּנְחָס: כְּשֵׁם שֶׁאֵין פַּרְצוּפֵיהֶן שֶׁל אָדָם שָׁוִין
זֶה לָזֶה, כַּךְ אֵין דַעְתָּם שָׁוִין זֶה לָזֶה.

כְּשֵׁם שֶׁהִנְךָ יָכוֹל לִסְבּוֹל שֶׁפַּרְצוּפוֹ שֶׁל אָדָם אַחֵר אֵינוֹ דוֹמֶה
לְשֶׁלְךָ, כַּךְ תִּסְבּוֹל אִם דֵעוֹתָיו שֶׁל אַחֵר אֵינָן דוֹמוֹת לְדֵעוֹתֶיךָ.

Midrash Tanchuma teaches, "Just as people's faces are different from each other, so their minds are different from each other."

The implication is that just as you tolerate other people who *look* different from you, so you should tolerate others who *think* differently than you do.

RABBI MENACHEM MENDEL MORGENSTERN
1787–1859

Chasidic rabbi and leader. Born near Lublin, Poland, Rabbi Menachem Mendel went on to succeed the Chozeh (Seer) of Lublin and Rabbi Simchah Bunim of Peshischa as a Chasidic rebbe in Kotsk. His teachings, some of which are gathered in *Ohel Torah* and *Emet Ve'emunah*, are well known in the Chasidic world for their sharpness.

Text 8

JOSEPH TELUSHKIN, *REBBE: THE LIFE AND TEACHINGS OF MENACHEM M. SCHNEERSON, THE MOST INFLUENTIAL RABBI IN MODERN HISTORY* (NEW YORK: HARPERCOLLINS, 2014), P. 134

What further fortified the Rebbe in his affection for those with whom he had differing views was a carefully cultivated consciousness of the areas in which he and his opponents agreed.

To a rabbi who expressed deep disagreement with him over a certain religious issue, the Rebbe noted that even if they disagreed on this matter, there still remained 612 issues on which they could work together—a reminder to the letter's recipient that they were two allies having a disagreement, not two opponents having a feud (the number 612 was of course a figurative reference to the Torah's 613 commandments, minus one). In this instance, he also reminded Rabbi Shmuel Lew, who had ongoing dealings with the same rabbi, "how positive a person this man and his family were, and how they can be forces for good [so] let's look [therefore] for the unifying force."

For Lew, the Rebbe's approach became a general directive for how to conduct his life: "Look always for that which you have in common with the other person and build that up." This was a good way, Lew came to understand, to avoid alienating potential allies and avoid living an existence filled with needless enmity.

RABBI JOSEPH TELUSHKIN
1948–

Rabbi and author. Telushkin received his ordination at Yeshiva University and a Jewish history degree at Columbia University. He has written many popular books about Judaism, including the best-selling *Jewish Literacy*, and *Rebbe*, a biography of the Lubavitcher Rebbe.

Text 9

TALMUD, BAVA METSI'A 84A ⚏

נָח נַפְשֵׁיה דְּרַבִּי שִׁמְעוֹן בֶּן לָקִישׁ וַהֲוָה קָא מִצְטַעֵר רַבִּי יוֹחָנָן בַּתְרֵיה טוּבָא. אָמְרוּ רַבָּנָן, "מַאן לֵיזִיל לֵיתְבֵיה לְדַעְתֵּיה? נֵיזִיל רַבִּי אֶלְעָזָר בֶּן פְּדָת דִּמְחַדְּדִין שְׁמַעְתָּתֵיה".

אֲזַל יָתִיב קַמֵּיה. כָּל מִילְּתָא דַּהֲוָה אֲמַר רַבִּי יוֹחָנָן, אֲמַר לֵיה: "תַּנְיָא דִּמְסַיְּיעָא לָךְ".

אֲמַר: "אַתְּ כְּבַר לָקִישָׁא? בַּר לָקִישָׁא כִּי הֲוָה אֲמֵינָא מִילְּתָא הֲוָה מַקְשֵׁי לִי עֶשְׂרִין וְאַרְבַּע קוּשְׁיָיתָא וּמְפָרִיקְנָא לֵיה עֶשְׂרִין וְאַרְבְּעָה פְרוּקֵי, וּמִמֵּילָא רַוְוחָא שְׁמַעְתָּא. וְאַתְּ אָמְרַתְּ תַּנְיָא דִּמְסַיַּיע לָךְ? אַטּוּ לֹא יָדַעְנָא דְּשַׁפִּיר קָאֲמִינָא?"

הֲוָה קָא אָזִיל וְקָרַע מָאנֵיה וְקָא בָּכֵי וְאָמַר, "הֵיכָא אַתְּ בַּר לָקִישָׁא? הֵיכָא אַתְּ בַּר לָקִישָׁא?" וַהֲוָה קָא צָוַח עַד דְּשַׁף דַּעְתֵּיה.

Reish Lakish died and Rabbi Yochanan grieved after him greatly. The rabbis said, "Rabbi Elazar ben Pedat should go to comfort him, for he is a brilliant scholar."

Rabbi Elazar ben Pedat went and sat before Rabbi Yochanan. To every idea Rabbi Yochanan taught, Rabbi Elazar ben Pedat responded, "There is an earlier teaching that supports your opinion."

Rabbi Yochanan said to him, "Are you supposed to be like Reish Lakish? In my discussions with Reish Lakish, whenever I would say something, he would raise twenty-four objections, and I would offer twenty-four responses. As a result of the give and take, the subject was crystalized. You, however, constantly say, 'There is an earlier teaching that supports your opinion.' Do I not already know that my ideas are sound?"

Rabbi Yochanan went about and tore his clothes, crying and saying, "Where are you, Reish Lakish? Where are you, Reish Lakish?" He screamed until he lost his sanity.

Exercise 6.5

1. During the coming week, spend some time with someone who disagrees with you. Focus on things that unite the two of you.

2. During the coming week, discuss with another something that you and the other disagree on. Stay focused throughout on deepening your understanding of the given issue.

LISTENING

Text 10

EXODUS 6:9

> וַיְדַבֵּר מֹשֶׁה כֵּן אֶל בְּנֵי יִשְׂרָאֵל, וְלֹא שָׁמְעוּ אֶל מֹשֶׁה מִקֹּצֶר
> רוּחַ וּמֵעֲבֹדָה קָשָׁה.

Moses spoke these words to the Children of Israel, but they did not hearken to Moses because of their suffering and their hard labor.

Question for Discussion

Have you ever had a conversation with someone and felt that the other *heard* you but didn't *listen* to you? How would you describe the difference?

Text 11

RABBI YEHOSHUA FALK KATZ, *SEFER ME'IRAT EINAYIM, CHOSHEN MISHPAT* 17:15 ⚎

וּסְבָרָא הוּא, כְּדֵי שֶׁיְּהֵא נוֹחַ דַּעַת בַּעֲלֵי דִין, וְלֹא יַעֲלֶה עַל לִבָּם
שֶׁמָּא הַדַּיָּינִים יִשְׂאוּ וְיִתְּנוּ בַּדִּין וְלֹא הֵבִינוּ טַעֲנָתָן . . .
וְעוֹד, שֶׁמָּא בֶּאֱמֶת הַדַּיָּינִים לֹא עָמְדוּ הֵיטֵב עַל דִּבְרֵי טַעֲנוֹתָן,
וּבְשֶׁנּוֹתָן לִפְנֵי הַבַּעֲלֵי דִין יְעוֹרְרוּ אוֹתָן לוֹמַר כֹּה וְכֹה הָיוּ
טַעֲנוֹתֵיהֶם.

RABBI YEHOSHUA FALK HAKOHEN KATZ

1555–1614

Polish rabbi, Talmudist, and authority on Jewish law. Rabbi Falk is best known for his *Perishah* and *Derishah* commentaries on the *Arbaah Turim*, as well as *Sefer Me'irat Einayim* on the Code of Jewish Law. Rabbi Falk was a pupil of Rabbi Moshe Isserlis and served as head of the yeshiva in Lemberg, as well as on the Council of Four Lands, a central body of Jewish authority in Poland.

The judges need to restate the arguments in order to put the litigants' minds at ease, so that they will not worry that the judges are deliberating the case without having properly understood their respective claims. . . .

Moreover, it is entirely possible that the judges misunderstood the arguments. If this occurred, when the judges restate the arguments, the litigants will have the opportunity to correct the misunderstanding.

Exercise 6.6

During the coming month, engage in at least three conversations where you:

1. take a moment before the conversation to remind yourself that listening is a skill that requires effort;

2. refrain from thinking about what you want to say while the other is talking;

3. invite the speaker, who has already completed the point, to elaborate on his or her experience or point of view; and

4. acknowledge and restate what the speaker said before offering your point of view.

THE ROOT ISSUE

Text 12

ORECHOT TSADIKIM, INTRODUCTION TO
THE PORTAL OF ARROGANCE 👥

הַשַּׁעַר הָרִאשׁוֹן, נְדַבֵּר בּוֹ עַל מִדַּת הַגַּאֲוָה. וּמַה טּוֹב שֶׁנִּזְדַּמֵּן
תְּחִלָּה לְכָל הַשְּׁעָרִים, מִפְּנֵי חִיּוּב הָאָדָם לְהִיבָּדֵל מִמֶּנָּה. כִּי
הִיא פֶּתַח לְרָעוֹת רַבּוֹת, וְלֹא רָאִינוּ כָּזֹאת לְרָעָה בְּכָל הַמִּדּוֹת.

The first portal [of this work] explores arrogance.
How appropriate it is to open with this topic,
given the necessity to distance oneself from this
trait. Arrogance is the gateway to all other character flaws; no other negative trait is its equal.

ORECHOT TSADIKIM

A classic work on Jewish ethics. The
identity of the author is unknown,
but it is believed to have been written
by a French scholar, probably in
the 14th century. Drawing much
from earlier ethicists Solomon ibn
Gabirol, Maimonides, and Bachya
ibn Pakudah, *Orechot Tsadikim* ("The
Ways of the Righteous") focuses
on refining character traits and
maintaining a balance in all matters.

Question for Discussion

Can you explain how any of the three negative
traits discussed in this lesson—cynicism, being
disagreeable, and failing to listen to others—results from excessive self-absorption?

CONCLUSION

Text 13

MIDRASH, *PESIKTA RABATI* 9 🎚️

אָמַר הַקָדוֹשׁ בָּרוּךְ הוּא: כְּשֶׁאֲנִי נוֹצֵחַ אֲנִי מַפְסִיד וּכְשֶׁאֲנִי
נָצוּחַ אֲנִי מִשְׂתַּכֵּר.
נִצַּחְתִּי אֶת דּוֹר הַמַּבּוּל לֹא אֲנִי הִפְסַדְתִּי שֶׁהֶחֱרַבְתִּי עוֹלָמִי?
שֶׁנֶּאֱמַר "וַיִּמַח אֶת כָּל הַיְקוּם" (בְּרֵאשִׁית ז, כג). וְכֵן דּוֹר
הַפְלָגָה וּסְדוֹמִיִּים.
אֲבָל בִּימֵי מֹשֶׁה שֶׁנּוּצַּחְתִּי עָשִׂיתִי שָׂכָר, שֶׁלֹּא כִּלִּיתִי אֶת
יִשְׂרָאֵל.
הֲוֵי לַמְנַצֵּחַ - לְמִי שֶׁהוּא מְבַקֵּשׁ לְהִינָצֵחַ.

PESIKTA RABATI

A Midrash divided into a series of sections, as indicated by its title *Pesikta*, which means "section." It differs in structure from most other Midrashic texts, which are continuous commentaries to the Bible. It is called *Rabati* ("the greater"), probably in contrast to *Pesikta DeRav Kahana*. The opening of *Pesikta Rabati* indicates that it was compiled 777 years after the destruction of the Temple, circa 845.

G-d said, "When I am triumphant, I lose, and when I am triumphed over, I gain.

"I triumphed over the generation of the Flood, but I lost, for I destroyed My world. As it states, 'And [the Flood] blotted out all that there was' (Genesis 7:23). The same was true concerning the generation of the dispersion and the city of Sodom.

"However, in the days of Moses, I was triumphed over, but I gained in that I did not destroy Israel."

This is the meaning of the word, "*Lamenatse'ach*," ["to the choirmaster"]. Let it be read as, "To Him Who desires to be triumphed over."

Key Points

1. Successful relationships are crucial to our happiness and they lie at the core of human identity. This is true for both extroverts and introverts.

2. Many Jewish observances are imbued with an ethos of genuine social connection. By embracing these, we open ourselves to more of the well-being that is derived from community and friendship.

3. Jewish sources are replete with teachings about working on our character. The underlying premise of these teachings is that we can choose to behave in specific ways even if our character predisposes us to act differently. Further, when we act a certain way multiple times, our disposition and character traits are eventually able to undergo change.

4. A number of traits hinder our ability to connect with others. Among them are

   a. the tendency to be cynical about the motives of others;

   b. the inability to tolerate those who have differing views; and

   c. the unwillingness to genuinely listen to others.

5. If we want to build good relationships with others, we should get better at

   a. attributing noble motives to people's behavior;

   b. connecting with people who disagree with us by focusing on areas of agreement; and

   c. listening when people speak to us and demonstrating our attentiveness by rephrasing what they have said.

6. Instead of regarding our opinions as absolute truths and fixed definitions of our personality, we can regard them as our current best attempt to arrive at the truth. This leaves us open to hearing a different

perspective. With this mindset, disagreements can become productive links within a relationship.

7. Arrogance is the gateway to many character flaws. It is one of the causes of cynicism, being disagreeable, and the unwillingness to listen. By becoming less self-absorbed, there is more room for others and the happiness we can find by connecting with them.

APPENDIX
ADDITIONAL TRAITS
ROOTED IN HUMILITY

Text 14

TALMUD, MEGILAH 28A

שָׁאֲלוּ תַּלְמִידָיו אֶת רַבִּי נְחוּנְיָא בֶּן הַקָּנָה: בַּמֶּה הֶאֱרַכְתָּ יָמִים? אָמַר לָהֶם: מִיָּמַי לֹא נִתְכַּבַּדְתִּי בִּקְלוֹן חֲבֵרִי. וְלֹא עָלְתָה עַל מִטָּתִי קִלְלַת חֲבֵרִי. וְוַתְרָן בְּמָמוֹנִי הָיִיתִי.

לֹא נִתְכַּבַּדְתִּי בִּקְלוֹן חֲבֵרִי: כִּי הָא דְרַב הוּנָא דָּרֵי מָרָא אַכַּתְפֵיה, אֲתָא רַב חָנָא בַּר חֲנִילַאי וְקָא דָּרֵי מִינֵּיה. אָמַר לֵיה: אִי רְגִילַתְּ דְּדָרִית בְּמָאתִיךְ דָּרֵי, וְאִי לָא, אִתְיַיקּוּרֵי אֲנָא בְּזִילוּתָא דִידָךְ לָא נִיחָא לִי.

וְלֹא עָלְתָה עַל מִטָּתִי קִלְלַת חֲבֵרִי: כִּי הָא דְּמַר זוּטְרָא כִּי הֲוָה סָלִיק לְפוּרְיֵיה, אָמַר: שָׁרֵי לֵיה לְכָל מַאן דְּצַעֲרַן.

וְוַתְרָן בְּמָמוֹנִי הָיִיתִי: דְּאָמַר מַר: אִיּוֹב וַתְרָן בְּמָמוֹנֵיה הֲוָה, שֶׁהָיָה מֵנִיחַ פְּרוּטָה לַחֶנְוָנִי מִמָּמוֹנֵיה.

Rabbi Nechunia ben Hakanah was asked by his disciples, "By what virtue have you reached such old age?"

He replied, "Never in my life have I sought respect through the degradation of my fellow. Nor have I ever gone to bed harboring animosity toward another. And I have been generous with my money."

[The Talmud explains these virtues:]

"I have not sought respect through the degradation of my fellow." This was illustrated by Rav Huna, who was once carrying a spade on his shoulder and Rav Chana bar Chanilai wanted to

carry it for him. Rav Huna said to him, "If you are accustomed to carrying things in your own town, take it; if not, I do not want to be respected through your degradation."

"Nor have I ever gone to bed harboring animosity toward another." This was illustrated by Mar Zutra, who, when he climbed into bed, would say, "I forgive all who vexed me."

"I have been generous with my money." This was illustrated by Job, who used to leave the shopkeeper with a coin [of his change].

ADDITIONAL READINGS

CONFLICT RESOLUTION

By Rabbi Lord Jonathan Sacks

One of the hardest tasks of a leader—from prime ministers to parents—is conflict resolution. Yet it is also the most vital. Where there is leadership, there is long-term cohesiveness within the group, whatever the short-term problems. Where there is a lack of leadership—where leaders lack authority, grace, generosity of spirit and the ability to respect positions other than their own—then there is divisiveness, rancor, backbiting, resentment, internal politics and a lack of trust. Leaders are people who put the interests of the group above those of any subsection of the group. They care for, and inspire others to care for, the common good.

That is why an episode in this week's Parshah is of the highest consequence. It arose like this. The Israelites were on the last stage of their journey to the Promised Land. They were now situated on the east bank of the Jordan, within sight of their destination. Two of the tribes, Reuben and Gad, who had large herds and flocks of cattle, felt that the land they were currently on was ideal for their purposes. It was good grazing country. So they approached Moses and asked for permission to stay there rather than take up their share in the Land of Israel. They said: "If we have found favor in your eyes, let this land be given to your servants as our possession. Do not make us cross the Jordan."[1]

RABBI LORD JONATHAN SACKS, PHD
1948–

Former chief rabbi of the United Kingdom. Rabbi Sacks attended Cambridge University and received his doctorate from King's College, London. A prolific and influential author, his books include *Will We Have Jewish Grandchildren?* and *The Dignity of Difference.* He received the Jerusalem Prize in 1995 for his contributions to enhancing Jewish life in the Diaspora, was knighted and made a life peer in 2005, and became Baron Sacks of Aldridge in 2009.

Moses was instantly alert to the danger. The two tribes were putting their own interests above those of the nation as a whole. They would be seen as abandoning the nation at the very time they were needed most. There was a war—in fact, a series of wars—to be fought if the Israelites were to inherit the Promised Land. As Moses put it to the tribes: "Should your fellow Israelites go to war while you sit here? Why do you discourage the Israelites from crossing over into the land the L-rd has given them?"[2]

The proposal was potentially disastrous. Moses reminded the men of Reuben and Gad what had happened in the incident of the spies. The spies demoralized the people, ten of them saying that they could not conquer the land. The inhabitants were too strong. The cities were impregnable. The result of that one moment was to condemn an entire generation to die in the wilderness and to delay the eventual conquest by forty years. "And here you are, a brood of sinners, standing in the place of your fathers and making the L-rd even more angry with Israel. If you turn away from following Him, He will again leave all this people in the wilderness, and you will be the cause of their destruction."[3] Moses was blunt, honest and confrontational.

What then followed is a role model in negotiation and conflict resolution. The Reubenites and Gadites recognized the claims of the people as a whole and the justice of Moses' concerns. They propose a compromise. Let us make provisions for our cattle and our families, they say, and the men will then accompany the other tribes across the Jordan. They will fight alongside them. They will even go ahead of them. They will not return to their cattle and families until all the battles have been fought, the land has been conquered and the other tribes have received their inheritance. Essentially, they invoke what would later become a principle of Jewish law: *zeh neheneh ve-zeh lo chaser*, meaning that an act is permissible if "one side gains and the other side does not lose."[4] We will gain, say the two tribes, by having land good for our cattle, but the nation as a whole will not lose because we will be in the army, we will be in the front line, and we will stay there until the war has been won.

Moses recognizes the fact that they have met his objections. He restates their position to make sure he and they have understood the proposal and they are ready to stand by it. He extracts from them agreement to a *tenai kaful*, a double condition, both positive and negative: If we do this, these will be the consequences, but if we fail to do this, those will be the consequences. He leaves them no escape from their commitment. The two tribes agree. Conflict has been averted. The Reubenites and Gadites achieve what they want, but the interests of the other tribes and of the nation as a whole have been secured. It was a model negotiation.

Quite how justified were Moses' concerns became apparent many years later. The Reubenites and Gadites did indeed fulfill their promise in the days of Joshua. The rest of the tribes conquered and settled Israel, while they (together with half the tribe of Manasseh) established their presence in Trans-Jordan. Despite this, within a brief space of time there was almost civil war.

Joshua 22 describes how, returning to their families and settling their land, the Reubenites and Gadites built "an altar to the L-rd" on the east side of the Jordan. Seeing this as an act of secession, the rest of the Israelites prepared to do battle against them. Joshua, in a striking act of diplomacy, sent Pinchas, the former zealot, now man of peace, to negotiate. He warned them of the terrible consequences of what they had done by, in effect, creating a religious center outside the Land of Israel. It would split the nation in two.

The Reubenites and Gadites made it clear that this was not their intention at all. To the contrary, they themselves were worried that in the future, the rest of the Israelites would see them living across the Jordan and conclude that they no longer wanted to be part of the nation. That is why they had built the altar, not to offer

sacrifices, not as a rival to the nation's sanctuary, but merely as a symbol and a sign to future generations that they too were Israelites. Pinchas and the rest of the delegation were satisfied with this answer, and once again civil war was averted.

The negotiation between Moses and the two tribes in our Parshah follows closely the principles arrived at by the Harvard Negotiation Project, set out by Roger Fisher and William Ury in their classic text, *Getting to Yes*.[5] Essentially, they came to the conclusion that a successful negotiation must involve four processes:

1. *Separate the people from the problem.* There are all sorts of personal tensions in any negotiation. It is essential that these be cleared away first, so that the problem can be addressed objectively.

2. *Focus on interests, not positions.* It is easy for any conflict to turn into a zero-sum game: if I win, you lose. If you win, I lose. That is what happens when you focus on positions and the question becomes, "Who wins?" By focusing not on positions but on interests, the question becomes, "Is there a way of achieving what each of us wants?"

3. *Invent options for mutual gain.* This is the idea expressed halakhically as *zeh neheneh ve-zeh neheneh*, "both sides benefit." This comes about because the two sides usually have different objectives, neither of which excludes the other.

4. *Insist on objective criteria.* Make sure that both sides agree in advance to the use of objective, impartial criteria to judge whether what has been agreed has been achieved. Otherwise, despite all apparent agreement, the dispute will continue, both sides insisting that the other has not done what was promised.

Moses does all four. First he separates the people from the problem by making it clear to the Reubenites and Gadites that the issue has nothing to do with who they are, and everything to do with the Israelites' experience in the past, specifically the episode of the spies. Regardless of who the ten negative spies were and which tribes they came from, everyone suffered. No one gained. The problem is not about this tribe or that, but about the nation as a whole.

Second, he focused on interests, not positions. The two tribes had an interest in the fate of the nation as a whole. If they put their personal interests first, G-d would become angry and the entire people would be punished, the Reubenites and Gadites among them. It is striking how different this negotiation was from that of Korach and his followers. There, the whole argument was about positions, not interests—about who was entitled to be a leader. The result was collective tragedy.

Third, the Reubenites and Gadites then invented an option for mutual gain. If you allow us to make temporary provisions for our cattle and children, they said, we will not only fight in the army; we will be its advance guard. We will benefit, knowing that our request has been granted. The nation will benefit by our willingness to take on the most demanding military task.

Fourth, there was an agreement on objective criteria. The Reubenites and Gadites would not return to the east bank of the Jordan until all the other tribes were safely settled in their territories. And so it happened, as narrated in the book of Joshua:

Then Joshua summoned the Reubenites, the Gadites and the half-tribe of Manasseh, and said to them, "You have done all that Moses the servant of the L-rd commanded, and you have obeyed me in everything I commanded. For a long time now—to this very day—you have not deserted your fellow Israelites, but have carried out the mission the L-rd your G-d gave you. Now that the L-rd your G-d has given them rest as He promised, return to your homes in the land that Moses the servant of the L-rd gave you on the other side of the Jordan."[6]

This was, in short, a model negotiation, a sign of hope after the many destructive conflicts in the book of Bamidbar, as well as a standing alternative to the many later conflicts in Jewish history that had such appalling outcomes.

Note that Moses succeeds, not because he is weak, not because he is willing to compromise on the integrity of the nation as a whole, not because he uses honeyed words and diplomatic evasions, but because he is honest, principled, and focused on the common good. We all face conflicts in our lives. This is how to resolve them.

Rabbisacks.org
Reprinted with permission of the author

Endotes

[1] Numbers 32:5.
[2] Numbers 32:6–7.
[3] Numbers 32:14–15.
[4] Talmud, Bava Kamma 20b.
[5] Roger Fisher and William Ury, *Getting to Yes: Negotiating Agreement Without Giving In* (Random House Business, 2011).
[6] Joshua 22:1–4.

Jew's Ongoing Yearning

DISCOVERING A DEEPER HAPPINESS

This lesson introduces a more transcendent form of joy that is available to each of us. Although more difficult to achieve, it is crucial to our happiness, because it allows for true self-actualization.

INTRODUCTION

Text 1

ED DIENER AND ROBERT BISWAS-DIENER, *HAPPINESS: UNLOCKING THE MYSTERIES OF PSYCHOLOGICAL WEALTH* (MALDEN, MASS.: BLACKWELL PUBLISHING, 2008), PP. 114–125

Psychologists who have studied whether religious people are happy or unhappy have often reached a general conclusion—religious people are on the whole happier than the non-religious. In the vast majority of studies, religious people report higher well-being than their nonbelieving counterparts. Even when researchers define religiosity in various ways—such as attending church or having self-professed spiritual beliefs—studies show that religious people are, on average, mildly happier.

In one study, conducted by one of the authors (Ed) and the Gallup Organization, about a thousand people living in St. Louis were contacted through random-digit telephone dialing and asked to answer a survey related to spiritual beliefs and satisfaction. It was found that respondents who believed in G-d and in an afterlife were more likely to be satisfied with their lives. . . .

Some scholars have accused us of pushing religion, and of not being objective scientists. Our response is that whether people are religious or secular, they can learn something about how to practice happiness from the findings on religion and happiness.

ED DIENER, PHD
1946–

Psychologist and professor. Dr. Diener is a leading researcher in positive psychology who coined the expression "subjective well-being," or SWB, as the aspect of happiness that can be empirically measured. Noted for his research on happiness, he has earned the nickname "Dr. Happiness."

ROBERT BISWAS-DIENER, PHD
1972–

Positive psychologist. Biswas-Diener is the son of Ed Diener and is an instructor at Portland State University. Biswas-Diener's research focuses on income and happiness, culture and happiness, and positive psychology. Biswas-Diener's research has led him to areas such as India, Greenland, Israel, Kenya, and Spain, and he has been called the "Indiana Jones of positive psychology." He sits on the editorial boards of the *Journal of Happiness Studies* and the *Journal of Positive Psychology*.

Question for Discussion

Why is religion beneficial for mental health and happiness?

MITZVOT
MITZVAH JOY

Text 2a
PSALMS 100:2

עִבְדוּ אֶת ה׳ בְּשִׂמְחָה, בֹּאוּ לְפָנָיו בִּרְנָנָה.

Serve G-d with joy; approach Him with joyful song.

Text 2b

MAIMONIDES, *MISHNEH TORAH*, LAWS OF THE *LULAV* 8:15 ⊞

הַשִּׂמְחָה שֶׁיִּשְׂמַח אָדָם בַּעֲשִׂיַּת הַמִּצְוָה וּבְאַהֲבַת הָאֵ-ל
שֶׁצִּוָּה בָּהֶן - עֲבוֹדָה גְדוֹלָה הִיא.

It is crucial that we experience joy in performing a mitzvah and in loving G-d.

RABBI MOSHE BEN MAIMON (MAIMONIDES, RAMBAM)
1135–1204

Halachist, philosopher, author, and physician. Maimonides was born in Córdoba, Spain. After the conquest of Córdoba by the Almohads, he fled Spain and eventually settled in Cairo, Egypt. There, he became the leader of the Jewish community and served as court physician to the vizier of Egypt. He is most noted for authoring the *Mishneh Torah*, an encyclopedic arrangement of Jewish law; and for his philosophical work, *Guide for the Perplexed*. His rulings on Jewish law are integral to the formation of halachic consensus.

Question for Discussion

Why should the performance of a mitzvah make us happy?

A RELATIONSHIP

Text 3
PSALMS 42:2–3 🎚️

> כְּאַיָּל תַּעֲרֹג עַל אֲפִיקֵי מָיִם, כֵּן נַפְשִׁי תַעֲרֹג אֵלֶיךָ אֱלֹקִים.
> צָמְאָה נַפְשִׁי לֵאלֹקִים לְאֵ-ל חָי מָתַי אָבוֹא, וְאֵרָאֶה פְּנֵי אֱלֹקִים.

As the deer longs for streams of water, so I long for You, O G-d.

I thirst for G-d, the living G-d. When can I come and appear in G-d's presence?

Text 4

MAIMONIDES, *MISHNEH TORAH*, LAWS OF THE
FOUNDATIONS OF THE TORAH 2:2 ⊞

בְּשָׁעָה שֶׁיִּתְבּוֹנֵן הָאָדָם בְּמַעֲשָׂיו וּבְרוּאָיו הַנִּפְלָאִים
הַגְּדוֹלִים, וְיִרְאֶה מֵהֶן חָכְמָתוֹ שֶׁאֵין לָהּ עֵרֶךְ וְלֹא קֵץ,
מִיַּד הוּא אוֹהֵב וּמְשַׁבֵּחַ וּמְפָאֵר, וּמִתְאַוֶּה תַּאֲוָה גְדוֹלָה
לֵידַע הַשֵּׁם הַגָּדוֹל. כְּמוֹ שֶׁאָמַר דָּוִד: "צָמְאָה נַפְשִׁי לֵאלֹקִים
לְאֵ-ל חָי".

When we contemplate G-d's great and wondrous creations, and perceive thereby His infinite wisdom that surpasses all comparison, we will immediately love, praise, and acclaim G-d, and we will yearn with tremendous desire to know Him. As King David stated, "I thirst for G-d, the living G-d."

Text 5

LAMENTATIONS 3:24 ⊞

חֶלְקִי ה' אָמְרָה נַפְשִׁי עַל כֵּן אוֹחִיל לוֹ.

"G-d is my portion," says my soul, "therefore I will place my hope in Him."

BRIDGING THE GAP

Text 6

RABBI YOSEF YITSCHAK SCHNEERSOHN,
CITED IN *HAYOM YOM*, 8 CHESHVAN ⚏

מִצְוָה לְשׁוֹן צַוְותָא וְחִבּוּר. וְהָעוֹשֶׂה מִצְוָה מִתְחַבֵּר עִם
הָעַצְמוּת בָּרוּךְ הוּא, שֶׁהוּא הַמְצַוֶּה אֶת הַצִּיּוּי הַהוּא. וְזֶהוּ
"שְׂכַר מִצְוָה מִצְוָה" (אָבוֹת ד, ב), דְּזֶה מַה שֶּׁנִּתְחַבֵּר עִם
עַצְמוּת אוֹר אֵין סוֹף מִצַּד מִצְוַה הַצִּיּוּי, זֶהוּ שְׂכָרוֹ.

The word mitzvah is related to the [Aramaic] word *tsavta*, which means "connection." One who performs a mitzvah connects with G-d, the issuer of the commandment.

This is the meaning of [the Mishnaic phrase, *Ethics of the Fathers* 2:4], "The reward of a mitzvah is the mitzvah": the reward of the mitzvah is the connection (*tsavta*) it generates with G-d, Who issued the commandment.

**RABBI YOSEF
YITSCHAK SCHNEERSOHN
(RAYATS, FRIERDIKER REBBE,
PREVIOUS REBBE)**
1880–1950

Chasidic rebbe, prolific writer, and Jewish activist. Rabbi Yosef Yitschak, the sixth leader of the Chabad movement, actively promoted Jewish religious practice in Soviet Russia and was arrested for these activities. After his release from prison and exile, he settled in Warsaw, Poland, from where he fled Nazi occupation and arrived in New York in 1940. Settling in Brooklyn, Rabbi Schneersohn worked to revitalize American Jewish life. His son-in-law Rabbi Menachem Mendel Schneerson succeeded him as the leader of the Chabad movement.

Text 7

PSALMS 19:9, 11–12 ⊕

פִּקּוּדֵי ה׳ יְשָׁרִים מְשַׂמְּחֵי לֵב . . .
הַנֶּחֱמָדִים מִזָּהָב וּמִפַּז רָב, וּמְתוּקִים מִדְּבַשׁ וְנֹפֶת צוּפִים.
גַּם עַבְדְּךָ נִזְהָר בָּהֶם, בְּשָׁמְרָם עֵקֶב רָב.

G-d's commandments are upright, causing the heart to rejoice. . . .

They are more desirable than gold, even the finest gold. They are sweeter than honey and the drippings from the comb.

I, too, am careful about them; for in observing them there is great reward.

PURPOSE

Text 8

RABBI SHNE'UR ZALMAN OF LIADI, *TANYA*, CH. 33

וְזֶהוּ שֶׁכָּתוּב: "יִשְׂמַח יִשְׂרָאֵל בְּעוֹשָׂיו" (תְּהִילִים קמט, ב). פֵּירוּשׁ: שֶׁכָּל מִי שֶׁהוּא מִזֶּרַע יִשְׂרָאֵל יֵשׁ לוֹ לִשְׂמוֹחַ בְּשִׂמְחַת ה' אֲשֶׁר שָׂשׂ וְשָׂמֵחַ בְּדִירָתוֹ בַּתַּחְתּוֹנִים.

"Let Israel rejoice with its Maker" (Psalms 149:2). The meaning of this verse is that we ought to rejoice in G-d's own joy, for G-d rejoices and is happy to dwell in our physical world.

RABBI SHNE'UR ZALMAN OF LIADI (ALTER REBBE)
1745–1812

Chasidic rebbe, halachic authority, and founder of the Chabad movement. The Alter Rebbe was born in Liozna, Belarus, and was among the principal students of the Magid of Mezeritch. His numerous works include the *Tanya*, an early classic containing the fundamentals of Chabad Chasidism; and *Shulchan Aruch HaRav*, an expanded and reworked code of Jewish law.

CONSTANT JOY
IN EVERY MOMENT

Text 9

RABBI NACHMAN OF BRESLOV, *LIKUTEI MOHARAN* 2:24

מִצְוָה גְּדוֹלָה לִהְיוֹת בְּשִׂמְחָה תָּמִיד.

It is a great mitzvah to be happy all the time.

RABBI NACHMAN OF BRESLOV
1772–1810

Chasidic rebbe and thinker. Rabbi Nachman was a great-grandson of the Baal Shem Tov, the founder of the Chasidic movement. His magnum opus, *Likutei Moharan*, was published and disseminated by his disciple, Rabbi Noson Steinhartz. Reb Nachman died of tuberculosis at the age of 38, without appointing a successor. He is buried in Uman, Ukraine, where his followers continue to make pilgrimages, especially for Jewish holidays.

Text 10

MAIMONIDES, *MISHNEH TORAH,*
LAWS OF TEMPERAMENTS 3:2–3

צָרִיךְ הָאָדָם שֶׁיְּכַוֵּן לִבּוֹ וְכָל מַעֲשָׂיו כּוּלָם לֵידַע אֶת הַשֵּׁם בָּרוּךְ
הוּא בִּלְבָד . . . הַמְהַלֵּךְ בְּדֶרֶךְ זוֹ כָּל יָמָיו עוֹבֵד אֶת ה' תָּמִיד . . .
וְעַל עִנְיָן זֶה צִוּוּ חֲכָמִים וְאָמְרוּ (אָבוֹת ב, יב) "וְכָל מַעֲשֶׂיךָ יִהְיוּ
לְשֵׁם שָׁמַיִם", וְהוּא שֶׁאָמַר שְׁלֹמֹה בְּחָכְמָתוֹ (מִשְׁלֵי ג, ו) "בְּכָל
דְּרָכֶיךָ דָעֵהוּ".

We should direct our hearts and the totality of our actions to one goal: becoming aware of G-d. . . . One who always follows this path continually serves G-d. . . .

Our sages instructed us regarding this matter, saying (*Ethics of the Fathers* 2:13), "All your deeds should be for the sake of Heaven." King Solomon, too, declared in his wisdom, "Know Him in all your ways" (Proverbs 3:6).

INNER TRANQUILITY (OPTIONAL)

Text 11

THE REBBE, RABBI MENACHEM MENDEL SCHNEERSON,
SEFER HASICHOT 5751:2, P. 553 ⓘ

בְּשַׁעַת אַ מֶענְטְשׁ פִילְט נִיט דִי כַּוָונָה וְתַכְלִית אִין זַיין לֶעבְּן (אַז
"אֲנִי נִבְרֵאתִי לְשַׁמֵּשׁ אֶת קוֹנִי"), קֶען עֶר נִיט שְׁטֵיין מִיט אַן
אֱמֶת'ע מְנוּחָה וְהַתְיַישְׁבוּת, וָוארוּם דִי שִׁינוּיֵי הַזְמַן וְהַמָקוֹם
אוּן אַלְע רִיבּוּי פְּרָטִים וּפְרָטֵי פְּרָטִים פוּן זַיין לֶעבְּן זַיינֶען גוֹרֵם
אַ שְׁטֶענְדִיקֶע אוּמְרוּ, וָואס "שְׁפַּאלְט" אִים פַאנַאנְדֶער;
דַוְוקָא בְּשַׁעַת עֶר דֶערְהֶערְט דִי צִיל - דִי כַּוָונָה וְתַכְלִית - וָואס
לִיגְט בְּתוֹךְ דִי אַלְע פְּרָטִים, דֶעמוּלְט בְּרֶענְגְט עֶס אִים אַ
מְנוּחָה, וָואס אִיז הֶעכֶער פַאר דֶער תְּנוּעָה וְשִׁינוּי פוּן פְּרָטֵי
הַחַיִים, אוּן בְּמֵילָא - צוּ שְׁלֵימוּת הָאָדָם.

When we do not feel the purpose in our lives—that we were created to serve our Maker—we cannot have a true sense of inner peace and tranquility. The continuous changes of time and location, and the myriad details and sub-details within our lives, cause a constant unrest that fragments us in different directions.

When we acknowledge the purpose that lies within all of these details—which transcends the ebb and flow of life's changes and movements—it brings us tranquility and, thereby, human completion.

RABBI MENACHEM MENDEL SCHNEERSON
1902–1994

The towering Jewish leader of the 20th century, known as "the Lubavitcher Rebbe," or simply as "the Rebbe." Born in southern Ukraine, the Rebbe escaped Nazi-occupied Europe, arriving in the U.S. in June 1941. The Rebbe inspired and guided the revival of traditional Judaism after the European devastation, impacting virtually every Jewish community the world over. The Rebbe often emphasized that the performance of just one additional good deed could usher in the era of Mashiach. The Rebbe's scholarly talks and writings have been printed in more than 200 volumes.

SELF-EXPRESSION

Text 12

THE REBBE, RABBI MENACHEM MENDEL SCHNEERSON,
IGROT KODESH 17, PP. 32–33 🔊

צוֹמֵחַ, וֶוען אַלֶעס וָואס אִיז נוֹיטיג צוּם וואקסן, עֶרד, וואסֶער,
לוּפט א.ד.ג. אִיז צוּגֶעשטֶעלט גֶעוואָרֶען אִין דֶער פוּלֶער
מָאס – אִיז דֶער צוֹמֵחַ "בַּאפרַייט" פוּן אַלֶע זַיינֶע "זָארג"
אוּן שטֶערוּנגֶען. אוּן כָאטש עֶר קֶען ניט אַוועק פוּן זַיין אָרט,
עֶר אִיז "פַארְאוּרטֵיילט" צוּ בְּלַייבְּן דָארט זַיינֶע אַלֶע יָארן –
הָאט עֶר דִי פוּלֶע פרַייהַייט פוּן אַ צוֹמֵחַ. כָּל זְמַן עֶר אִיז ניט
מֶער ווי אַ צוֹמֵחַ – אִיז עֶר בֶּאֱמֶת פרַיי.

אָבֶּער אַ **חַי**, וֶוען עֶר אִיז אֲפילוּ בֶּאזָארגט מיט אַלֶע זַיינֶע
בֶּאדֶערפָענישֶען פוּן עֶסֶען, טרינקֶען אוּן אַזוֹי ווַייטֶער, אָבֶּער
עֶר אִיז גֶעצוואוּנגֶען צוּ זַיין אוֹיף אַיין אָרט, אִיז דָאס בַּא אִים
דִי גרֶעסטֶע בֶּאשרֶענקוּנג – אַ תְּפִיסָה, דִי שרֶעקלִיכְסטֶע
תְּפִיסָה, ווַייל עֶס פֶּעלט עֶם דֶער **עִיקָר** פוּן זַיין מַהוּת (וֶועזן).

אַ מֶענטש, וָואס עֶר אִיז דָאך אַ שֵׂכְלִי, אֲפילוּ אַז עֶר הָאט דִי
פוּלֶע פרַייהַייט פוּן בֶּעוועגוּנג, אָבֶּער אַז מֶען שליסט עֶם אָפ
פוּן שֵׂכֶל-לֶעבְּן – גֶעפִינט עֶר זִיך אִין תְּפִיסָה, אִין אַ תְּפִיסָה
ווֶעלְכֶע בַּארוֹיבְּט עֶם פוּן זַיין **עִיקָר מַהוּת.**

When a plant is fully provided with all that it requires for growth—earth, water, air, etc., it is liberated from all of its worries and concerns, so-to-speak. Although it is immobile, doomed to remain rooted in place for its entire lifespan, it nevertheless enjoys the full freedom that a plant can experience. It is truly free—despite its lack of mobility.

An animal, however, is different. Even if its needs for food, drink, etc., were to be provided, it would feel horribly restricted—imprisoned in the harshest manner—if it were to be immobilized and forced to forever remain in one place. For it would be denied one of the primary features of its existence.

The primary feature of a human being is intelligence. Humans would feel imprisoned even if granted full freedom of mobility, if they were denied their primary aspect of being—the freedom to utilize their intelligence and live mindfully.

COURSE CONCLUSION

Exercise 7.1

Choose a mitzvah that you will perform during this coming week.

In the box below, write a short meditation, as eloquently as you can, that describes the reasons why you consider this particular mitzvah a beautiful gift. What aspects of the mitzvah do you particularly enjoy?

During the coming week, designate several minutes to read your meditation, slowly and with concentration, before you perform this mitzvah.

Text 13

RABBI MENACHEM MENDEL OF LUBAVITCH, *IGROT KODESH*, P. 21

לְהַרְאוֹת בְּעַצְמוֹ תָּמִיד תְּנוּעוֹת מְשַׂמְּחוֹת כְּאִלּוּ הוּא מָלֵא שִׂמְחָה בְּלִבּוֹ, אַף עַל פִּי שֶׁאֵין בְּלִבּוֹ כֵּן בִּשְׁעַת מַעֲשֶׂה, וְסוֹפוֹ לִהְיוֹת כֵּן. וְהַטַּעַם בָּזֶה הוּא כִּי לְפִי הַמַּעֲשִׂים וְהַפְּעוּלוֹת אֲשֶׁר הָאָדָם עוֹשֶׂה, נִקְבָּע אַחַר כָּךְ בְּלְבָבוֹ.

RABBI MENACHEM MENDEL OF LUBAVITCH
(*TSEMACH TSEDEK*)
1789–1866

Chasidic rebbe and noted author. The *Tsemach Tsedek* was the third leader of the Chabad Chasidic movement and a noted authority on Jewish law. His numerous works include halachic responsa, Chasidic discourses, and kabbalistic writings. Active in the communal affairs of Russian Jewry, he worked to alleviate the plight of the cantonists, Jewish children kidnapped to serve in the Czar's army. He passed away in Lubavitch, leaving seven sons and two daughters.

At all times, assume a demeanor as if your heart were full of joy, even if at the moment this is far from the case. Such behavior will eventually lead you to truly feel happy, because behavior and action impact the heart.

Key Points

1. Many psychological studies suggest that religion and spirituality can have positive effects on one's happiness. These findings can be explained by many of the ideas explored in this course.

2. When we have an accurate and mature definition of G-d, and when we recognize His greatness and our essential bond with Him, we begin to crave a connection with G-d.

3. When we shift our mitzvah-perspective from "commands" to "connections," we cease to see *mitzvot* solely as duties and perceive them as relationship builders. Each mitzvah provides us with an opportunity to engage in a relationship with G-d, thus constituting the fulfillment of a spiritual dream—truly a joy-inspiring opportunity.

4. Another function of *mitzvot* is to fulfill G-d's ultimate purpose for which He created us: to reveal how each of the many details of this fragmented world is (a) an expression of Him, and (b) a part of His purpose. Awareness of our role in this task, and the divine joy we cause by engaging in this project, leads us to immense happiness.

5. It is important to be happy about performing a mitzvah. This happiness, or lack thereof, is the measure whether, and to what degree, we appreciate and value the mitzvah.

6. The blessings we recite upon performing *mitzvot* help us become more mindful of their value.

7. There is never a moment in life that is devoid of meaning. Every moment of life can become a moment of connecting with G-d, fulfilling the cosmic purpose, and bringing G-d immense joy.

8. Although the joy in mitzvah performance is more abstract and more difficult to achieve, it is not

something to avoid; it nourishes and actualizes our higher needs—especially the needs of the G-dly soul within us that lies at the core of our identity.

9. Going through the motions of happiness can trigger emotions of happiness.

ADDITIONAL READINGS

TAKING CARE OF YOUR BODY AND YOUR SOUL

Sonja Lyubomirsky, Phd

PRACTICING RELIGION AND SPIRITUALITY

Psychological researchers have often been hesitant to study spirituality and religion. On the face of it, science and religion cannot mix. G-d cannot be investigated in the laboratory, and the sacred cannot be quantified. Just because religious beliefs can't be empirically tested or falsified, however, doesn't mean that the *consequences* of having religious beliefs, participating in religious life, or searching for the sacred cannot be studied. Indeed, a growing body of psychological science is suggesting that religious people are happier, healthier, and recover better after traumas than nonreligious people.[1] In one study, parents who had lost a baby to sudden infant death syndrome were interviewed three weeks after their loss and then again after eighteen months.[2] Those who attended religious services frequently and who reported religion as being important to them were better able to cope eighteen months after the loss, showing relatively less depression at this time and greater well-being than nonreligious parents. Two reasons were found to underlie the benefit of religion on adjustment: Those active in their churches reported greater social support (perhaps through the church itself) and were able to find some meaning, however elusive, in their children's deaths.

RELIGIOUS RETURNS FOR HEALTH AND WELL-BEING

Other studies have shown that relative to nonreligious folks, those active in their religions live longer with a variety of diseases and are healthier in general.[3] For example, if you are having serious cardiac surgery and receive strength and comfort from your religious faith, you'll be almost three times more likely to be

---

SONJA LYUBOMIRSKY, PHD.

Leading expert in positive psychology. Lyubomirsky is professor of psychology at the University of California, Riverside. Originally from Russia, she received her PhD in social/personality psychology from Stanford University. Her research on the possibility of permanently increasing happiness has been honored with various grants, including a million-dollar grant from the National Institute of Mental Health. She has authored *The How of Happiness* and, more recently, *The Myths of Happiness*.

---

1 For an excellent review, see Ellison, C. G., and Levin, J. S. (1998). The religion-health connection: Evidence, theory, and future directions. *Health Education and Behavior*, 25: 700–20. Another very readable review is Myers(2000), op. cit.
2 McIntosh, D. N., Silver, R. C., and Wortman, C. B. (1993). Religion's role in adjustment to a negative life event: coping with the loss of a child. *Journal of Personality and Social Psychology*, 65:812–21.
3 Examples of studies showing that religion is related to superior health include Oman, D., and Reed, D. (1998). Religion and mortality among the community dwelling elderly. *American Journal of Public Health*, 88:1469–75. Koenig, H. G., Hays, J. C., George, L. K., Blazer, D. G., Larson, D. B., and Landerman, L. R. (1997) Modeling the cross-sectional relationships between religion, physical health, social support, and depressive symptoms. *American Journal of Geriatric Psychology*, 5:131–44. Oxman, T. E., Freeman, D. H., and Manheimer, E. D. (1995). Lack of social participation or religious strength and comfort as risk factors for death after cardiac surgery in the elderly. *Psychosomatic Medicine*, 57:5–15. Strawbridge, W. J., Cohen, R. D., Shema, S. J., and Kaplan, G. A. (1997). Frequent attendance at religious services and mortality over 28 years. *American Journal of Public Health*, 87:957–61.

alive six months later.[4] The trouble is that we don't really know why. One seemingly obvious reason could be that religious people are more likely to practice healthy behaviors. Indeed, many religions prohibit such unhealthy practices as excessive drinking, drug use, promiscuous sex, and smoking. Religious people smoke and drink less than their less religious peers.[5] Certain religious groups (like Mormons and Seventh-Day Adventists), which encourage healthy diets and prohibit premarital sex, alcohol, tobacco, and drug use, are healthier than other groups.[6] Religious groups also encourage positive, low-stress lifestyles—for example, by advocating moderation (versus extreme, illegal, or risk-taking behavior) and by fostering a harmonious family life. Indeed, some studies show that religious involvement is related to reduced risk of crime, delinquency, and marital conflict.

This potentially explains the finding that religious people are physically healthier, but what about the fact that they're happier, more satisfied with their lives, and cope better with crises? For instance, 47 percent of people who report attending religious services several times a week describe themselves as "very happy," versus 28 percent of those who attend less than once a month.[7] The social support and sense of identity provided by belonging to a close-knit religious organization (church, temple, or mosque) could be the operative mechanisms. After all, religion is usually not practiced in isolation but within a "fellowship of kindred spirits," who share one another's burdens, reach out to those in need, and offer friendship and companionship. To be sure, people who attend religious services on a regular basis have larger social networks—that is, more friends and acquaintances on whom they can rely—and actually do receive tangible help from members of their religious group.[8] This isn't surprising: religious services and the

many activities associated with them (such as charities, volunteer programs, and outreach initiatives) bring together people who have a lot in common. Members share not only the basic assumptions and beliefs inherent in their religion but important political and social values. This fact enables one-to-one social, emotional, and material support, and creates a sense of community among the members of the church, synagogue, or mosque, leading people to feel appreciated, respected, and provided for. This sense reinforces your identity and affirms your lifestyle. After all, it feels good when people whom you respect and admire share similar roles and values and your approach to daily life.

So it's possible that the fact that religious people are happier than the nonreligious has nothing to do with the substance of their religious and spiritual beliefs—with G-d, with living life in accordance to their holy texts, with the sanctity of life, or with the sense of meaning that religious faith gives their lives—and everything to do with the simple fact that their religions bring them into contact with other similarly minded and caring people. It could be true, but I don't believe it.

First, we shouldn't ignore the one "ultimate" supportive relationship for many religious individuals, one that doesn't require any formal participation in religious services or programs, and that is their relationship with G-d. This relationship is not only a source of comfort in troubled times but a source of self-esteem, feeling unconditionally valued, loved, and cared for. Those of you who feel this way have a sense of security that others only wish for. Your belief that G-d will intervene when needed gives you a sense of peace and calm. Your identification with G-d or particular biblical figures can help you interpret and guide your own life (e.g., "What would the divine other do in this situation?") and even fuel a sense of vicarious control (i.e., "With an omniscient and omnipotent deity, all things are possible").[9]

Second, your sense that G-d has a purpose in everything helps you find meaning in ordinary

4 Oxman et al. (1995), op. cit.

5 Koenig et al. (1997), op. cit.

6 Ellison and Levin (1998), op.cit.

7 This finding comes from an analyses of National Opinion Research Center General Society Survey Data. Myers (2000), op. cit.

8 Ellison and Levin (1998), op. cit.

9 Pollner, M. (1989). Divine relations, social relations, and well-being. *Journal of Health and Social Behavior,* 30: 92–104.

life events as well as in traumatic ones. This is critical. Regardless of whether you are involved with a formal religious organization, your health and happiness may benefit simply (or perhaps not so simply) from your having religious faith. This becomes particularly important during challenging times. A health crisis or a death in the family, especially one that is unexpected or premature, may lack a clear secular explanation and can severely challenge your basic assumptions about the fairness and justice of the world. "Religious coping," which includes praying, reexamining one's sense of meaning, and collaborating with a divine other, can help you understand that the event *is* part of a broader divine plan or that it offers an opportunity for spiritual growth or that you have the ability to handle things. The sense of meaning that you derive from your religion can provide hope (e.g., "G-d will ensure that things will get better"), a satisfying explanation via a broader, benign purpose (e.g., "G-d brings hardship to make you strong" or "The will of a loving G-d cannot be fully understood"), and solace (e.g. "We are more than just a momentary blip in the universe"). Indeed, such religious coping is so powerful that during hard times it is the single most frequently used form of coping by older people.[10]

A mother who lost her firstborn son and later gave birth to a healthy second child was able to find meaning in the death in the following way: "They say there's a reason for G-d to do everything, you know. I think that's very true because I think I love [my second child] a lot more than I would [have] had our first son been here."[11] Similarly, studies show that "G-d had a reason" is one of the most common responses by victims of a range of traumas, such as paralysis, to the question, Why me? Furthermore, those of us who are able to apply benevolent religious frameworks generally adjust better to

our ordeals. For example, in a study of patients undergoing chemotherapy, those who believed that G-d had a measurable control over their cancers had higher self-esteem and were rated as better adjusted by their nurses (e.g., more happy, serene, and active, and relating better to others).[12] Interestingly, the belief in G-d as a controlling force helped these cancer patients cope better than did belief in their own personal control. But the control they were talking about wasn't a passive submission to an external force: rather, the patients spoke of using prayer and faith, as well as their own efforts at managing the disease, as a means of obtaining control from G-d. It was an active and interactive give-and-take process between the individual and a higher power.

Even beyond negative or traumatic life events—when our days are merely ordinary—religion and spirituality undoubtedly help us find meaning in life. Why do we need a sense of meaning? Because we need to feel that we matter, that our suffering and our hard work aren't futile, and that our life has a purpose. Because we need to feel a sense of control over our fates. Because we need to be able to justify our actions: why we should forgive, what we have to be grateful for, why we should turn the other cheek, and so on. Because we need a reason to focus beyond just ourselves. Finally, because a sense of meaning fuels our sense of self-worth. It makes us feel good about our belief systems, our identities, and the communities of like-minded individuals to which we belong.[13]

It's also worth noting that religious faith gives rise to a number of positive emotions and expediencies that are associated with happiness, and this in itself can partly explain why religious and pious people are happier than nonreligious ones. One such attribute is the disposition to forgive. A slew of studies has shown that highly religious and spiritual individuals see themselves as more forgiving and value forgiveness more than do

10 Koenig, H. G., George, L. K., and Siegler, I. C. (1998). The use of religion and other emotion-regulating coping strategies among older adults. *Gerontologist,* 28:303–10.
11 Quoted in Pargament, K. I., and Mahoney, A. (2002). Spirituality: Discovering and conserving the sacred. In Snyder and Lopez, op. cit., pp. 646–59.

12 Jenkins, R. A., and Pargament, K. I., (1988). Cognitive appraisals in cancer patients. *Social Science and Medicine,* 26: 625–33.
13 Baumeister, R. F. (1991). *Meanings of Life.* New York, Guilford.

their peers.[14] Finally, the practice of religion—private prayer, spiritual pursuit, and collective worship—can engender hope, gratitude, love, awe, compassion, joy, and even ecstasy, all being happiness-increasing feelings.[15]

BENEFITS OF SPIRITUALITY

So far I have been muddling a bit the words *spiritual* and *religious*. What's the difference? There is certainly a lot of overlap, but the overlap isn't complete.[16] *Spirituality* is defined as a "search for the sacred"[17]—that is, a search for meaning in life through something that is larger than the individual self ("self-transcendence" is a good label). Spiritual individuals refer to G-d or to related concepts like divine power or ultimate truth. Religion also involves a spiritual search, but this search usually takes place in a formal, institutional context. However, because the majority of spiritual people define themselves as also religious, the benefits of spirituality are essentially identical to the benefits of religion. Spiritual people are relatively happier than nonspiritual people, have superior mental health, cope better with stressors, have more satisfying marriages, use drugs and alcohol less often, are physically healthier, and live longer lives.[18] People who perceive the divine being as loving and responsive are happier than those who don't.[19]

However, those of you who do not believe in G-d may still be able to sanctify ordinary things on earth. If you think of your work as a calling (divine or not), if you perceive your children as blessings, if you understand love as eternal, or if you believe that the body is holy, you are imbuing aspects of life with sacred or divine qualities. Sanctification, it turns out, can provide motivation, meaning, and satisfaction. Couples who sanctify their marriage are more satisfied and invested, parents who sanctify parenting are more effective disciplinarians, and college students who pursue goals concerned with transcending the self and committing to a higher power (e.g., "Be aware of the spiritual meaningfulness of my life" or "Learn to tune into higher power throughout the day") are relatively happier.[20]

So spirituality offers something for those of us who are not, or do not want to be, affiliated with any formal religious institution. Instead of attending church or temple, we can work at searching for the sacred in many different ways—through meditation, prayer, or by instilling a spiritual dimension into our daily lives.

First, as I describe in the next section, meditation is a powerful technique that can boost both physical and psychological well-being, and many people who practice it do so by using a spiritual mantra. The ability to transcend your ordinary life through meditation appears to be one of the reasons for its many benefits.

Although undoubtedly there are different ways to pray, the type of prayer most closely linked with spiritual practice, and the most beneficial, is meditative prayer. This is a type of prayer through which you try to maintain a divine relationship. For example, you might spend time just being "in the presence" of G-d. People who practice meditative prayer are happier overall and feel closer to G-d than those who practice other kinds of prayer, such as petitioning for relief or beseeching for forgiveness.[21]

Finally, people for whom spirituality is important try to experience a sense of the divine in their day-to-day existence—for example, by cultivating feelings of awe, inspiration, and wholeness, by fostering a sense of the vastness of G-d's love, by nurturing belief in a power

14 McCullough, M. E., and Worthington, E. L., (1999). Religion and the forgiving personality. *Journal of Personality*, 74:1257–92.

15 Vaillant, G. E. (in press). *Spiritual Evolution: A Scientific Defense of Faith*. New York, Broadway Books.

16 Saucier, G. and Skrzypinska, K. (2006). Spiritual but not religious? Evidence for two independent dispositions. *Journal of Personality*, 74:1257–92.

17 Pargament, K. I. (1999) The psychology of religion and spirituality?: Yes and no. *International Journal for the Psychology of Religion*, 9:3–16.

18 Pargament and Mahoney (2002), op. cit.

19 Pollner, M. (1989). Divine relations, social relations, and well-being. *Journal of Health and Social Behavior*, 30:92–104.

20 Pargament and Mahoney (2002), op. cit.

21 Poloma, M. M. and Gallup, G. H. Jr. (1991). *Varieties of Prayer: A Survey Report*. Philadelphia: Trinity Press International.

greater than oneself, and by developing a connection with the transcendent. This sense of spirituality may come more easily with practice and during extraordinary circumstances, such as childbirth.

FOR WHOM ARE RELIGION AND SPIRITUALITY MOST BENEFICIAL?

The first answer to this question is consistent with a key theme of this book, which is that particular happiness-enhancing activities will be most effective for people who are open to them and are motivated to practice them with effort and commitment. In other words, if it feels natural to you to practice religion and spirituality, then by all means do it.

In addition, researchers have made several interesting discoveries, including the fact that religiosity is more strongly tied to happiness among women (relative to men), among African-Americans (relative to whites), among older people (relative to younger ones), and among North Americans (relative to Europeans), possibly because their religious faith is relatively stronger. Furthermore, people who actively and publicly participate in religious activities (e.g., attending church or praying) are happier than those who simply espouse religious beliefs. (This finding underscores the key role that a support community may play in the happiness-boosting effects of religion.) Finally, and not surprisingly, those who pursue religion for intrinsic reasons (i.e., as a way of life) are happier than those who pursue it as a means to an end (i.e., for instrumental, extrinsic reasons, such as career or status).[22]

ARE THERE DOWNSIDES TO RELIGION?

Freud argued that religion can create an "obsessional neurosis," whose symptoms include suppressed emotions, repressed sexuality, and guilt.[23] The popular media sometimes suggest that religious people are more prejudiced and closed-minded than their less religious peers, or are rather passive about their lives and health (relinquishing all control to G-d), or are incapable of rational scientific thought, or have maladaptive beliefs in divine vengeance, "righteous anger," and original sin. Furthermore, just like intimate relationships, which can deliver a person's highest highs and lowest lows, religious congregations can similarly be a source of stress and conflict. They may demand a great deal of time, energy, money, sacrifice, and conformity to strict expectations for moral conduct and family life.

Do these represent genuine drawbacks and harms of a religion, or are they myths perpetuated by a secular public? Yes and no. Studies support some, but not all, of these observations. For example, people who strongly believe that prayer can cure their ills are less likely to exercise and are less involved in their own health care, and those who passively defer their problems to G-d show lower levels of mental health.[24] People who perceive G-d as distant and punitive are more likely to be distressed and ill, and individuals angry at G-d backslide in their health. Guilt, shame, and fear may be experienced when people believe that negative events represent G-d's punishment for their sins (or, worse, the work of demonic forces), and such beliefs are associated with greater depression and worse health and quality of life.[25] Finally, beliefs in original sin are associated with low self-esteem, perhaps because it's hard to feel good about yourself if you feel incompetent and shameful out of the conviction that you are inherently a wicked person.

Regarding the question of whether religious beliefs can foster prejudice, this has been found in some studies of religious fundamentalists, who sometimes agree with statements like "The

22 For a review of this research, see Compton, W. C. (2004). Religion, spirituality, and well-being. In *An Introduction to Positive Psychology* (pp. 196–216). Belmont, CA: Wadsworth.
23 Freud, S. (1964). *The Future of an Illusion*. Garden City, NY: Doubleday, p. 71. (Original work published in 1928).

24 For example, see Klonoff, E. A., and Landrine, H. (1996). Belief in the healing powers of prayer: Prevalence and health correlates for African-Americas. *Western Journal of Black Studies*, 20:207–10.
25 For example, see Koenig, H. G., Pargament, K. I., and Nielsen, J. (1998). Religious coping and health status in medically ill hospitalized older adults. *Journal of Mental and Nervous Disease*, 186: 513–21.

reason the Jews have so much trouble is because *[sic]* G-d is punishing them for rejecting Jesus"[26] and "The AIDS disease currently killing homosexuals is just what they deserve."[27] However, these findings are fairly weak and the results not very generalizable to today's diversity of views, indicating that the vast majority of religious and spiritual individuals are more likely to be inclusive, compassionate, and open-minded than the reverse.

Finally, the search for the sacred can be unsuccessful, triggering anxiety and distress, or, in rare cases, can lead to absolute submission to a cult or hostility toward nonbelievers. To be sure, these are extreme examples. If you choose religion and spirituality as one of the activities to increase and sustain your happiness, you're unlikely to confront such problems. As with all the happiness-boosting strategies I have discussed, moderation and common sense are wisest.

PRACTICING RELIGION AND SPIRITUALITY

I had considered leaving this section blank, as most people who are religious or spiritual have a pretty good idea of how to observe their faith. But perhaps a few suggestions can galvanize someone who is uncertain, at a loss, or feeling despondent and inert. I'll start with a brief list and expand on a couple of strategies in detail. For now, for today, you need choose only **one** activity to try. Join (or recommit to) a temple, church, or mosque, a spiritual program, or a Bible study group. Set as your goal attending a religious service once a week or even daily. Spend fifteen minutes every day reading a spiritually themed or religious book, flipping through a volume of affirmations, listening to a spiritual radio program, or watching a religious show. Volunteer for a faith-based charity. Finally, learn about other religions by doing research at the library or on the Web or by talking to friends and acquaintances about their faiths. Not only

will you be enlightened and perhaps stirred to try something new, but you may end up building or strengthening friendships.

Seek meaning and purpose. Researchers believe that a genuine sense of meaning in life must be rooted in a person's own thoughts, feelings, and experiences. Blindly embracing someone else's sense of meaning won't bring about happiness and growth. Creating meaning is one of the most difficult things that you can do, and the meaning that you do create is likely to change over the course of your life. Here are six suggestions from researchers on how to strive to find it.[28]

First, life is more meaningful when you are pursuing goals that are harmonious and within reach—for example, when you have the time, the ability, and the energy to devote to your most important goals, whether those goals involve rearing children or developing as a writer. If you're not sure what your goals are or how to follow them, read Chapter 8.

Second, greater meaning comes from having a coherent life scheme. Sit back and write down, or share with someone, your own life story. Who are you now, and who were you before? What future do you imagine for yourself? What are the obstacles in your path? What assumptions do you hold about the world and why things are the way they are?

Third, creativity—in the arts, humanities, *and* sciences and even in self-discovery—can impart a sense of meaning to many people's lives. Here again, self-transcendence may be critical. What you create may be not only a joyful process for you personally, which lends your life significance, but something, if you're lucky, you may pass on to others—for today and for future generations.

Fourth, for many, there is sometimes powerful meaning in anguish and trauma (see chapter 6). Suffering may bring about posttraumatic growth, including spiritual growth, a timeless perspective on possible life paths, and a sense that life has renewed meaning.

Fifth, at the heart of religion and spirituality are strong emotional experiences, like the

26 Glock, C. Y., and Stark, R. (1996). *Christian Beliefs and Anti-Semitism.* New York: Harper & Row.
27 Altemayer, B., and Hunsberger, B. (1992). Authoritarianism, religious fundamentalism, quest, and prejudice. *International Journal for the Psychology of Religion,* 2:113–33.

28 Compton (2004), op. cit.

comfort you feel at a religious service or the awe and wonder you feel when in the presence of the mystery and majesty of the divine or when confronted with the intensity of love, the immensity of the universe, or scenes of exquisite natural beauty. Such religious expediencies, including conversion and near-death experiences, which may contain profound feelings of spiritual awakening, ecstasy, or being "bathed in light," all serve to deepen your faith and endow your life with greater meaning.

Finally, an essential path to finding meaning in your life is, almost by definition, to work on developing your faith. In a sense, faith provides the answer to the "big" questions: Who am I? What is my life for? Where do I fit in? Who is the creator? How do I live a virtuous life and improve the world around me?

Pray. A universal way to practice religion and spirituality is through prayer. Indeed, almost seven out of ten Americans report praying every single day, and only 6 percent report never praying.[29] Every religion has its own form and tradition of prayer, its own ways of communicating with G-d or the divine. The following ideas are for how to make prayer a bigger part of life.

- *Dedicate a period of time each day—from five minutes to an hour—to prayer. You may use the time to petition G-d for something for yourself or others or simply to be "in his presence," or to read a prayer book.*
- *Alternatively, you may choose to pray spontaneously throughout the day and in specific situations—for example, when you feel depressed or tense or judgmental, or when you witness a beautiful object or a kind act, or when something particularly good (or bad) has happened.*
- *Say a prayer upon waking or before bedtime or prior to each meal. A prayer of gratitude, if you are so inclined, may be particularly comforting and happiness-inducing (see Chapter 4).*

Rosa, a young woman I met at my university, decided to change her life by actively practicing prayer. Although she was raised to believe in G-d and to attend church on Sundays, she told me that she did it only because she was dragged there. When she became an adult, she had stopped doing something that she used to do a lot, and that was praying. This is how Rosa describes her experience of trying to accomplish her new goal and the multiple benefits she incurs:

The past week I have been praying when I go to bed and when I wake up. I pray for my day, and I give thanks for everything that has happened. I tell G-d of all the things that have bothered me during the day, finding myself wiser and happier when I finish praying, as if I had just told a friend everything that has bothered me for a while. Before I started praying, I felt awkward, as I had to do it in front of my roommate and I did not know how she would take it, yet when I engaged in praying to G-d and closed my eyes, I stopped being aware of my surroundings. I completely let myself free of all opinions and biases and thanked him for my day, thanked him for all he had done for me, and prayed for strength to continue in his path in the following days. As I finished praying, I felt relieved, as if a huge weight had left me, and I felt satisfied.

The activity itself was not hard per se, but doing something I have not done in many years was hard to pick up, especially since I started doing it every morning and every night. However, I enjoyed doing it. . . . I did not feel alone anymore. . . . I have and will make a habit of repeating my prayers every day, as I know that every time I do, I engage in better conversations with people, act more thankful, forgive easier, and make the ones around me feel like they are in good company. I believe that G-d is capable of many great things and he will watch over me wherever I am. He is my father, my friend, and my brother, and the feeling that I receive from talking to him is joyous as I get to share with him all my secrets, and he rids me of all my doubts and anxieties. I am definitely going to continue doing this every day as it gives me strength when I wake up and I rest easier as I go to sleep.

29 Blanton, D. (2005, December 1). 12/01/05 FOX poll: Courts driving religion out of public life; Christianity under attack. Retrieved June 26, 2006, from the World Wide Web: http://www.foxnews.com/story/0,2933,177355,00.html

30 Hoge, D. R. (1996). Religion in America: The demographics of belief and affiliation. In Shafranske, E. P., (ed.). *Religion and*

Find the sacred in ordinary life. Develop an ability to see holiness in everyday things, both beautiful and plain. A meal can be holy, and so can a child's laugh or a new snowfall. The big sky above Montana looks to many people as if it has G-d's fingerprints on it, but so can ordinary scenes and situations. Sanctifying day-to-day objects, experiences, and struggles takes a great deal of practice, but it's at the heart of spirituality and its rewards.

CLOSING

Scientists can no longer ignore the powerful influences of spirituality and religion on health and well-being. If nothing else, the statistics should compel them. In the United States alone the vast majority of individuals, about 95 percent, believe in G-d.[30] If you so choose, and in your own way, you can harness the benefits of faith to improve your happiness and your life.

The How of Happiness (New York, Penguin Press, 2008), pp. 228–244
Reprinted with permission

the Clinical Practice of Psychology (pp. 21–42). Washington, DC: American Psychological Association. Johnson, B., Bader, C., Dougherty, F., Froese, P., Stark, R., Mencken, C., and Park, J. (2006, September 11). Losing my religion? No, says Baylor religion survey. Retrieved from the World Wide Web: http://www.baylor.edu/pr/new.php?action=story&story=41678

ACKNOWLEDGMENTS

Seldom does one have the opportunity to seamlessly fuse a life's mission and a labor of love. These acknowledgments are a public affirmation of the incredible blessings I experience daily.

Extreme appreciation is owed to the course author, **Rabbi Mordechai Dinerman**, for his dedication, talent, and skillful ability in bringing this project to fruition, and to **Dr. David Pelcovitz** for his professional, wise, and indispensable counsel. I am deeply grateful to our gifted course development team, **Mrs. Mushka Grossbaum, Mrs. Rochel Holzkenner**, **Rabbi Yanky Raskin**, **Rabbi Naftali Silberberg**, **Dr. Casey Skvorc**, and **Rabbi Yanky Tauber**, for contributing to this course in so many important ways. **Mrs. Rivki Mockin**, our curriculum coordinator, I am grateful for your sensibilities in every aspect of book production, which are commendable and worthy of special mention. To each of you I say: Thank you for so generously sharing your expertise. It has been a true pleasure and joy to collaborate with you every step of the way, and I consider myself exceedingly fortunate to reap the rewards of this quintessential dream team. The Rosh Chodesh Society is indeed blessed.

Mrs. Malky Bitton, **Mrs. Shula Bryski**, **Mrs. Chanie Wilhelm**, and **Mrs. Yehudis Wolvovsky** graciously agreed to lend their know-how and experience—from reviewing curricula, to aiding in general course development, to piloting the course so that others may benefit. We acknowledge their pedagogic and instructional skills and thank them on behalf of the entire Rosh Chodesh Society.

Our talented teams have expended numerous hours to bring our materials to production. **Mrs. Ya'akovah Weber** and **Mimi Palace** meticulously copyedited and proofread the textbooks with attention and dedication. **Mrs. Mush Kanner** created the beautiful book design, and **Rabbi Zalman Korf** and **Mrs. Shayna Grosh** are responsible for the textbooks' professional layout. I am deeply thankful to all of you. You always rise to the occasion.

We laud our design and marketing teams for producing our beautiful materials with creative vision and attentiveness to the finest of details. Thank you **Mrs. Mush Kanner**, **Mrs. Shifra Tauber, Rabbi Levi Weingarten**, and **Rabbi Boruch Werdiger** for your artfulness, brilliant creativity, proficiency, and grace. Accolades to **Rabbi Aron Lieberow**, who oversees and ensures the integrity of our cyberspace field, and a shout-out to **Mendel Grossbaum** and **Moshe Levin** for their competence and resourceful tech assistance.

Special mention must be made regarding our very gifted multimedia team. Thank you, **Mrs. Mushka Druk,** for leading the magnificent PowerPoint presentations—a wonderful asset to each lesson. Kudos as well to **Mrs. Baila Goldstein** for your stunning creations. Having the good fortune to work with **Moshe and Getzy Raskin** of Swish Media, who are simply so good at all things video, is a blessing I'm sure many would wish for.

Many thanks to **Mr. Shimon Leib Jacobs** and to **Mary Stevens** for the printing and distribution of our books. Much gratitude to **Rabbi Mendel Sirota**, who oversees production, shipping, and handling. You always go the extra mile, and we acknowledge your efforts.

It is with heartfelt gratitude that I recognize **Zehava Krafchik,** who, while overseeing many other responsibilities, always managed to seamlessly keep things moving forward.

Kudos to **Mrs. Baila Goldstein**, an administrator and single-handed project manager par excellence. She is much more than her title can ever tell you, and my appreciation for her knows no bounds. Her wise contributions, in so many areas, are immeasurable.

I pay tribute to **Mrs. Shaina B. Mintz** for everything she does to keep the many parts of our organization's machine oiled and for ensuring that every day is an A-to-Z, all-systems-go day—a stunning accomplishment.

The Rosh Chodesh Society is enormously grateful for the encouragement of **Rabbi Moshe Kotlarsky**, chairman of the Rohr Jewish Learning Institute and vice chairman of Merkos L'Inyonei Chinuch—Lubavitch World Headquarters.

We are fortuitously blessed with the unwavering support of JLI's principal benefactors, **Mr. and Mrs. George and Pamela Rohr**, who have staunchly spearheaded and invested in the growth of the organization with an unparalleled commitment. Their dedication is evident and alive within the tens of thousands of Jewish students studying Torah around the globe. May your merit stand you—and all of us—in good stead, and may you reap bountiful blessings all the days of your long, happy, and healthy lives.

Heartfelt acclamation to **Mr. and Mrs. Yitzchak and Julie Gniwisch** for their steadfast support and resolute belief in us, always. May the goodness you bring to the world be returned to you ten thousandfold.

JLI's devoted executive board—**Rabbi Chaim Block**, **Rabbi Hesh Epstein**, **Rabbi Ronnie Fine**, **Rabbi Yosef Gansburg**, **Rabbi Shmuel Kaplan**, **Rabbi Yisrael Rice**, and **Rabbi Avrohom Sternberg**—give countless hours to the development of JLI. Their dedication, commitment, and sage advice have helped the organization grow and flourish.

The constant progress of JLI is a testament to the visionary leadership of our director, **Rabbi Efraim Mintz**, who is never content with the status quo, boldly encourages unbridled innovation and forward thinking, and embodies successful accomplishment. You are an example to many. On this auspicious day, I thank you publicly, both personally and professionally, for this benevolent, outstanding, and truly wonderful opportunity. Directing the Rosh Chodesh Society is the calling of my heart and the journey of my soul. It is a gift that keeps on giving eternal blessings. May all who read this be equally blessed. Your merit is great. Thank you for sharing it with me.

The Rosh Chodesh Society, JLI's women's division, was launched on the anniversary of the first *yahrtzeits* of **Rabbi Gavriel Noach and Rebbetzin Rivkah Holtzberg, *H"YD***, devoted Chabad emissaries to Mumbai, India. May the merit of the countless Jewish women who are engaged in these Torah studies serve as a testament to the heroic lives the Holtzbergs led and continue to perpetuate their noble deeds.

On behalf of all the individuals who play a role in the Rosh Chodesh Society, particularly our affiliates out there on the front lines fulfilling their positions, I offer up a prayer to Almighty G-d: may He actualize the hope of the Jewish nation, as repeatedly expressed by the Lubavitcher Rebbe, of righteous memory, and may we very soon experience the world as it will be, filled with the knowledge of G-d as the waters cover the sea. Amen.

Shluchos! It is solely thanks to you that we will merit the fulfillment of our mandate, *No Jewish Woman Will Be Left Behind*. We could never do it without you. You continue to change the world for the better and certainly make it a happier place! Thank you for allowing us to partner with you. You are the heart and soul of the Jewish nation. Indeed, this is the ultimate acknowledgment.

Shaindy Jacobson
Director, Rosh Chodesh Society
Brooklyn, New York
Chai (18) Elul 5780

The Rohr
JEWISH LEARNING INSTITUTE

An affiliate of **MERKOS L'INYONEI CHINUCH**
The Educational Arm of The Chabad Lubavitch Movement
822 Eastern Parkway, Brooklyn, NY 11213

ROSHCHODESH society FACULTY

UNITED STATES

BIRMINGHAM, AL
Mrs. Frumie Posner
Chabad of Alabama
205.970.0100
cyfposner@aol.com

CHANDLER, AZ
Mrs. Shternie Deitsch
Chabad of the East Valley
4808554333
mycmommy@gmail.com

FOUNTAIN HILLS, AZ
Mrs. Tzipi Lipskier
Chabad of Fountain Hills
480.776.4763
tzipi@jewishfountainhills.com

ORO VALLEY, AZ
Mrs. Mushkie Zimmerman
Chabad of Oro Valley
3475265967
mushkie@jewishorovalley.com

PARADISE VALLEY, AZ
Mrs. Chaya Levertov
Chabad of Paradise Valley
3054799686
chaya@jewishparadisevalley.com

TUCSON, AZ
Mrs. Feigie Ceitlin
Chabad Lubavitch of Tucson
520.869.4971
FeigieCeitlin@gmail.com

LITTLE ROCK, AR
Mrs. Estie Ciment
Lubavitch of Arkansas
501.221.7940
Estie@arjewishcenter.com

NORTHWEST AR
Dobie Greisman
Chabad of Northwest Arkansas
479.464.7999
dobi@jewishnwa.org

ARCATA, CA
Mrs. Mushkie Cowen
Chabad of Humboldt
412.390.6481
mushkiecowen@gmail.com

BAKERSFIELD, CA
Mrs. Esther Malka Schlanger
Chabad of Bakersfield
661.835.8381
estherm@bak.rr.com

BERKELEY, CA
Mrs. Miriam Chaya Ferris
Chabad of the East Bay
510.684.5292
miriamferris@gmail.com

BEVERLY HILLS, CA
Mrs. Devorah Leah Illulian
One Lev Women's Circle
310.927.3362
dltraxler@gmail.com

BRENTWOOD, CA
Mrs. Mashie Goldshmid
Chabad of the Delta
718.812.1425
mashie@JewishDelta.com

BURBANK, CA
Mrs Elana Kornfeld
Chabad of Burbank
1.8187.491.592
elanakornfeld@gmail.com

CALABASAS, CA
Mrs. Shaina Friedman
Chabad of Calabasas
818.222.3838
shaini@jewishcalabasas.com

DANVILLE, CA
Mrs Mushky Raitman
Chabad of Danville
213.447.6694
chabaddsr@gmail.com

ENCINO, CA
Mrs. Chana Herzog
Chabad of Encino
818.784.9986
JLI@chabadofthevalley.com

FOLSOM, CA
Mrs. Goldie Grossbaum
Chabad Folsom
916.608.9811
info@jewishfolsom.org

FREMONT, CA
Mrs. Chaya Fuss
Chabad of Fremont
510.300.4090
chaya@chabadfremont.com

FRESNO, CA
Mrs. Chanie Zirkind
Chabad of Fresno
559.432.2770
chabadfresno@sbcglobal.net

GLENDALE, CA
Mrs. Shterny Backman
Chabad of Glendale
818.240.2750
shterny@chabadcenter.org

GOLETA, CA
Mrs. Devorah Loschak
Chabad of S. Barbara
805.324.3584
dloschak@gmail.com

GRANITE BAY, CA
Mrs. Malkie Korik
Chabad of Roseville
9165004522
rabbi@jewishroseville.com

HUNTINGTON BEACH, CA
Mrs Rochel Berkowitz
Chabad of West Orange County
714.846.0675
adbralp@verizon.net

HUNTINGTON BEACH, CA
Mrs. Susha Alperowitz
Chabad of West Orange County
714.846.2285
chabadhb@verizon.net

IRVINE, CA
Mrs. Binie Tenenbaum
Chabad of Irvine
949.786.5000
binie@chabadirvine.org

LAGUNA NIGUEL, CA
Mrs. Kreinie Paltiel
Chabad of Laguna Niguel
949.831.7701
Krein-ie@ChabadLagunaNiguel.com

LONG BEACH, CA
Mrs. Amina Newman
Congregation Lubavitch
562.596.1681
info@longbeachshul.com

LOS ALTOS, CA
Mrs. Nechama Schusterman
Chabad Los Altos
650.858.6990
nechama@bayareafc.org

LOS ANGELES, CA
Mrs. Chanie Levin
Beis Bezalel Chabad
310.385.2222
administration@baisbezalel.org

LOS ANGELES, CA
Mrs. Channa Hecht
Chabad Jewish Center of Brentwood
310.826.4453
channa@chabadbw.com

LOS ANGELES, CA
Mrs. Dvonye Korf
Chabad of Greater Los Feliz
323.660.5177
rabbi@chabadlosfeliz.org

LOS ANGELES, CA
Mrs Runya Wagner
Chabad Jewish Student Center at USC
213.748.5884
runya@usc.edu

LOS ANGELES, CA
Mrs. Shterny Gurary
Chabad Jewish Center of Hancock Park
323.939.5138
rabbi@jewishhp.com

LOS ANGELES CA
Simons
YJP Los Angeles
310.595.5490
mendel@yjplosangeles.com

MALIBU, CA
Mrs. Sarah Cunin
Chabad of Malibu
310.456.6588
sarah@ganmalibu.com

MILL VALLEY, CA
Mrs. Chana Scop
Chabad of Mill Valley
415.419.7296
chanascop@comcast.net

NEWBURY PARK, CA
Mrs. Tzippy Schneerson
Chabad of Newbury Park
805.499.7051
sschneerson@gmail.com

NEWHALL, CA
Mrs Frumi Marozov
Chabad of SCV
6616445734
frumim@gmail.com

OAKLAND, CA
Mrs. Shulamis Labkowski
Chabad of Oakland
510.545.6770
info@jewishoakland.org

OCEANSIDE, CA
Mrs. Nechama Greenberg
Chabad Jewish Center Oceanside
760.806.7765
info@jewishoceanside.com

PACIFIC PALISADES, CA
Mrs. Zisi Cunin
Chabad of Pacific Palisades
310.454.7783
info@chabadpalisades.com

PALO ALTO, CA
Mrs. Devory Levin
Chabad Palo Alto
650.561.6013
devory@chabadpaloalto.com

PASADENA, CA
Mrs. Chana Hanoka
Chabad of Pasadena
626.564.8820
hanoka@sbcglobal.net

PLEASANTON, CA
Mrs. Fruma Resnick
Chabad of the Tri-Valley
925.846.0700
Fruma@JewishTriValley.com

RANCHO MIRAGE, CA
Mrs. Chaya Posner
Chabad of Rancho Mirage
760.770.7785
info@chabadrm.com

REDONDO BEACH, CA
Mrs. Sara Mintz
Chabad Jewish Community Center
310.214.4999
laya0208@gmail.com

REDWOOD CITY, CA
Mrs. Ella Potash
Chabad of Redwood City
650.232.0995
ella@jewishredwoodcity.com

SACRAMENTO, CA
Mrs. Dinie Cohen
Chabad of Sacramento
916.455.1400
chabadsac@aol.com

S. CLARA, CA
Mrs. Elana Rosenberg
Chabad S. Clara
4087189074
elana@jewishsantaclara.com

S. DIEGO, CA
Mrs. Leah Fradkin
Chabad of S. Diego
858.547.0076
lfradkin@chasd.org

S. DIEGO, CA
Mrs. Nechama Dina Carlebach
Chabad of Downtown
(619).289.8770
info@ChabadDowntown.com

S. FRANCISCO, CA
Mrs. Sara Hecht
RTC-Chabad
415.386.8123
office@rtchabad.org

S. FRANCISCO, CA
Mrs. Mattie Pil
Schneerson Center
415.933.4310
mattieplot@gmail.com

S. MONICA, CA
Mrs. Sara Levitansky
Bais Chabad of Simcha Monica
310.829.5620
soriandisaac@gmail.com

S. MONICA, CA
Mrs. Rivka Rabinowitz
Chabad Living Torah Center
310.394.5699
rabbi@livingtorahcenter.com

S. ROSA, CA
Mrs. Altie Wolvovsky
Chabad Jewish Center
707.577.0277
rabbi@jewishsonoma.com

SEAL BEACH, CA
Mrs. Bluma Marcus
Chabad of Cypress
714.828.1851
shmuelmarcus@yahoo.com

SHERMAN OAKS, CA
Mrs. Ruth Weiss
Chabad of Sherman Oaks Mishkan Sholom
818.789.0850
hmweiss@hotmail.com

SIMI VALLEY, CA
Mrs. Bassie Gurary
Chabad of Simi Valley
805.577.0573
bassie@chabadsimi.org

STOCKTON, CA
Mrs. Nechamie Brod
Chabad of Stockton
209.471.2154
nechamie@gmail.com

TEMECULA, CA
Mrs. Dina Hurwitz
Chabad Jewish Center Temecula Valley
951.813.1401
jewishtemecula@gmail.com

THOUSAND OAKS, CA
Mrs. Shula Bryski
Chabad of Thousand Oaks
805.493.7776
shula@jewishto.org

TOLUCA LAKE, CA
Mrs. Michal Carlebach
Chabad of Toluca Lake
818.308.4118
chabadtl@gmail.com

VACAVILLE, CA
Mrs. Aidel Zaklos
Chabad of Solano County
707.592.5300
rabbi@jewishsolano.com

VENTURA, CA
Mrs. Sarah Miriam Latowicz
Chabad of Ventura
805.658.7441
chabadventura@aol.com

DENVER, CO
Mrs Devora Lea Popack
Chabad Lubavitch of Colorado
720.224.8484
dpopack@gmail.com

DENVER, CO
Mrs. Elka Popack
Chabad Lubavitch of Colorado
303.780.0537
elkapopack@gmail.com

LONE TREE, CO
Mrs. Hindy Mintz
Chabad Jewish Center - South Metro Denver
303.694.9119
Hindy@DenverJewishCenter.com

WESTMINSTER, CO
Mrs. Leah Brackman
Chabad of NW Metro Denver
303.429.5177
Leahbrackman9@gmail.com

FAIRFIELD, CT
Mrs Miriam Landa
Chabad of Fairfield
203.373.7551
miriam@chabadff.com

GLASTONBURY, CT
Mrs. Yehudis Wolvovsky
Chabad Jewish Center
8608336451
yehudis@chabader.com

GREENWICH, CT
Mrs. Maryashie Deren
Chabad Lubavitch of Greenwich
203.629.9059
info@chabadgreenwich.org

GUILFORD, CT
Mrs. Rochel Baila Yaffe
Chabad of the Shoreline
203.453.5580
chabad@snet.net

MILFORD, CT
Mrs. Chanie Wilhelm
Chabad Jewish Center of Milford
203.878.4569
chanie@jewishmilford.com

ORANGE, CT
Mrs. Bluma Hecht
Chabad of Orange
203.795.5261
blumahecht@gmail.com

RIDGEFIELD, CT
Mrs. Chana Deitsch
Chabad of Ridgefield
203.438.4421
ChabadRidgefield@aol.com

WEST HARTFORD, CT
Mrs. Shayna Gopin
Chabad House of Greater Hartford
860.232.1116
info@chabadhartford.com

WILMINGTON, DE
Mrs. Rochel Flikshtein
Chabad of Delaware
302.529.9900
Office@ChabadDE.com

BOCA RATON, FL
Mrs. Ahuva New
Chabad of East Boca Raton
561.417.7797
Office@chabadbocabeaches.com

BOCA RATON, FL
Mrs Chanie Bukiet
Chabad of West Boca Raton
561.487.2934
cbukiet@bellsouth.net

BOCA RATON, FL
Mrs Rivkah Denburg
Chabad of Central Boca Raton
561.526.5738
rivkahden@gmail.com

BOYNTON BEACH, FL
Mrs. Dina Ciment
Chabad of Boynton
561.732.4633
ciments@gmail.com

BOYNTON BEACH, FL
Mrs Shaina Raichik
Chabad of West Boynton
33.472.4418
shainyraichik@gmail.com

BRADENTON, FL
Mrs. Chanie Bukiet
Chabad of Bradenton and Lakewood Ranch
941.752.3030
Chanie@chabadofbradenton.com

CLEARWATER, FL
Chabad of Clearwater
Miriam Hodakov
727.265.2770
miriamhodakov@gmail.com

CORAL SPRINGS, FL
Mrs. Chaya Mushka Yaras
Chabad of Coral Springs
9548674684
chayamushkaf@gmail.com

FORT LAUDERDALE, FL
Mrs. Rochel Holzkenner
Chabad of Las Olas
954.224.7162
rochelholzkenner@gmail.com

HOLLYWOOD, FL
Mrs Sheina Kudan
Chabad Ocean Drive
954.457.8080
sheina@chabadoceandrive.com

JUPITER, FL
Mrs. Sarah Barash
Chabad Jewish Center of Jupiter
561.222.4083
sarah@jewishjupiter.com

KEY BISCAYNE, FL
Mrs Zeldy Caroline
Chabad of Key Biscayne
305.725.8758
avremel.caroline@gmail.com

LAKE MARY, FL
Mrs. Chanshy Majesky
Chabad-Lubavitch of North Orlando
407.878.3011
chanshy@JewishNorthOrlando.com

LAKE WORTH, FL
Mrs. Leah Rosenfeld
Chabad Lake Worth
561.649.8468
Chabadlakeworth@gmail.com

LAKELAND, FL
Mrs. Libby Lazaros
Chabad of Lakeland
863.510.5968
mendel@chabadlakeland.org

MIAMI, FL
Mrs. Chana Gopin
Chabad at Midtown
305.573.9995
info@maormiami.org

MIAMI, FL
Mrs. Gutal Fellig
Chabad of South Dade
305.445.5444
info@chabadmiami.com

MIAMI BEACH, FL
Mrs. Chani Katz
Chabad House in Miami Beach
305.505.9065
rabbi@mbjewish.com

MIAMI BEACH, FL
Mrs. Tzippy Mann
Chabad of Venetian & Sunset Islands
305.674.8400
tzippymann@gmail.com

PALM BEACH, FL
Mrs. Hindel Levitin
Chabad of Northern Palm Beach Island
561.659.3884
hindelle@gmail.com

PALM COAST, FL
Mrs. Tzivie Ezagui
Chabad of Palm Coast
386.453.7107
lyezag@gmail.com

PALM HARBOR, FL
Mrs. Mushky Adler
Chabad of Pinellas County
248.305.0462
emailmushka@gmail.com

PALMETTO BAY, FL
Mrs. Chani Gansburg
Chabad of Palmetto Bay
786.282.0413
chabadpalmettobay@gmail.com

PUNTA GORDA, FL
Mrs. Sheina Jacobson
Chabad of Charlotte County
941.833.3381
chabadpg@yahoo.com

ROYAL PALM BEACH, FL
Mrs. Leah Schtroks
Chabad of Royal Palm Beach
561.795.1534
rabbizevis@gmail.com

S. PETERSBURG, FL
Mrs. Chaya Korf
Chabad Jewish Center
727.344.4900
chaya@chabadsp.com

SARASOTA, FL
Mrs. Sara Steinmetz
Chabad of Sarasota
941.925.0770
steinmetz.sara@gmail.com

SUNNY ISLES BEACH, FL
Mrs. Chanie Kaller
Chabad Russian Center
305.803.5315
Rabbi@chabadrc.org

SURFSIDE, FL
Mrs. Chani Lipskar
The Shul of Bal Harbour
305.868.1411
info@theshul.org

TRINITY, FL
Mrs. Dina Eber
Chabad of West Pasco
727.376.3366
lubavitcher@gmail.com

TAMPA, FL
Mrs. Sulha Dubrowski
Chabad of Tampa Bay
813.963.2317
lamplightersd@gmail.com

VALRICO, FL
Mrs. Tzippy Rubashkin
Chabad of Brandon
813.571.8100
tzipsor@gmail.com

WESLEY CHAPEL, FL
Mrs Chanie Yarmush
Chabad of East Pasco & New Tampa
813.642.3244
mmy613@aol.com

WEST PALM BEACH, FL
Mrs. Chaya Gancz
Chabad of West Palm Beach
561.659.7770
Rabbi@jewishwpb.com

WESTON, FL
Mrs. Leah Spalter
Chabad Lubavitch of Weston
954.349.6565
amychabadofweston@gmail.com

ATLANTA, GA
Mrs. Dassie New
Chabad of Georgia
404.843.2464 ext.102
office@chabadga.com

ATLANTA, GA
Mrs. Leah Sollish
Mrs. Dena Schusterman
Chabad In-town
404.898.0434
leah@chabadintown.org

KENNESAW, GA
Mrs. Nechami Charytan
Chabad Jewish Center
678.460.7702
info@jewishwestcobb.com

PEACHTREE CORNERS, GA
Mrs Esther Lerman
Chabad of Gwinnett
6785950196
esther@chabadofgwinnett.org

KAPA'A, HI
Mrs. Zisel Goldman
Chabad Kauai
808.647.4293
jewishkauai@gmail.com

BOISE, ID
Mrs. Esther M. Lifshitz
Chabad Lubavitch of Idaho
208.841.9927
esther@jewishidaho.com

CHICAGO, IL
Mrs. Chaya Epstein
Women to Women
773.875.9147
w2wchaya@gmail.com

CHICAGO, IL
Mrs. Dinie Cohen
Jewish Women's Group
773.262.1381
ndcohen@sbcglobal.net

GLENVIEW, IL
Mrs. Sara Benjaminson
Rohr Chabad Center of Glenview
847.998.0770
Chabad@ChabadofGlenview.com

HIGHLAND PARK, IL
Mrs. Michla Schanowitz
North Suburban Chabad
847.433.1567
yschanow@sbcglobal.net

NORTHBROOK, IL
Mrs. Esther Rochel Moscowitz
Lubavitch Chabad of Northbrook
847.564.8770
info@chabadnorthbrook.com

RIVERWOODS, IL
Mrs. Sarale Notik
Chabad Riverwoods Initiative
224.415.4896
saralepruss@gmail.com

SKOKIE, IL
Mrs. Elka Wolf
Seymour J. Abrams Cheder Lubavitch Hebrew Day School
847.675.6777
elkiewolf@gmail.com

DAVENPORT, IA
Mrs. Chana Cadaner
Chabad Lubavitch of the Quad Cities
563.355.1065
Chana@Chabadquadcities.com

IOWA CITY, IA
Mrs. Chaya Blesofsky
Chabad Lubavitch of Iowa City
319.358.1323
chabadiowa@msn.com

LAWRENCE, KS
Tiechtel
Chabad at KU & the Capital District
785.832.8672
info@jewishku.com

OVERLAND PARK, KS
Mrs. Blumah Wineberg
Neshei Chabad of KC
913.649.4852
nesheichabad@gmail.com

LEXINGTON, KY
Mrs. Shoshi Litvin
Chabad of the Bluegrass
502.576.0392
chabadofthebluegrass@gmail.com

METAIRIE, LA
Mrs. Chanie Nemes
Chabad Jewish Center
504.957.4987
chanienemes@gmail.com

ANNAPOLIS, MD
Mrs. Hindy Light
Chabad of Anne Arundel County
443.321.9859
hindy@chabadaac.com

BALTIMORE, MD
Mrs. Rochelle Kaplan
Aleph Learning Institute
410.486.2666 ext.2
alephjli@gmail.com

BEL AIR, MD
Mrs. Fraida Malka Schusterman
Chabad of Harford County
443.353.9718
Chabad@HarfordJewish.com

COLUMBIA, MD
Mrs. Chaya Sufrin
Lubavitch Center of Howard County
443.474.0340
rabbi@chabadclarksville.org

GAITHERSBURG, MD
Mrs. Chana Raichik
Chabad Upper Montgomery County
301.537.0068
chana@ourshul.org

OLNEY, MD
Mrs. Devorah Stolik
Chabad of Olney
301.660.6770
info@jewisholney.com

OWINGS MILLS, MD
Mrs. Chanie Katsenelenbogen
chabad Owings Mills
410.356.5156
chanie@chabadom.com

POTOMAC, MD
Mrs. Chana Kaplan
Chabad of the Village
301.433.4524
villagechabad@gmail.com

POTOMAC, MD
Mrs. Sarale Bluming
Chabad of Potomac
240.621.0770
sara@chabadpotomac.com

SILVER SPRING, MD
Mrs. Chaya Wolvovsky
Chabad of Silver Spring
301.593.1117
chayawolvovsky@gmail.com

ANDOVER, MA
Mrs Faigy Bronstein
Chabad Lubavitch Jewish Center of Merrimack Valley
978.470.2288
Bronstein08@gmail.com

CHESTNUT HILL, MA
Mrs. Grunie Uminer
Chabad at Chestnut Hill
617.738.9770
grunie@chabadch.com

MILFORD, MA
Mrs Rochy Kivman
Chabad Lubavitch of Greater Milford
508.473.9724
rochykivman@gmail.com

NATICK, MA
Mrs. Chanie Fogelman
Chabad Center of Natick
508.202.2283
education@chabadnatick.com

PEABODY, MA
Mrs. Raizel Schusterman
Chabad of Peabody
978.977.9111
raizel@jewishpeabody.com

STOUGHTON, MA
Mrs. Chana Gurkow
Shaloh House
781.344.6334
rabbi@shalohhouse.com

SUDBURY, MA
Mrs. Shayna Freeman
Chabad Center of Sudbury
978.443.0110
info@chabadsudbury.com

WELLESLEY, MA
Mrs. Geni Bleich
Wellesley Weston Chabad House
781.239.1066
JewishWomenRgr8@aol.com

SUDBURY, MA
Mrs. Rochel Freeman
Chabad of Sudbury
978.443.0110
rabbi@chabadsudbury.com

WORCESTER, MA
Mrs. Sarah Fogelman
Chabad of UMASS Medical School
518.947.1165
sarahcohen97@gmail.com

COMMERCE, MI
Mrs. Estie Greenberg
Chabad Jewish Center of Commerce
248.363.3644
estie@jewishcommerce.org

SOUTHFIELD, MI
Mrs. Tzippy Misholovin
FREE of Michigan
248.569.8514
free.michigan@yahoo.com

WEST BLOOMFIELD, MI
Mrs. Itty Shemtov
The Shul
248.788.4000
itty@theshul.net

MINNEAPOLIS, MN
Mrs. Mushky Brook
CYP Minneapolis
612.405.6967
rabbi@cypminneapolis.com

MINNETONKA, MN
Ms. Rivkie Grossbaum
Chabad Minneapolis
952.929.9922
rivka@ChabadMinneapolis.com

S. PAUL, MN
Mrs. Nechama Bendet
Chabad Lubavitch of Greater S. Paul
651.998.9298
jewishspaul@gmail.com

KANSAS CITY, MO
Mrs. Chana'le Itkin
Chabad on the Plaza
816.645.6610
chana@plazachabad.com

S. LOUIS, MO
Mrs. Shiffy Landa
Chabad of Greater St. Louis
314.725.0400
shiffyl@aol.com

BOZEMAN, MT
Mrs. Chavie Bruk
Chabad-Lubavitch of Montana
406.585.8770
chavs84@yahoo.com

MISSOULA, MT
Mrs. Shayna Nash
Chabad Lubavitch of Missoula
406.529.3196
berrynash@gmail.com

MANCHESTER, NH
Mrs. Shternie Krinsky
Chabad Center For Jewish Living
603.647.0204
Info@chabadofnh.com

BOONTON, NJ
Mrs. Rivky Dubinsky
Chabad of Mountain Lakes
347.967.7720
rivkydubinsky@gmail.com

CHERRY HILL, NJ
Mrs. Dinie Mangel
Chabad Lubavitch in Cherry Hill
856.874.1500
Dinie@TheChabadCenter.org

CLINTON, NJ
Mrs. Rachel Kornfeld
Chabad of Hunterdon County
908.238.9002
rachel@jewishhunterdon.com

FAIR LAWN, NJ
Mrs. Rivkah Bergstein
Anshei Lubavitch Outreach Center
201.794.3770
rivky@flchabad.com

FLANDERS, NJ
Mrs. Fraida Shusterman
Chabad of Northwest NJ - Western Region
973.927.3531
fmshust@gmail.com

FRANKLIN LAKES, NJ
Mrs. Mimi Kaplan
Chabad of NW Bergen County – Franklin Lakes
201.848.0449
kaplanmimi@gmail.com

FREEHOLD, NJ
Mrs. Zisi Bernstein
Chabad of Freehold
732.972.3687
zisinj@gmail.com

HOBOKEN, NJ
Mrs. Shaindel Schapiro
Chabad Hoboken
201.386.5222
chabadhoboken@gmail.com

MONTVILLE, NJ
Mrs. Chaya Schera Spalter
Chabad of Montville Township
973.727.8824
chayasspalter@aol.com

MORRISTOWN, NJ
Mrs Chaya Gurevitz
Chabad Young Morristown
973.216.8077
mushkie@cypmorristown.com

MORRISTOWN, NJ
Mrs. Gani Goodman
Morristown RCA
917.860.0146
jdomber@gmail.com

RANDOLPH, NJ
Mrs. Chava Bekhor
Chabad of Randolph
973.895.3070
info@chabadrandolph.com

TOMS RIVER, NJ
Mrs. Chanie Gourarie
Chabad Toms River
732.349.4199
chanie@chabadtomsriver.com

VINELAND, NJ
Mrs. Nechama Rapoport
Chabad of Cumberland County
856.207.3797
yohama1@verizon.net

WEST ORANGE, NJ
Mrs. Altie Kasowitz
Lubavitch Center
973.486.2362
altiekas@yahoo.com

WEST WINDSOR, N.J.
Mrs. Aliza Leverton
Chabad of the Windsors
609.638.2935
alileverton@gmail.com

WOODCLIFF LAKE, NJ
Mrs. Hindy Drizin
Valley Chabad
201.476.0157
hindy@valleychabad.org

LAS CRUCES, NM
Mrs. Chenchie Schmukler
Chabad of Las Cruces
575.524.1330
chenchie@ymail.com

LAS VEGAS, NV
Mrs. Binie Rivkin
Chabad of Red Rock
7022172170
binie@chabadredrock.com

BAYSIDE, NY
Mrs. Chany Pinson
Chabad of northeast queens
718.877.9389
Cfuterfas@gmail.com

BEDFORD HILLS, NY
Mrs. Sara Wolf
Chabad of Bedford & Pound Ridge Towns
914.666.6065
sara@chabadbedford.com

BRONX, NY
Mrs. Sorah Shemtov
Chabad of Riverdale / Bronx
718.549.1100 ext. 15
sorahshmtv@gmail.com

BRONXVILLE, NY
Mrs. Mushka Deitsch
Chabad of Bronxville
347.623.0449
mushka@jewishbronxville.com

BROOKLYN, NY
Mrs. Chana'le Levin
Chabad of Ditmas Park
347.850.2255
ChabadofDitmasPark@gmail.com

BROOKLYN, NY
Mrs. Chanel Lipskier
Mrs. Dvora Lakein
The Beis Medrash Women's Circle
718.778.6712
WC@thebeismedrash.com

BROOKLYN, NY
Mrs. Devorah Marosov
Chabad of Midwood
718.338.3324
dmarsow@gmail.com

BROOKLYN, NY
Mrs. Esther Abramowitz
Chabad-Lubavitch of Clinton Hill
718.974.9472
esther@greenechabad.com

BROOKLYN, NY
Mrs. Esther Winner
Chabad Neshama
718.946.9833 ext.104
estherwinner@gmail.com

BROOKLYN, NY
Mrs. Hadassah Stroh
Chabad of Bay Ridge
718.974.6366
hadassahstroh@gmail.com

BROOKLYN, NY
Mrs. Sarah Hecht
Chabad of Park Slope
718.965.9836
shconquer@aol.com

BROOKLYN, NY
Mrs. Tzippy Vigler
Mayan Yisroel Chassidus Center
718.677.0030
tv@mayanyisroel.net

BROOKLYN, NY
Raichik
Chabad at BC
323.3605.480
rabbi@chabadatbc.com

CEDARHURST, NY
Mrs. Chana Wolowik
Sara Blau
Chabad of the Five Towns
516.295.2478
chanie@chabad5towns.com

DOBBS FERRY, NY
Mrs. Hinda Silverman
Chabad of the River Towns
914.693.6100
office@chabadrt.org

EAST NORWICH, N.Y.
Chana Shain
Chabad of Oyster Bay and Jericho
203.901.7206
chabadmn@gmail.com

FLUSHING, NY
Mrs. Chanie Zalmanov
Chabad of Eastern Queens
718.464.0778
chaniezalmanov@gmail.com

FOREST HILLS, NY
Mrs. Mushky Mendelson
Congregation Machane Chodosh
347.867.8672
rabbi@machanechodosh.org

GREAT NECK, NY
Mrs. Chanie Geisinsky
Chabad of Great Neck
516.528.6033
cgeisinsky@gmail.com

LONG BEACH, NY
Mrs. Baila Goodman
Chabad of the Beaches
516.897.2473
chabadofthebeaches@gmail.com

MAMARONECK, NY
Mrs. Chana Silberstein
Jewish Women's Circle
914.834.8000
chana@jewishlarchmont.com

MERRICK, N.Y.
Chanie Kramer
Chabad of Merrick, L.I.
516.833.3057
campgi@jewishelc.org

NEW YORK, NY
Mrs. Chana Paris
Chabad of Tribeca
212.566.6764
info@chabadoftribeca.com

NEW YORK, NY
Mrs. Chanie Krasnianski
Chabad Upper East Side
212.717.4613
ckrasnianski@gmail.com

NEW YORK, NY
Mrs. Devora Wilhelm
Chabad Young Professionals UES
347.451.4375
chabadyp@gmail.com

NEW YORK, NY
Mrs Elisheva Kirshenbaum
Chabad of Washington Heights
718.913.7900
osherelc@gmail.com

NEW YORK, NY
Mrs. Frumie Weitman
Chabad Jewish Latin Center
646.678.3569
jewishlatincenternyc@gmail.com

NEW YORK, NY
Mrs. Gillie Shanowitz
New York Hebrew
646.573.6773
gillie@nychebrewschool.org

NEW YORK, NY
Mrs. Mushka Zaklos
Chabad of Battery Park
646.770.3636
jewishbpc@gmail.com

NEW YORK, NY
Mrs. Rachel Benchimol
Aleph Learning
646.827.9181
info@alephlearning.org

NEW YORK, NY
Mrs. Raizy Metzger
Upper Midtown Chabad
212.758.3770
raizymetzger@yahoo.com

NEW YORK, NY
Mrs. Sarah Alevsky
Chabad of the West Side
2128645010
sarah@chabadwestside.org

PORT WASHINGTON , N.Y.
Mrs. Esti Paltiel
Chabad of Port Washington
516.767.8672
esti@chabadpw.org

POUGHKEEPSIE, NEW YORK
Mrs Dalia Sanoff
Chabad on Fulton
8452146286
dalia@chabadonfulton.org

ROCHESTER, NY
Mrs. Chany Mochkin
Chabad Lubavitch of Rochester
585.981.0477
chanymo@yahoo.com

STONY BROOK, NY
Mrs. Chanie Cohen
Neshei Chabad Woman's Club
631.585.521
chanie@chabadsb.com

STONY BROOK, NY
Mrs. Chaya Grossbaum
Chabad Stony Brook
631.585.0521
Chaya@ChabadSB.com

SUFFERN, NY
Mrs. Esty Weber
NCFJE
443.418.4336
Estherweber7@gmail.com

BEACHWOOD, OH
Mrs. Rivky Friedman
Jewish Learning Institute
216.282.0112
jli@enrichingjudaism.com

CINCINNATI, OH
Mrs. Chana Mangel
Chabad Jewish Center
513.793.5200
office@chabadba.com

CLEVELAND, OH
Mrs. Estie Marozov
Friendship Circle
216.377.3000
RabbiYossi@ChabadofCleveland.com

DAYTON, OH
Mrs. Devorah Leah Mangel
Chabad of Greater Dayton
937.643.0770
chabad@chabaddayton.com

NEW ALBANY, OH
Mrs. Esther Kaltmann
Chabad of Columbus
614.610.4293
esther.kaltmann@sbcglobal.net

TOLEDO, OH
Mrs. Raizel Shemtov
Chabad of Toledo
4192703548
morahraizel@gmail.com

OKLAHOMA CITY, OK
Mrs. Nechama Goldman
Chabad of Oklahoma City
405.524.4800
chabadokc@gmail.com

HILLSBORO, OR
Mrs Chaya Rivkin
Chabad of Hillsbro
503.747.5363
chaikyr@gmail.com

PORTLAND, OR
Mrs. Mushka Wilhelm
Chabad of Northeast Portland
971.402.9395
mushkawilhelm@gmail.com

SALEM, OR
Mrs. Fruma Perlstein
Chabad Jewish Center of Salem
503.383.9569
Fruma@chabadsalem.com

ALLENTOWN, PA
Mrs. Devorah Halperin
Chabad of the Lehigh Valley
610.351.6511
Rabbi@chabadlehighvalley.com

FORT WASHINGTON, PA
Mrs. Devorah Leah Deitsch
Lubavitch of Montgomery County
215.591.9310
devorah@jewishmc.com

MERION STATION, PA
Mrs. Michal Sherman
Chabad of the Main Line
610.660.9900
michal@chabadmainline.org

NEWTOWN, PA
Mrs. Rosie Weinstein
Lubavitch of Bucks County
215.497.9925
rosie@jewishcenter.info

PHILADELPHIA, PA
Mrs Reuvena Grodnitzky
Chabad Young Philly
856.308.9930
rlgrod36@gmail.com

PHILADELPHIA, PA
Mrs Shevy Lowenstein
Jewish Center Northern Liberties
610.203.0996
shevy.lowenstein@gmail.com

PITTSBURGH, PA
Mrs Batya Rosenblum
Chabad of the South Hill
412.344.2424
batya812@gmail.com

PITTSBURGH, PA
Mrs. Chani Altein
Chabad of Pittsburgh
412.421.3561
jli@chabadpgh.com

PITTSBURGH, PA
Mrs. Chasi Rothstein
Chabad at Pitt
443.525.4212
chasirothstein@gmail.com

RYDAL, PA
Mrs. Nechama Dina Gurevitz
Chabad Lubavitch Jewish Center
267.536.5757
zusheg@gmail.com

STATE COLLEGE, PA
Mrs. Miri Gourarie
Chabad of the Undergrad
814.409.8130
mirigourarie@gmail.com

STATE COLLEGE, PA
Mrs. Sarah Meretsky
Chabad of Penn State
814.861.8063
sarahitameretsky@comcast.net

YARDLEY, PA
Mrs. Chaya Blecher
Lubavitch of Yardley
215.666.0698
rabbi@jewishyardley.com

ASHVILLE, SC
Mrs. Chana Susskind
Chabad House of Ashville
828.505.0746
chana@chabadasheville.org

COLUMBIA, SC
Mrs. Devorah Leah Marrus
The Chabad-Alef House
803.237.6084
devorahld@gmail.com

GREENVILLE, SC
Mrs. Musie Kesselman
Chabad of Greenville
864.256.1770
chabadgreenville@gmail.com

MYRTLE BEACH, SC
Mrs. Leah Aizenmen
Chabad of Myrtle Beach
843.448.0035
laizenman@gmail.com

MEMPHIS, TN
Mrs. Rivky Klein
Chabad Lubavitch of Tennessee
901.754.0404
Info@JewishMemphis.com

NASHVILLE, TN
Mrs. Esther Tiechtel
Chabad of Nashville
615.646.5750
rabbi@chabadnashville.com

ARLINGTON, TX
Mrs. Risha Gurevitch
Chabad of Arlington
817.451.1171
rishi@arlingtonchabad.org

AUSTIN, TX
Mrs. Mussy Levertov
Chabad Young Professionals
512.905.2778
Mendyaustin@gmail.com

BELLAIRE, TX
Mrs. Esty Zaklikofsky
The Shul of Bellaire
713.484.9887
estyzak@gmail.com

DALLAS, TX
Mrs. Michal Shapiro
Chabad of Dallas
972.818.0770
moshenaparstek@gmail.com

DALLAS, TX
Mrs Rivka Goldschmidt
Chabad of Dallas
972.818.0770
shikoon@aol.com

FORT WORTH, TX
Mrs. Chana Tovah Mandel
Chabad of Fort Worth
817.263.7701
Cgi@chabadfortworth.com

FRISCO, TX
Mrs. Mushkie Kesselman
Chabad of Frisco
214.460.7773
chabadgreenville@gmail.com

HOUSTON, TX
Mrs. Leah Marinovsky
Chabad Lubavitch
713.541.1774
leahfeige2@aim.com

HOUSTON, TX
Mrs. Rochel Lazaroff
Chabad at Rice
713.522.2004
Rochel@aishelhouse.org

MISSOURI CITY, TX
Mrs Chaya Feigenson
Chabad of Sugar Land
8327580685
cbfeigenson@gmail.com

PLANO, TX
Mrs. Sara Block
Chabad at Legacy West
214.620.4083
chabadlw@gmail.com

S. ANTONIO, TX
Mrs. Rivkie Block
Chabad Lubavitch
210.492.1085
chabadsa@sbcglobal.net

SALT LAKE CITY, UT
Mrs. Sheina Zippel
Chabad Lubavitch of Utah
801.414.3377
sheina@jewishutah.com

SALT LAKE CITY, UT
Zippel
Chaabd Lubavitch of Utah
801.414.3377
avremi@jewishutah.com

BURLINGTON, VT
Mrs. Draizy Junik
Chabad of Vermont
802.658.5770
chabad@chabadvt.org

ARLINGTON, VA
Mrs. Yehudis Newman
Chabad Lubavitch of Alexandria-Arlington
703.820.2770
yehudisnewman@gmail.com

FAIRFAX, VA
Raizel Deitch
Chabad of George Mason University
5712792587
raizelg@gmail.com

NORFOLK, VA
Mrs. Rashi Brashevitzky
Chabad of Tidewater
757.616.0770
Rabbilevi@chabadoftidewater.com

BELLINGHAM, WA
Mrs. Noa-Miriam Truxton
Rohr Center for Jewish Life
360.393.3845
rabbi@jewishbellingham.com

MERCER ISLAND, WA
Mrs. Devorah Kornfeld
Chabad of Mercer Island
206.679.9117
y-kornfeld2@yahoo.com

OLYMPIA, WA
Mrs. Chava Edelman
Chabad of Olympia
360.584.4306
info@jewisholympia.com

SEATTLE, WA
Mrs. Chana Levitin
Chabad of the Pacific Northwest
206.931.4100
chanielevitin@gmail.com

SPOKANE, WA
Mrs. Chaya Sarah Hahn
Chabad of Spokane
509.443.0770
rabbihahn@gmail.com

VANCOUVER, WA
Mrs. Tzivie Greenberg
Chabad Jewish Center
360.326.5923
info@jewishclarkcounty.com

KENOSHA, WI
Mrs. Rivkie Wilschanski
Chabad of Kenosha
262.359.0770
rabbitzali@jewishkenosha.com

MADISON, WI
Mrs. Henya Matusof
Rohr Chabad House at University of Wisconsin-Madison
608.257.1757
Info@jewishuwmadison.com

MEQUON, WI
Mrs. Dinie Rapoport
Center for Jewish Life
262.242.2235
dinie@chabadmequon.com

US VIRGIN ISLANDS

S. THOMAS
Mrs. Henya Federman
Chabad Lubavitch of the Virgin Islands
340.714.2770
henya@jewishvirginislands.com

AUSTRALIA

SYDNEY, NSW
Dina Koncepolski
Cremorne Synagogue
+614.108.40009
rabbi@cremornessynagogue.com

SYDNEY, NSW
Mrs Esther Feldman
*Beis Menachem Chabad - Dover Heights
Shule*
+61.2.9731.8682
esterke_f@hotmail.com

SYDNEY, NSW
Mrs. Henya Milecki
South Head Synagogue
+61.4.2361.3770
henyam@me.com

SYDNEY, NSW
Mrs. Sara-Tova Yaffe
CBD Chabad
+61.4.2247.0655
saratova613@gmail.com

MELBOURNE, VIC
Nathanson
Jewish Melbourne
+613.9636.3321
jewishmelbourne@gmail.com

MELBOURNE, VIC
Mrs. Sara Rosenfeld
Beis Chabad Ohel Devorah
+61.3.9525.9014
rivkah.groner@gmail.com

BELGIUM

BRUSSELS
Mrs. Nehama Tawil
EJCC
+32.2.231.1770
ntawil@ejcc.eu

BRUSSELS
Mrs. Shulamit Pinson
Chabad of Brussels
+32.47.621.7445
shulamitpinson@gmail.com

EDEGEM, ANTWERPEN
Mrs. Chaya Hertz
Chai Center
+32.3.288.7970
chajah@gmail.com

ANTWERPEN
Mrs. Debbie Rabenou
JLI Antwerp
+32477700538
debbie@rabenou.com

BRAZIL

MANAUS
Mrs. Dvorah Lea Raichman
Chabad-Lubavitch of Manaus
+55.92.3088.3302
Zagudeby@hotmail.com

S. PAULO
Mrs. Rivka Rosenfeld
Sinagoga Beit Menachem
+55.11.3816.6216
rivkyrosenfeld@hotmail.com

S. PAULO
Mrs. Sarah Steinmetz
Beit Chabad Central
+55.11.3081.3081
sarah.a.steinmetz@gmail.com

CANADA

RICHMOND, BC
Mrs. Chanie Baitelman
Chabad of Richmond
604.277.6427
admin@chabadrichmond.com

VANCOUVER, BC
Mrs. Chaya Rosenfeld
Lubavitch of British Columbia
604.266.1313
esti@lubavitchbc.com

VANCOUVER, BC
Mrs. Malky Bitton
Chabad of Downtown
778.688.1273
malky@chabadcitycentre.com

HAMILTON, ON
Mrs. Shaina Rosenfeld
Chabad Lubavitch Hamilton
905.529.7458
shaina@chabadhamilton.com

LONDON, ON
Mrs. Basie Gurkow
Congregation Beth Tefilah
2262345022
bgurkow@gmail.com

MAPLE, ON
Mrs. Toby Bernstein
Chabad Romano Centre
905.303.1880
chabad@chabadrc.org

OTTAWA, ON
Mrs. Devora Caytak
Jewish Youth Library of Ottawa
613.729.1619
Dev18@sympatico.ca

S. CATHARINES, ON
Mrs. Perla Zaltzman
Chabad at Brock
905.401.6281
perla@Jewishniagara.com

THORNHILL, ON
Mrs. Chanah Leah Beckerman
Chabad at York
905.771.6359
bekermans@gmail.com

THORNHILL, ON
Mrs. Chanie Hildeshaim
Chabad Russian Center of Thornhill Woods
905.326.9258
chanie@jewishthornhillwoods.org

THORNHILL, ON
Mrs. Faygie Kaplan
Chabad @ Flamingo
905.763.4040
faygie@chabadflamingo.com

THORNHILL, ON
Mrs. Goldie Plotkin
Chabad Lubavitch of Markham
905.886.0420
rabbi@chabadmarkham.org

TORONTO, ON
Bais Chomesh High School
Bais Chomesh High School
416.631.0585
baischomesh@gmail.com

TORONTO, ON
Mrs. Chana Gansburg
Chabad on the Avenue
416.546.8770
chana@chabadavenue.com

TORONTO, ON
Mrs. Chanie Zaltzman
JRCC of East Thornhill
416.222.7812
Chanie.zaltzman@jrcc.org

TORONTO, ON
Mrs. Mushky Blau
JRCC South Thornhill
6477095770
Mushka.Blau@jrcc.org

TORONTO, ON
Mrs. Nechama Dina Jacobson
JRCC West Thornhill
416.902.9254
ndjacobson@rogers.com

TORONTO, ON
Mrs. Rivka Gansburg
Chabad Lubavitch of York Mills
416.551.9391
rivky@chabadyorkmills.com

TORONTO, ON
Mrs. Yehudis Steiner
Uptown Chabad
416.635.9696
yehudissteiner@gmail.com

WATERLOO, ON
Mrs. Rivky Goldman
Chabad Lubavitch of the Waterloo Region
519.725.4289
rmg@jewishwaterloo.com

WHITBY, ON
Mrs. Chana Borenstein
Chabad Jewish Centre of Durham Region
905.493.9007
info@jewishdurham.com

MONTREAL, QC
Mrs. Chanie Gansbourg
Chabad of Old Montreal
514.907.8778
chabadofoldmtl@gmail.com

MONTREAL, QC
Mrs. Rashi Weiss
Chabad Student Centre
514.845.4443
rashi@chabadmcgill.com

MONTREAL, QC
Mrs. Simcha Fine
Chabad Zichron Kedoshim
514.738.3434
simchafine@gmail.com

MONTREAL, QC
Mrs. Zeldie Treitel
Montreal Torah Center
514.739.0770
zeldie@themtc.com

VILLE S. LAURENT, QC
Mrs. Leah Silberstein
Chabad Ville S. Laurent
514.747.1199
info@chabadvsl.com

SASKATOON, SK
Mrs. Sarah Kats
Chabad Lubavitch of Saskatoon
306.384.4370
rabbi@jewishsask.com

GRAND CAYMAN
Mrs. Rikal Pewzner
Chabad Cayman
717.798.1040
rikal@jewishcayman.com

PUDONG
Mrs. Nechama Greenberg
Chabad of Pudong
+86.21.1780.0791
nechamieg@gmail.com

COPENHAGEN
Mrs. Rochel Loewenthal
ChabaDanmark
+45.3316.1850
Info@chabad.dk

ANTIBES JUAN-LES-PINS
Mrs. Hanna Sebag
Habad Loubavitch d'Antibes Juan-les-Pins
+336.37.72.14.18
habadantibes@gmail.com

ARCUEIL
Mrs. Haya Goldberg
Beth Loubavitch d'Arcueil
+336.95.39.84.55
haya.mouchka@gmail.com

AUBERVILLIERS
Mrs. Rivky Belinow
Beth Habad S. Denis
+336.09.49.23.87
rivky-belinow@hotmail.fr

BOIS-COLOMBES
Mrs. Hanna Gershovitz
Beth Loubavitch Bois-Colombes
+336.30.46.94.05
sgershovitz@gmail.com

CERGY-PONTOISE
Mrs. Nehama Dawidowicz
Beth Loubavitch de Cergy Pontoise, S. Ouen L'aumône
+336.95.06.04.64
nehama770@hotmail.com

LA VARENNE S. HILAIRE
Mrs. Haya Benelbaz
Beth Habad La Varenne S. Hilaire
+336.28.53.53.17
mbenelbaz@gmail.com

LYON
Mrs. Devorah Gurewitz
Beth Habad Centre Ville
+336.14.52.27.03
dl.gurewitz@gmail.com

MARSEILLE 5ÈME
Mrs. Sarah Bard
Beth Habad Marseille 5ème
+336.20.32.71.52
habadmarseille5@gmail.com

MARSEILLE 8ÈME
Mrs. Rivka Altabé
Beth Habad Marseille 8ème
+336.25.47.37.66
vivialtabe@gmail.com

NICE
Mrs. Dvora Nidam
Habad Loubavitch Nice Côte d'Azur
+336.13.12.89.88
adnidam@gmail.com

PANTIN
Mrs. Rivka Balouka
Beth Loubavitch Pantin
+336.13.32.55.49
activiteblp@gmail.com

PARIS 7ÈME
Mrs. Sarah Mergui
Beth Loubavitch Paris 7ème
+336.27.47.34.45
yymergui@gmail.com

PARIS 9ÈME
Mrs. Cheina Asseraf
Beth Loubavitch Paris 9ème
+336.03.36.35.86
cheina@asseraf.net

PARIS 17ÈME
Mrs. Haya Elbaz
Habad Loubavitch Batignolles—DCJB
+336.50.07.01.40
yacovielbaz@gmail.com

PARIS
Mrs. Mushky Lachkar
Habad Bercy 13
+33.6.63.025.430
mushky92@gmail.com

PAU
Mrs. Shayna Matusof
Habad des Pyrenees-Atlantiques
+33.6.22.107.549
habadpyrenees@gmail.com

STRASBOURG
Mrs. Tehila Samama
Beth Habad Strasbourg
+336.64.86.99.20
tehilasamama@gmail.com

GUATEMALA CITY
Mrs. Yael Pelman
Chabad of Guatemala
718.504.7344
yaell@hotmail.com

JERUSALEM
Mrs. Chana Canterman
Chabad Center of Talbiya
+972.54.682.3737
chabadtalbiya@gmail.com

TZFAT
Mrs. Chaya Bracha Leiter
Ascent
+972.52.677.0142
cb@ascent.co.il

FIRENZE
Mrs. Sonia Wolvovsky
Chabad of Tuscany
+39.38.9595.2034
jewishtuscany@gmail.com

MEXICO

SAN MIGUEL DE ALLENDE
Mrs. Raizel Huebner
Chabad of SMA
+52.425.181.8091
raizel@chabadsma.com

RUSSIAN FEDERATION

MOSCOW
Mrs. Rivky Wilansky
Chabad of Moscow
+7.495.645.5000
doamitzvah@gmail.com

SOUTH AFRICA

SEA POINT, CAPE TOWN
Mrs. Avigail Popack
Chabad Center of Cape Town
+27.21.434.3740
avipopack@gmail.com

SWEDEN

MALMÖ
Mrs. Reizel Kesselman
Chabad Malmo
+46.40.979.358
chabadmalmo@gmail.com

SWITZERLAND

LUGANO
Mrs. Yuti Kantor
Chabad Lugano
+41.91.921.3720
Yuti@jewishlugano.com

LUZERN
Mrs. Rivky Drukman
Chabad of Central Switzerland
+41.41.361.1770
Info@ChabadLuzern.com

TASMANIA

SOUTH LAUNCESTON
Mrs. Rochel Gordon
Chabad of Tasmania
+61.363.449.129
rochel@chabadtas.com

UNITED KINGDOM

BIRMINGHAM, ENGLAND
Mrs. Rivky Cheruff
Chabad on Campus Birmingham
+44.78.05092236
dercheruff@gmail.com

EDGWARE, MIDDX, ENGLAND
Mrs. Sarah Jacobs
Lubavitch of Edgware
+44.20.8905.4141
sarahjacobs@loe.org.uk

EDGWARE, MIDDX, ENGLAND
Mrs. Shterna Sudak
Lubavitch Foundation
+44.20.8800.0022
Shternasudak@yahoo.com

BUCKHURST HILL, ESSEX, ENGLAND
Mrs. Henny Brandman
Chabad Buckhurst Hill
+442089262376
Henny@chabadonthehill.co.uk

ILFORD, ESSEX, ENGLAND
Mrs. Devorah Sufrin
Chabad Lubavitch Centres Essex
+44.20.8554.1624
mrssufrin@chabadilford.co.uk

LEEDS, ENGLAND
Mrs. Dabrushy Pink
Chabad Lubavitch of Leeds
+44.113.266.3311
jwc@judaismlive.com

LONDON, ENGLAND
Mrs. Chai Cohen
Chabad-Lubavitch of Shoreditch
+44.77.7261.2661
cohenchai@gmail.com

LONDON, ENGLAND
Mrs Leah Moscowitz
Chabad of South London
+44.7490.519.619
leahzlata@gmail.com

LONDON, ENGLAND
Mrs. Devora Lew
Chabad of Bloomsbury - Central London
+44.20.7060.9770
info@bloomsburychabad.org

LONDON, ENGLAND
Mrs. Devorah Leah Weisz
Chabad of Hampstead Village
+44.79.7652.2807
Shulinhampstead@gmail.com

LONDON, ENGLAND
Mrs. Hadasa Korer
Chabad Lubavitch of Islington
+44.20.7688.0169
mkorer@gmail.com

LONDON, ENGLAND
Mrs. Kezi Levin
Brondesbury Park Synagogue
+44.20.8451.0091
kezi@bark.org

LONDON, ENGLAND
Mrs. Roizy Gancz
Chabad of Finchley
+44.203.7192.231
roizygancz@gmail.com

LONDON, ENGLAND
Mrs Shira Lebhar
Chabad of West Hampstead
+44.208.7868.741.235
shiramail2@gmail.com

MANCHESTER, ENGLAND
Mrs. Shaina Cohen
Lchaim Chabad Manchester
+44.16.1792.6335
Shaina@Lchaim.org.uk

SHEFFIELD, ENGLAND
Mrs. Faiga Rochel Golomb
Chabad of Sheffield
+44.114.281.7459
rabbijgolomb@blueyonder.co.uk

WESTMINSTER, LONDON, ENGLAND
Mrs. Chana Kalmenson
Chabad of Belgravia
+44.75.8592.0195
jewishbelgravia@gmail.com

URUGUAY

MONTEVIDEO
Mrs. Musya Shemtov
Beit Jabad Uruguay
+598.2709.3444
rmusyashemtov@gmail.com

VENEZUELA

CARACAS
Mrs. Chani Rosenblum
Hogar Jabad Lubavitch
+58.212.264.7011
chaniros1@gmail.com

The Jewish Learning Multiplex

Brought to you by the Rohr Jewish Learning Institute

In fulfillment of the Mandate of the Lubavitcher Rebbe, of blessed memory, whose leadership guides every step of our work, the mission of the Rohr Jewish Learning Institute is to transform Jewish life and the greater community through the study of Torah, connecting each Jew to our shared heritage of Jewish learning.

While our flagship program remains the cornerstone of our organization, JLI is proud to feature additional divisions catering to specific populations, in order to meet a wide array of educational needs.

The Rohr **JEWISH LEARNING INSTITUTE**

A subsidiary of **Merkos L'Inyonei Chinuch**,
the adult educational arm of the Chabad-Lubavitch movement.

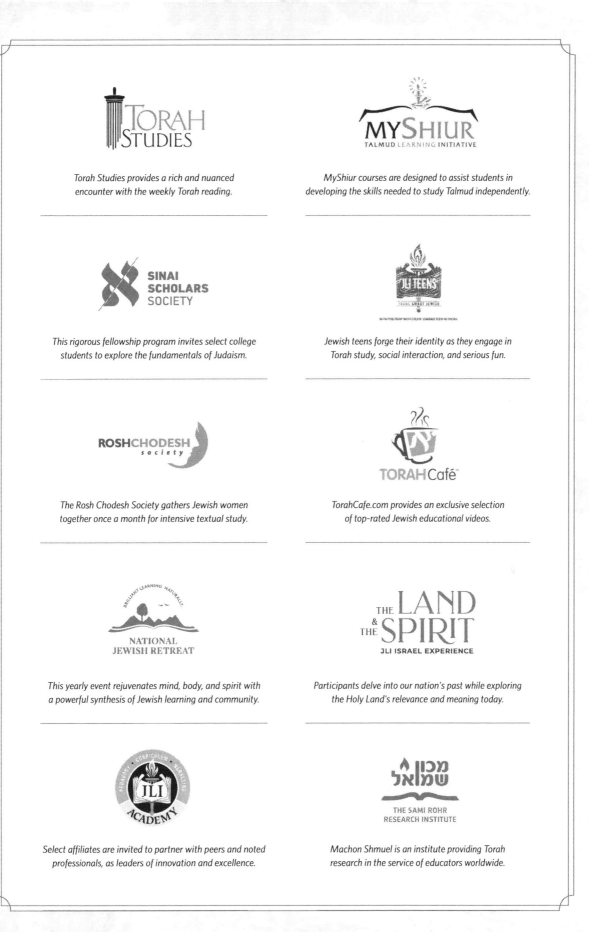

TORAH STUDIES

Torah Studies provides a rich and nuanced encounter with the weekly Torah reading.

MYSHIUR
TALMUD LEARNING INITIATIVE

MyShiur courses are designed to assist students in developing the skills needed to study Talmud independently.

SINAI SCHOLARS SOCIETY

This rigorous fellowship program invites select college students to explore the fundamentals of Judaism.

JLI TEENS
YOUNG SMART JEWISH
IN PARTNERSHIP WITH CTEEN CHABAD TEEN NETWORK

Jewish teens forge their identity as they engage in Torah study, social interaction, and serious fun.

ROSHCHODESH society

The Rosh Chodesh Society gathers Jewish women together once a month for intensive textual study.

TORAHCafé

TorahCafe.com provides an exclusive selection of top-rated Jewish educational videos.

BRILLIANT LEARNING. NATURALLY.
NATIONAL JEWISH RETREAT

This yearly event rejuvenates mind, body, and spirit with a powerful synthesis of Jewish learning and community.

THE LAND & THE SPIRIT
JLI ISRAEL EXPERIENCE

Participants delve into our nation's past while exploring the Holy Land's relevance and meaning today.

JLI ACADEMY

Select affiliates are invited to partner with peers and noted professionals, as leaders of innovation and excellence.

מכון שמואל
THE SAMI ROHR RESEARCH INSTITUTE

Machon Shmuel is an institute providing Torah research in the service of educators worldwide.

Made in the USA
Las Vegas, NV
22 October 2020